DESTINATION MARKETING ORGANISATIONS

ADVANCES IN TOURISM RESEARCH

Series Editor: Professor Stephen J. Page
University of Sterling, U.K.
s.j.page@stir.ac.uk

Advances in Tourism Research series publishes monographs and edited volumes that comprise state-of-the-art research findings, written and edited by leading researchers working in the wider field of tourism studies. The series has been designed to provide a cutting edge focus for researchers interested in tourism, particularly the management issues now facing decision-makers, policy analysts and the public sector. The audience is much wider than just academics and each book seeks to make a significant contribution to the literature in the field of study by not only reviewing the state of knowledge relating to each topic but also questioning some of the prevailing assumptions and research paradigms which currently exist in tourism research. The series also aims to provide a platform for further studies in each area by highlighting key research agendas which will stimulate further debate and interest in the expanding area of tourism research. The series is always willing to consider new ideas for innovative and scholarly books, inquiries should be made directly to the Series Editor.

Published:

WILKS & PAGE
Managing Tourist Health and Safety in the New Millennium

BAUM & LUNDTORP
Seasonality in Tourism

ASHWORTH & TUNBRIDGE
The Tourist-Historic City: Retrospect and Prospect of Managing the Heritage City

RYAN & PAGE
Tourism Management: Towards the New Millennium

SONG & WITT
Tourism Demand Modelling and Forecasting: Modern Econometric Approaches

TEO, CHANG & HO
Interconnected Worlds: Tourism in Southeast Asia

KERR
Tourism Public Policy and the Strategic Management of Failure

THOMAS
Small Firms in Tourism: International Perspectives

LUMSDON & PAGE
Tourism and Transport

Forthcoming titles include:

SIMPSON
Back to the Future: In Search of an Effective Tourism Planning Model

RYAN
Tourism and the Culture of Indigenous Peoples

Related Elsevier Journals - sample copies available on request
Air(line) Transport Journal
Annals of Tourism Research
International Journal of Hospitality Management
International Journal of Intercultural Relations
Tourism Management
World Development

DESTINATION MARKETING ORGANISATIONS

BY

STEVEN PIKE

School of Advertising, Marketing & Public Relations,
Queensland University of Technology, Australia

2004

ELSEVIER

Amsterdam – Boston – Heidelberg – London – New York – Oxford
Paris – San Diego – San Francisco – Singapore – Sydney – Tokyo

ELSEVIER B.V.
Radarweg 29
P.O. Box 211
1000 AE Amsterdam
The Netherlands

ELSEVIER Inc.
525 B Street, Suite 1900
San Diego
CA 92101-4495
USA

ELSEVIER Ltd
The Boulevard, Langford
Lane, Kidlington
Oxford OX5 1GB
UK

ELSEVIER Ltd
84 Theobalds Road
London
WC1X 8RR
UK

First edition 2004

Library of Congress Cataloging in Publication Data
A catalog record is available from the Library of Congress.

British Library Cataloguing in Publication Data
A catalogue record is available from the British Library.

ISBN: 0-08-044306-0

♾ The paper used in this publication meets the requirements of ANSI/NISO Z39.48-1992 (Permanence of Paper). Printed in The Netherlands.

To Louise, Jesse and Alex
Arohanui – your patience really is a virtue
With thanks to Ben

Contents

Chapter 1

Introduction to Destination Marketing Organisations

> In higher education it is important that the sometimes unfashionable public sector is included in programs. This allows students to gain an understanding of the roles and structures of tourism organizations at all levels ... what is critical is that students have a thorough understanding of issues of globalization, the public and private sector structures and policies that are in place to both capitalize and protect nations from its effects, and are equipped to enter the work force at a senior level 'surprise free' in terms of such issues (Fayos-Solá 2002).

Most tourism activities take place at destinations, and so the destination forms a pillar in any modelling of the tourism "system" (e.g. Leiper 1979). It has even been suggested that destinations have emerged as "the fundamental unit of analysis in tourism" (WTO 2002). Travellers are now spoilt for choice of destinations, which must compete for attention in a market place cluttered with the messages of substitute products as well as rival regions. As their title clearly indicates, destination marketing organisations (DMOs) are concerned with the selling of places, a field of study that has only relatively recently attracted significant research attention. Given the prominent place of destinations in the tourism system it is surprising there have been few texts to date that have focused on the operations of DMOs. Tourism has been around, in an organised form at least, since the late 19th century, and for most of that time DMOs have played an active role in the development of tourism worldwide. However, texts concerned with destination planning, marketing and management have only emerged in earnest since the 1990s. Contributions have included: destination planning and management (Godfrey & Clarke 2000; Howie 2003; Laws 1995; Lickorish 1992; WTO 1994), urban destinations (Page 1995), case studies of "tourist organizations" (Pearce 1992), destination marketing (Ashworth & Goodall 1990a; Goodall & Ashworth 1990; Heath & Wall 1992; Nykiel & Jascolt 1998; Wahab *et al.* 1976), the promotion of places (Ashworth & Voogd 1990; Gold & Ward 1994), destination branding (Morgan *et al.* 2002), and destination crisis marketing (Beirman 2003a).

A growing number of academic conferences have also featured the destination marketing theme in recent years. In 1990 the topic of the third international tourism workshop organised by the Geographical Institutes of the University of Groningen and the University of Reading was "selling" tourism destinations (Ashworth & Goodall 1990). The 1993 Association Internationale d'Experts Scientific du Tourisme (AIEST) conference addressed the issue of the competitiveness of long haul destinations (Ritchie & Crouch 2000a). In 1996 the Fundacion Cavanilles for Advanced Studies in Tourism organised the Second International Forum on Tourism, themed "the future of traditional tourist destinations" (Buhalis & Cooper 1998). In 1998 the 48th Congress of the International Association of Scientific Experts in Tourism (AIEST) focused on "Destination marketing — scopes and limitations" (Keller 1998). The 1999 TTRA Europe conference was themed "Tourism Destination Marketing — Gaining the Competitive Edge" (see Ruddy & Flanagan 1999). Also in 1999, the Centro Internazionale di Studi Économia Turitica (CISET) conference on destination marketing and management was held in Venice.

There has also been a wealth of material related to destination marketing published in academic tourism journals. For example, Pike (2002a) reviewed 142 papers published in the literature between 1973 and 2000 that were concerned with just one aspect of destination marketing — that of destination image analysis. The purpose of the text is to synthesis the current extent of knowledge in the field, and in doing so highlight research gaps relating to destination marketing management issues. These include a lack of DMO research attention towards:

- governance and the politics of decision making
- organisational structure
- alternative funding sources
- strategic planning and implementation
- destination competitiveness
- destination positioning
- human resource management
- relationships between national, state and regional DMOs
- destination brand management
- integrated marketing communication (IMC) implementation
- performance measures.

This text is primarily designed for use by undergraduate students of tourism, travel and hospitality. The rationale is that an understanding of the nature of DMO operations and challenges should not only be a prerequisite for those seeking a career in destination marketing, but should also be regarded as essential for those who will become active stakeholders of such organisations. As future managers, students will almost definitely interact with DMOs at national, state and/or local levels during their career. Opportunities exist for even the smallest of tourism operators to participate in, benefit from, and contribute to DMO planning and operations in some way. All DMOs share a common range of political and resource-based challenges not faced by private sector tourism businesses. Understanding these constraints and challenges will be of benefit to those who will be dealing with DMOs. Without this knowledge, initial encounters with DMO staff can be frustrating, which can then inhibit a long term relationship with the organisation marketing their region. Private sector tourism managers must understand that the principles guiding public sector managers, such as in DMOs, are often quite different to their own, and that by understanding these they will be able to work more effectively work with them (Elliott 1997). The aim should be to develop relationships that both create opportunities to further their own business interests more effectively, as well as contribute positively to the competitiveness of the destination. After all the success of these individual tourism businesses will ultimately be reliant to a large extent on the attractiveness of the destination. At one extreme the very viability of tourism enterprises at destinations in crisis, such as Fiji, Beirut, the former Yugoslavia and Bali, have been wiped out by exogenous events, such as war and terrorism, which have rendered the destination uncompetitive overnight. The key learning outcomes of the text are to aid the development of an understanding of the fundamental issues relating to:

* The rationale for the establishment of DMOs
* The structure, roles, goals and functions of DMOs
* The key opportunities, challenges and constraints facing DMOs
* The complexities of marketing destinations as tourism brands.

Two clear themes underpin the discussion throughout the text. The first, involving both the demand-side and supply-side perspectives of marketing, is concerned with the challenges involved in promoting multi-attributed destinations in heterogeneous and dynamic markets. The second theme concerns the need to provide more effective bridges linking academic theory and research outputs with "real world" DMO practise.

Marketing Multi-Attributed Destinations in Heterogeneous Markets

> The tourism industry (in New Zealand) is so fragmented, diverse, unfocused, self seeking and disorganised that Ph.D. theses have been written on its structural complexities. It's got more separate working parts than a 747's Rolls Royce engine and only some of them are vaguely headed in the same direction (Chamberlain 1992).

While Chamberlain's observations clearly referred to the New Zealand tourism industry, there are few if any countries where a multiplicity of divergent tourism interests does not exist. Consider also the small scale of the New Zealand tourism industry, with an estimated 13,500–18,000 small businesses (OTSP 2001), compared to Europe with an estimated 1.5 million tourism businesses, of which 95% employ less than 10 people (Wason 1998) and the issue is magnified. The first key theme underpinning the text is the DMO challenge of marketing a multi-attributed destination in a heterogeneous and dynamic global market place. From the supply-side marketing perspective, a DMO often represents a large and diverse range of destination attributes, including natural features, commercial and not-for-profit facilities and amenities, and people. Consider the following for example:

* commercial visitor attractions such as theme parks
* accommodation
* outdoor adventure activities such as white water rafting
* dining and nightlife
* shopping precincts and craft markets
* historic sites and scenes of disaster

- beaches
- museums
- picnic and barbecue amenities
- children's playgrounds
- forests and parklands
- landscape vistas
- climate
- flora and fauna
- host population characteristics such as language and indigenous culture.

The key tenet of this theme is that a DMO usually has no direct control over the products they represent nor the packaged offerings of intermediaries such as airlines, tour wholesalers and travel agencies. From the supply perspective the often eclectic collection of destination features must somehow be presented to the market in a way that not only cuts through the clutter of crowded markets to offer benefits desired by travellers, but also satisfies the interests of the host community, local businesses and travel intermediaries. DMO and stakeholder opinions on how this can be achieved are rarely congruent. It is not being cynical to suggest the natural self-interest of many small businesses will instinctively be to expect their market of interest to be the target of promotions, which in turn feature their product or product class. The politics of DMO decision making can, and does, inhibit implementation of marketing theory.

On the demand-side of destination marketing, the global market of consumer-travellers is not homogenous in terms of needs (Wahab *et al.* 1976). Travellers from different geographic areas, socio-demographic groups, and lifestyle clusters will respond to different offers, for a complex array of reasons, including the purpose of travel, individual motivation(s), time available, the time of year, and availability of other discretionary spending opportunities. Thousands of DMOs now compete for the attention of busy consumers through communication channels cluttered with noise from rival and substitute offerings. Not even the largest NTOs have the funds to match the promotional spending of corporate heavyweights from other product categories, such as Coke, Sony and BMW. Marketers must communicate meaningful but focused messages at the right time and place to gain "cut through" to the right people. How can a DMO produce succinct messages that: (i) encapsulate the essence of place; (ii) differentiate the destination from the myriad of competitors offering the same features; and (iii) be meaningful to heterogeneous and dynamic markets? Destination marketing is not for the faint hearted, and this core challenge, faced by every destination globally, has implications for every aspect of DMO operations, including: funding, strategy, organisation, politics, finance and budgeting, human resources, crisis management, branding, communication, market research, promotions and performance measures.

Bridging Theory and Practise

Information that has a limited audience is bound by formal considerations. Scientific information appears in scholarly monographs; political information in speeches, pamphlets, editorials and wall posters; commercial information in advertisements and catalogues; news in reports. Each special informational format presupposes a set of methods and has its own version of reliability, validity and completeness. Becoming a scientist or a politician means, in part, learning and adhering to, even "believing in," the standards and techniques of one's profession (MacCannell 1976: 135).

This statement, from MacCannell's seminal work *The Tourist*, suggested the process of becoming a tourist was akin to the learning process involved in becoming a member of a profession. The statement also serves to introduce the second key theme underpinning the text, which is the divide between tourism academics and practitioners (perhaps ironically the term "practitioner" is not one used by members of the tourism industry to describe themselves). Admittedly, this mention of a divide is a generalisation and is likely to be a contentious point, since many tourism academics engage in research with tourism organisations. In an ideal world the academic literature would inform industry while DMO best practise would inform the literature, in a mutually beneficial cycle. However, a significant divide does exist. Academics have written about the problem (e.g. Ryan 2002), and practitioners have spoken about it. For example, in a plenary session at the 2004 Council for Australian University Tourism and Hospitality Education (CAUTHE) conference, Managing Director of Brisbane's *The Day Tour Company* Wayne Clift lamented:

In the aftermath of September 11 and the Ansett collapse, we nearly drowned in a sea of research data and information churned out by every well-intentioned organisation known to man . . . As an industry we certainly said enough is enough, we cant handle it — we don't have time to read all this stuff! And therein lies the problem. We don't see the benefits — therefore we don't make the time.

As observed by MacCannell, different professions have different requirements in terms of the ways in which information is controlled and disseminated. Therefore it could be expected that, if tourism is now a profession [it was only as recently as 1976 that MacCannell (176) referred to the new term "the tourist industry" being used at the time], then it would be fair to assume that all those associated with this profession would confer using a common dialogue. The reality is the information needs of tourism academics and practitioners are often quite different, and are provided for in different types of forums and publications. It is suggested therefore, MacCannell's statement also applies to the difference in discourse between tourism academics and practitioners. While the work of many academics and practitioners could be subsumed under the terms "tourism," "travel," "leisure" and "hospitality," the assumption should not be made that academics and practitioners work together in some sort of organised and symbiotic fashion. There is no common tourism discourse. Calls have been made for more engagement between tourism academics and practitioners, particularly at a destination level:

. . . our understanding of place promotion is, like the activity itself, partial and fragmentary . . . yet if place promotion is to become an established and

useful practise, it requires some real intellectual engagement between critic
and practitioner (Ward & Gold 1994: 15).

In this regard, the World Tourism Organisation (WTO 2002a) noted their 2002 think tank on destination competitiveness was the first time that a group of practitioners and knowledge experts had met in a WTO forum on destination management. For the most part, separate conferences are held for the two groups, often with only small overlaps in attendance by the other.

Academics must publish to gain recognition from peers, in an environment of "publish or perish." Even though many studies in the tourism literature have practical implications for practitioners, the vast majority of practitioners will never actually read the academic papers relevant to their business operations. Academics gain credibility by being published in textbooks, peer reviewed academic journals and in academic conference proceedings. Increasingly, due to the proliferation of publishing opportunities, papers must be seen to be in the "right" journals. Fortunately, for practitioners used to the confidentiality of privately commissioned research reports, these journals are in the public domain, available by subscription. Also, the blind-refereed rigour of the academic literature is one of the very reasons for its value. However the process results in lengthy delays between manuscript submission and journal publication, and it is not unusual for data reported to be three or four or more years old by the time it is published. The practical downside is that these papers usually involve lengthy theoretical and methodological discussions, with complicated formulae and terminology that will be unfamiliar to those without research training, such as "epistemology," "periodicity," "multivariate analysis," and "principal components analysis with orthogonal rotation." The reality is that practitioners, particularly those in small businesses that make up the majority of the tourism industry, have a busy operational focus. Tomorrow's cash flow concentrates the mind in the fiercely competitive market place. Realistically, how many practitioners are aware of, let alone have time to keep up to date with, the extant literature?

For busy practitioners, the expanse and variety of the tourism literature can be overwhelming. If they are aware in the first place, the difficulty lies in the complex, multidisciplinary and fragmented nature of the tourism system as well as the sometimes turgid nature of academic writing, relative to other information sources. Clift summarised industry's view of research in general as: "We don't believe it, we don't know where to look, and we're not sure how to use it." However, there should be anticipation that the value of the literature will be more widely accepted by the next generation of tourism managers, as a higher percentage will have had exposure to tourism theory through participation in the tourism and hospitality degree courses that have only emerged in recent years. In New Zealand, Coventry (1998) cited an RTO spokesperson from the country's leading resort destination who was particularly critical of an academic destination image report by Kearsley *et al.* (1998):

> Why don't academics produce meaningful research which adds value to debate . . . they just produce this academic, trite stuff which simply occupies shelves and gives academics something to do.

This type of comment is surprising given the richness of academic tourism marketing information, including the aforementioned report. For example, Ritchie (1996: 51–52) argued that tourism research "from its very beginning, has been driven by individuals having a strong market orientation." Nevertheless, in the example above, this was a "real world" belief held by a destination marketer. The issue has also been raised in other parts of the world. Three decades ago in the U.K., Riley & Palmer (1975) lamented their study recommendations had not been adopted by destination marketers. They suggested market research must therefore be better marketed to industry. Others have also suggested more research needs to provide practical recommendations for tourism practitioners (Baker *et al.* 1994; Nickerson & Moisey 1999; Selby & Morgan 1996; Taylor *et al.* 1994). In discussing the gap between researchers and practitioners, Taylor *et al.* suggested the key to research not ending up collecting dust on a shelf, as was much of what was produced by Canada's tourism researchers, lay in improving interpretation and presentation. Similarly, Hall (1998) claimed Australia was yet to develop close ties between the tourism industry and academia. In the USA, Plog (2000) lamented the lack of consulting opportunities for tourism academics, observing it was amazing the number of tourism operators who make continue to make decisions "by the seat of their pants" instead of based on research. In terms of the converse situation of reporting DMO best practise in the literature there are also constraints. For example, why should DMOs share confidential insights based on their own significant investment of resources? What incentives exist for busy practitioners to prepare detailed case studies? Even if there were more case collaboration by academics and practitioner, one journal editor privately regretted to the author the decreasing space available for case studies in tourism journals.

Notable recent initiatives in the attempt to bridge the academic/practitioner discourse divide include on-line publications with academic contributions designed for both researchers and academics. *Eclipse* is a periodic publication for DMOs edited by former destination marketer Ivan Polunin, which contains contributions from academics in as succinct a form as would be expected in any trade publication. Additionally, in November 2003 the publishers of *Eclipse* launched a new discussion forum on destination marketing topics at www.moonshinetravel.com/paginas/eclipse/foindex.html. The *e-Review of Tourism Research (eRTR)*, launched in April 2003, is a cooperative venture between Texas A & M University, the Travel & Tourism Research Association (TTRA), and the Canadian Tourism Commission. The publishers promote *eRTR* as creating a platform for the dissemination of ideas and research in a "user friendly manner." The journal focuses on presenting short pieces, of less than 1000 words, which have an applied focus. Contributions in the following areas have been particularly encouraged (see http://ertr.tamu.edu):

- non-technical summaries of current research
- applied tourism research notes
- practitioner perspectives on tourism research
- best practises
- case studies
- conference reports.

Recognising the practical value of so much of the academic literature, the second theme of this text therefore is an attempt to present a synthesis of the literature relating to DMOs, in a manner that will be of value to, and decipherable by, students and practitioners of tourism alike.

Defining Key Terms

Tourism

> All tourism involves travel, yet not all travel is tourism. All vacation travel involves recreation, yet not all tourism is recreation. All tourism occurs during leisure time, but not all leisure time is spent on tourism activities (Mill & Morrison 2002: 1).

A WWW search of the word "tourism" using a search engine such as www.google.com will generate over one million references in less than a second. Tourism is a word that is so often used in everyday language, that few adults in the developed world would have difficulty articulating some interpretation of its meaning. All of us have been somewhere on holiday, know someone working in hospitality, travel or tourism, and have seen coach loads of visitors from other parts. So it is a surprise for many students to learn that there is no universally accepted definition of tourism. Instead, there have been almost as many different definitions as there are researchers (Smith 2001). It has even been suggested that defining tourism is almost conceptually impossible (Holloway 1994; Smith 1988). Complications arise from the multidisciplinary nature of tourism research, the ambiguity of what constitutes a "tourist" and "tourism business," and overlaps with the concepts of travel, hospitality and leisure. Tourism is a relatively new academic discipline, and as such Leiper (1979: 392) found few academics had devoted effort towards defining tourism:

> The study of tourism as a focal subject has sometimes been treated with derision in academic circles, perhaps because of its novelty, perhaps because of its superficial fragmentation, perhaps because it cuts across established disciplines.

Tourism research has drawn extensively from theories in other disciplines such as geography, economics, sociology, psychology, business and anthropology (Gilbert 1990). Thus, as has been pointed out by Hall (1998) and Leiper (1995), most tourism texts offer a different definition. Table 1 presents a selection of tourism definitions from the academic literature.

The definition used will also depend on the purpose for which it is to be applied, which is commonly to define markets and analyse statistics. For DMOs these include for example reports that seek to:

- promote the economic and social benefits of tourism to a community in a bid to enlist government funds for destination promotion
- promote the scale and growth of tourism in a business investment prospectus
- highlight potentially negative environmental impacts at a proposed development site
- report negative socio-cultural impacts at a destination.

Table 1: Definitions of tourism.

Author	Definition
Hunziker (1951, in Collier 1997: 2)	. . . the sum of the phenomena and relationships arising from the travel and stay of non-residents, in so far as they do not lead to permanent residence and are not connected with any earning activity.
Leiper (1979: 403–404)	It is the system involving the discretionary travel and temporary stay of persons away from their usual place of residence for one or more nights, excepting tours made for the primary purpose of earning remuneration from points en route.
Ryan (1991: 6)	. . . holiday tourism may be defined as the means by which people seek psychological benefits that arise from experiencing new places, and new situations that are of a temporary duration, whilst free of the constraints of work, or normal patterns of daily life at home.
Mill & Morrison (1992: 9)	Tourism is the term given to the activity that occurs when people travel. This encompasses everything from the planning of the trip, the travel to the destination area, the stay itself, the return and the reminiscences about it afterward. It includes the activities the traveller undertakes as part of the trip, the purchases made, and the interactions that occur between host and guest in the destination area. In sum it is all of the activities and impacts that occur when a visitor travels.
Heath & Wall (1992: 4)	The study of tourism is the study of people away from their usual habitat, of the establishments that respond to the requirements of travellers, and of the impacts they have on the economic, physical, and social well-being of their hosts. It involves the motivations and experiences of the tourists, the expectations of and adjustments made by residents of reception areas, and the roles played by the numerous agencies and institutions that intercede between them.
Holloway (1994: 3)	. . . someone who travels to see something different, and then complains when he finds things are not the same!
Gunn (1994: 4)	. . . tourism is defined as encompassing *all travel* with the exception of commuting.
WTO (1995: 12)	. . . the activities of persons traveling to and staying in places outside their usual environment for not more than one consecutive year for leisure, business and other purposes.
Hall (1998: 6)	Tourism is a commercial phenomenon of industrial society which involves a person, either individually or in a group, travelling from place to place (the physical component of tourism), and/or journeying from one psychological state to another (the re-creating component of tourism).
Sharpley (2002: 22)	It is, in short, a social phenomenon which involves the movement of people to various destinations and their (temporary) stay there.

Following Buck's (1978) assertion that tourism scholarship was organised across two distinctive streams, economic development and tourism impacts, Leiper (1979) sought to develop a general framework for tourism that would bridge this divide. In reviewing previous attempts at defining tourism, Leiper identified three approaches. The first was "economic," where definitions only recognised business and economic aspects, such as:

> Tourism is an identifiable nationally important industry. The industry involves a wide cross section of component activities including the provision of transportation, accommodation, recreation, food, and related services (Australia Department of Tourism & Recreation 1975, in Leiper 1979: 392).

Leiper's criticism of this approach was that it clearly lacks a number of elements, the most important being the human dimension. The second approach was "technical," where the interest was in monitoring the characteristics of tourism markets, such as describing tourists, travel purpose, distance travelled and length of time away. For example, the first of these was that adopted by the League of Nations Statistical Committee in 1937, which defined an international tourist as someone who "visits a country other than that in which he habitually lives for a period of at least twenty-four hours (OECD 1974, in Leiper 1979: 393). Most definitions have used this approach, usually as a basis for collection of comparable statistics. The third approach was "holistic," where the attempt was made to capture the whole essence of tourism, such as:

> Tourism is the study of man away from his usual habitat, of the industry which responds to his needs, and of the impacts that both he and the industry have on the host's socio-cultural, economic and physical environments (Jafari 1977, in Leiper 1979: 394).

While this approach is notable for embracing a wider frame of reference than "the tourist," this type of definition has been criticised as being too broad in definitions of sub-elements such as "tourist."

According to Sigaux' (1966: 6) overview of the history of tourism, the word first appeared in the 19th century. Sigaux cited the *Dictionnaire Universal du XIX Siecle of 1876*, which defined tourists as "people who travel for the pleasure of travelling, out of curiosity and because they have nothing better to do." Sigaux (92) also limited the scope of tourism to preclude domestic travel: "One can almost say that national tourism, at home in one's own country, hardly counts as tourism." Such perspectives clearly don't encompass all categories of temporary "visitors" to a destination, who would otherwise still contribute to the coffers of businesses whose managers consider themselves to be in the tourism industry. Other than travel for general pleasure, many other types of tourism, for example, which may or may not fit the category of a holiday, have been documented. These include:

- business travel, including attendance at conferences or exhibition or trade fair
- attendance or participation at special events, the arts and entertainment
- visiting friends or relatives
- sex and romance
- educational field trips
- adventure sports

- hunting and fishing
- spiritual events and pilgrimages
- day excursions.

Although some of the above could be subsumed under the heading of "pleasure travel," it is doubtful whether all participants would regard themselves as "tourists." Consider the case of travel for health or recuperation such as spa visits. For example, a report in the *News-Mail* (22/1/04: 18–19), entitled "Nip and Tuck Holiday," discussed the potential of Queensland coastal resort Noosa to become Australia's cosmetic surgery capital. Leading Melbourne cosmetic surgeon Professor Gerard Sormann spends 12 days a month at his practise in Noosa to cope with demand from visitors from around Australia and overseas:

> I should be nominated for a Noosa tourism award. Why wouldn't people who want cosmetic surgery come here, it's a fantastic destination and only makes sense to combine the two — surgery and holiday.

Tourism then is concerned with the "activities" of "people," as they "visit" different "places." Importantly, people not only include travellers, but also the travel trade at the origin and host destinations and residents of the host communities. Visiting encompasses involves travel by various modes while transiting and temporarily residing. Places include destinations at various levels from continents to visitor attractions. That there is no commonly accepted definition is neither problematic, nor unique to tourism (Leiper 1995). For the purpose of this text, no new definition is offered, other than to state an interest in:

> The activities of people, other than regular commuters, and the resultant impacts on both the demand and supply sides, while visiting places away from home.

Destination

Destinations are places that attract visitors for a temporary stay, and range from continents to countries to states and provinces to cities to villages to purpose built resort areas. At the foundation level destinations are essentially communities based on local government boundaries. With regard to the multidimensional nature of destinations, it has been suggested that the smaller the destination region, the greater the likelihood of internal homogeneity (Kelly & Nankervis 2001). Intuitively this appears logical since a town or city would likely be more compact and less geographically diverse than an entire country. However, a diversity of natural features and tourism facilities also represents both a strength and a challenge for many smaller regions. In fact, the RTO operating environment is a microcosm of that faced by NTOs. The WTO (2002a) think tank offered the following working definition of a "local tourism destination":

A local tourism destination is a physical space in which a visitor spends at least one overnight. It includes tourism products such as support services and attractions, and tourism resources within one day's return travel time. It has physical and administrative boundaries defining its management, and images and perceptions defining its market competitiveness. Local destinations incorporate various stakeholders often including a host community, and can nest and network to form larger destinations.

Logically, since the majority of tourism activity takes place at destinations, they can be described as:

... a place at which visitors temporarily base themselves to participate in tourism related activities or non-activities.

Marketing

Tourism features a negotiation between two forces — a supply-side and a demand-side (Murphy 1985). The supply-side is the travel and tourism industry, which seeks to stimulate demand for products and services. The demand-side represents consumer-travellers, who seek travel products and services to meet certain needs. Marketing is an exchange process between the two forces:

Marketing is a social and managerial process by which individuals and groups obtain what they need through creating and exchanging products and value with others (Kotler *et al.* 1999: 12).

What is not explicit in many definitions or discussion about marketing is whether marketing is a strategy, a series of processes, or a philosophy? Ideally marketing should be viewed as an organisational philosophy, not the sole responsibility of the marketing department. A market orientation should pervade the entire organisation. After all if a firm fails to sell its wares, there won't be any need for accountants or human resource managers, except to close the business. On this basis it could be argued that marketing is the most important function of organisations. Since the 1960s the "market concept" has dominated marketing thinking (Urde 1999). The focus in this approach is based on the principle of making decisions with the customer's needs in mind:

A marketing orientation is a philosophy that recognizes the achievement of organizational goals requires an understanding of the needs and wants of the target market, and then delivering satisfaction more effectively than rivals (Kotler *et al.* 2003).

This represents the third stage in the evolution of marketing by firms. Medlik and Middleton (1973) proposed tourism was following the traditional three stage process towards a market orientation, which had been experienced by other industries. The three stages were identified as:

- *Production orientation.* This stage is characterised by a shortage of available goods and services, and is therefore a seller's market. The main problem is to increase the output. Until the 1950s tourism was, in general, at this stage.
- *Selling orientation.* This occurs when technological progress enables mass production, leading to increased competition, lower prices and a supply in excess of demand. This is therefore a buyer's market with a sales orientation from the producer to sell the increased output. The development of wide bodied jets and large hotels in the 1960s and 1970s are examples of the second phase in tourism.
- *Marketing orientation.* Increased competition and sophistication of buyers in an affluent society leads to the recognition of the necessity to identify consumer needs. Selling will not be sufficient by itself since consumer needs become the starting point for what is produced. "Modern marketing is designed to achieve optimal satisfaction of the consumer and to do so at an appropriate return to the producer" (34). Tourism has been slow to achieve the full potential from moving from the selling orientation to a marketing orientation.

A fourth level that has since been introduced to the hierarchy is the societal marketing approach, which dictates a market orientation, but operationalised in a way that also considers the well being of society and the environment. DMOs, as representatives of a host community and natural environment as well as commercial tourism services, have such a wider societal obligation. Wahab *et al.* (1976: 24) offered the following definition of tourism destination marketing:

> The management process through which the National Tourist Organisations and/or tourist enterprises identify their selected tourists, actual and potential, communicate with them to ascertain and influence their wishes, needs, motivations, likes and dislikes, on local, regional, national and international levels, and to formulate and adapt their tourist products accordingly in view of achieving optimal tourist satisfaction thereby fulfilling their objectives.

In other words, for DMOs, marketing may be considered as representing:

> ...the process of matching destination resources with environment opportunities.

Organisations

Organisations have been defined as "formal entities in which a complex interaction of people, materials, and money is used for the creation and distribution of goods and services" (Inkson & Kolb 1998: 6). All organisations, whether in business, the public sector, or not-for-profit sector, share a common set of characteristics. Each usually has a set of objectives, a chairperson and governing board, a chief executive officer, and staff. The study of organisational behaviour emerged during the 1940s, and was primarily undertaken by psychologists interested with job satisfaction (Lawrence 1987, in Kolb *et al.* 1995). Since then the field has expanded to cover a broad range of macro and micro issues relating to the external and internal environments in which organisations operate, such as: productivity, ethics, open systems, strategic management, innovation, leadership, governance, organisational culture, change management, human resource management, outsourcing, communication, networks, and organisational learning.

At a country level there are often three quite distinctive types of tourism organisations with interests in destination tourism development. These are a destination marketing organisation (DMO) responsible for promotion, a government ministry providing policy advice to government, and a private sector umbrella industry association that champions the causes of member organisations. The focus of the text is on the activities of organisations responsible for marketing the destination. These most commonly include the following:

• Destination Marketing Organisation (DMO).

A destination marketing organisation is:

> Any organisation, at any level, which is responsible for the marketing of an identifiable destination. This therefore excludes separate government departments that are responsible for planning and policy.

• National Tourism Office (NTO).

The WTO (1979: ii) introduced the term national tourism administration (NTA) as: "the authorities in the central state administration, or other official organisation, in charge of tourism development at the national level." The term NTA was used to distinguish from national tourist organisation and national tourist office:

> ... to reflect the new concept of tourism management at national level and to stress that the majority of countries are moving away from the traditional system, where the national tourist organization is essentially a central publicity body, to the newer concept of a national tourism administration which sees promotion and marketing as one of many functions.

For consistency in the text, the term national tourism office (NTO) is used to represent:

> The entity with overall responsibility for marketing a country as a tourism destination, whether purely a DMO or an NTA.

• State Tourism Office (STO).

A state tourism office is:

> The organisation with overall responsibility for marketing a state (e.g. USA), province (e.g. Canada) or territory (e.g. Australia) as a tourism destination, in a country that has a federal political system.

* Regional Tourism Organisation (RTO).

The term "region" has a number of different meanings, ranging in geographic scope from a transnational area such as South East Asia to a local area. For the text the term is used to represent "concentrated tourism areas" (Prosser *et al.* 2000: 4), such as cities, towns, villages, coastal resort areas, islands and rural areas. This level of DMO is also known by other titles in different parts of the world, such as convention and visitor bureaus (CVBs) in the USA, regional tourism boards (RTBs) in the U.K. and area tourism boards (ATBs) in Scotland. Sheehan and Ritchie's (1997) survey of CVBs found host populations ranged from 50,000 to 1.5 million. In the U.K., Bramwell and Rawding (1994) reported the Birmingham RTO covered a geographic region of 25 miles around the city, while the Manchester RTO was established to market an area containing 10 district councils. Also, in some cases there may be more than one form of DMO operating within a city destination. In the U.K. for example, Bramwell and Rawding found Birmingham and Manchester both operated RTOs as well as local government tourism units. For the purpose of the text, a regional tourism organisation is defined as:

> The organisation responsible for marketing a concentrated tourism area as a tourism destination.

* Local Tourism Administration and Local Tourism Association (LTA).

Not all local tourism areas, as defined by a local authority boundary, have a stand alone RTO. Instead they may have an LTA, which is a term used to represent both a local tourism administration and a local tourism association. The former may be the local government authority, while the latter is a form of cooperative association of tourism businesses.

Position of the Author

The text has been motivated by first hand experience of the political and marketing challenges involved in marketing destinations at both the NTO and RTO levels. In January of 1989 I was allocated a desk and a phone in a quiet second floor corner of the Rotorua District Council's (RDC) Civic Centre, a local authority responsible for the public administration of one of New Zealand's leading tourism resort areas. A few months earlier, the board members of the district's poorly funded LTA, the Rotorua Promotions Society, had resigned en mass, effectively terminating a contract with the RDC to act as the DMO. RDC recognised the tourism community in Rotorua, for so long the flagship of New Zealand's tourism industry, was in crisis, and had committed to taking a more direct and proactive role in destination promotion. I had been employed, at age 28, to establish a new regional tourism organisation. Previously I had spent nine years with the New Zealand Tourism Department, in New Zealand and Australia.

My experience as the Tourism Rotorua CEO was never dull, due to local tourism industry politics and the challenges of marketing a multi-dimensional destination to a heterogeneous world. While the marketing challenges were exciting, the politics were frankly frustrating and boring. However, the two issues of marketing and politics are inextricably linked at the destination level. I recall the then Rotorua Mayor John Keaney counselling me that Rotorua tourism operators were like farmers, of which he was one, because they were "rugged individuals" with plenty of strong opinions. From experience I learnt that tourism operators are happy to be led during a crisis, but demand increasing involvement when progress is being made and the budget is increasing. The more operators are involved in destination marketing planning, the more they must be empowered in RTO decision-making. However, the more they are empowered the more bureaucratic the process, and the slower the decision making becomes. A fast moving entrepreneurial approach during a crisis (see Ateljevic & Doorne 2000) can evolve into a politically correct bureaucracy. This can in turn be a source of frustration for entrepreneurial RTO staff and the "rugged individuals" alike.

It would be an understatement to suggest the task of establishing the Rotorua RTO was recognised as representing a significant challenge. One senior airline official commented at the time: "If you can turn Rotorua around you will be able to write your own ticket!" With the benefit of hindsight, Wahab *et al.*'s (1976: 92) reflections on negative images were certainly appropriate in Rotorua's case:

> It is easy to downgrade a product or allow it to deteriorate; but it is the devil's own work to upgrade a low-image product.

Once proud Rotorua was suffering serious image problems, not only in the market place but within the host community. Aspects of the history leading to this crisis point have been reported previously (e.g. Ateljevic 1998; Ateljevic & Doorne 2000; Horn *et al.* 2000), and will be discussed in a section of the text addressing destination rejuvenation. One of the problems noted during my initial meetings with local industry groups was the disparate nature of the tourism community. In particular there was a strong feeling that RPS promotions had only focused on the larger tourism businesses, which were referred to as "the fat cats." The larger operators explained to me that since they contributed the majority of funding, it was only fair to expect more promotional exposure. It was also implied that any future destination promotions should continue to feature their product. Ironically, one of these businesses was from outside the district boundary, and therefore not a contributor to the local authority rates (tax) that funded the RTO. Another offered to provide a fund of $1,000 per month to the office to ensure their product featured in all destination advertising. I learnt from countless discussions with counterparts in New Zealand and overseas that this was certainly not a situation unique to Rotorua.

By the time I handed over the reins of the RTO, Tourism Rotorua (see www.rotoruanz.com), in 1996, the organisation had won two national tourism awards for "Best RTO." The office also won again in 1997 and became the first RTO to win a "distinction," which is granted to those organisations that have won an award category three times. Through a team effort between our staff and local tourism operators, Tourism Rotorua had progressed from being one of the lowest funded RTOs in New Zealand in 1989 to the best resourced in 1996.

Rotorua attracts approximately 1.3 million visitors each year, and tourism is the leading employer. This has always been a "tourist town," and most locals have an opinion on how tourism works, what the opportunities are, and how they should be delivered to the community. The range of RTO stakeholders is not therefore limited to those directly involved in the tourism industry. Everyone in Rotorua seems to knows someone in the tourism industry. In my case my mother Pearl worked at Rainbow Springs wildlife sanctuary for 30 years and my father-in-law Ben Hona has been the Kaumatua (elder) at the New Zealand Maori Arts and Crafts Institute since the early 1990s. I therefore felt it important to include this section to acknowledge the perspective from which I approached this text. I enjoyed 17 years experience as a tourism practitioner, in Australia and New Zealand, and have participated in destination promotions in North America, the Pacific, Asia and Europe. I have attempted to provide an objective analysis, but acknowledge that I have brought to the research my own experiences and potential biases.

I became an academic almost by accident. While completing an MBA as the Tourism Rotorua CEO I became impressed with the rich resource of information for destination marketers that existed in the literature, and I wondered why this was not being disseminated by academia to industry directly. I changed careers, became an academic, began consulting to RTOs, and completed a PhD in destination marketing. The text has therefore been written by someone who claims not to be an expert in the topic, but rather one who understands and appreciates, from experience, both sides of the "divide" — the perspectives of destination marketing "practitioners" and tourism academics.

While academic theory offers a wealth of opportunities for tourism practitioners, my own experience suggests that implementation for DMOs responsible for co-ordinating a diverse range of stakeholders in multiple markets is problematic. My interest in theory is motivated by the desire to identify practical solutions for DMOs. However, my recommendations to industry and students have always been made with the explicit acknowledgement that this is often "easier said than done."

Chapter 2

The Rationale for Destination Marketing Organisations

Chapter Perspective

Although the first DMOs were established over a century ago, most have only emerged in recent decades. While a myriad of private and public sector organisations have vested interests in different aspects of society relating to tourism, no other entity has such an active and holistic interest in the quality of the traveller experience, the host community's sense of place, and the profitability of tourism businesses. It is now difficult to imagine a tourism industry without DMOs. An important issue in the development of DMOs has been the role played by governments in their establishment, at national, state and local levels. While entrepreneurs in many areas have been catalysts for stimulating co-operative destination promotions, rarely have they become effective in the long term without government. A foundation of destination competitiveness is the establishment of a partnership approach between all those stakeholders with a vested interest in the impacts of temporary visitors.

A Brief History of DMO Development

National Tourism Offices

In the long history of tourism, the establishment of the New Zealand Department of Tourist and Health Resorts in February 1901, represented the world's first NTO (NZTPD 1976). This was a remarkably forward thinking initiative for a small, fledgling and far flung South Pacific colony, at a time when only four New Zealand towns had electricity. This was perhaps indicative of the type of creative thinking that Saatchi & Saatchi world-wide CEO Kevin Roberts referred to, at the 1999 New Zealand tourism conference, as being stimulated by the country's position "on the edge" of the world. Other examples of world tourism firsts for New Zealand include the first jet boat and first ski plane with retractable skies in the 1950s, and the first commercial bungee jump in the 1980s. New Zealand was also the first country to introduce government tourist bureaux (Coventry 2001), which were a combination of travel agent, tour wholesaler and visitor information centre. The first annual report of the New Zealand NTO, in July 1902, reported that tourist offices had been established in Auckland, Rotorua, Wellington, Christchurch and, perhaps surprisingly to anyone with a knowledge of New Zealand's major attractions, Invercargill:

As far as practicable these offices have been located in positions near the main business thoroughfares. They are intended primarily to afford information regarding New Zealand — such as where to go, when to go, how to go, what to pay — to all inquirers, whether residents in or tourists from outside the colony; particulars of hotel charges, routes, fares, time-tables, and other important matters in connection with travel being kept for the public benefit . . . the aim of the Department being to make them, as far as possible, bureaux of general information. The many thousands of inquiries which have been made at the various offices, both orally and in writing, show that they are filling the public requirement (New Zealand Department of Tourist and Health Resorts 1902: H-2).

In the first year of operation, the NTO received and dispatched 18,800 letters and distributed 4,300 pamphlets (TNZ 2001). However, the department's role was far more than promotion. One of the original aims was to stimulate the development of a New Zealand tourism industry. This was particularly pronounced in Rotorua, which had been identified as a potential tourism resort because of the district's geothermal resources and Maori culture. Central government funded almost everything concerned with the early development of Rotorua, with much of the work overseen by the Department of Tourist and Health Resorts. Indeed, under the Rotorua Town Bill of 1907, the town was to be managed by the department (Stafford 1986). In this regard it has been suggested Rotorua was the only town in the British Empire to have been completely controlled by central government (Braynart 1980). Rotorua did not have an independent local authority, devoid of government representatives, until 1950 (Stafford 1988; Tapsell 1972). During most of the 20th century, the government assumed wide-ranging responsibilities in the district, including: airports, drainage, water supply, roads, parks and gardens, railways, hotel development, spa facilities, electricity, visitor information, swimming pools, lake launches, deer and possum release, administration of Maori villages, licensing of tourist guides, development of the New Zealand Maori Arts and Crafts Institute, and geothermal tourist attractions. The first regional government tourist office was built in Rotorua, on the southern end of the district's current visitor information centre, and was funded and operated by the department for almost 90 years.

Overseas visitor arrival statistics in New Zealand were first recorded in 1903–04 (5,233 arrivals), and in 1906 the department opened an office in Australia (NZTPD 1976). The first overseas sales mission was a visit to the 1904 St. Louis Exposition, and by 1910 honorary agents had been appointed in England, USA, Canada and South Africa (TNZ 2001). Interestingly, it would be another fifty years before a national association of private sector tourism interests was formed in New Zealand (Staniford & Cheyne 1994).

In the century since its inception, New Zealand's NTO has undergone a number of name changes and restructures. The most significant was in 1991 when the department was disbanded and replaced by a private sector governed, but government owned, entity, the New Zealand Tourism Board. Under the provisions of the New Zealand Tourism Board Act (1991), the NTO was for the first time overseen by a board of private sector representatives who were appointed by, and responsible to, the Minister of Tourism. The NTO was later renamed Tourism New Zealand.

Disappointingly, the published literature on historical tourism is sparse, particularly in relation to the establishment of DMOs. However, what is evident from available information is that many nations did not establish an NTO until decades after New Zealand. For example, of the key international competitors to New Zealand for the European market, Australia's federal government became involved in tourism marketing for the first time in 1929 when a grant was provided to the newly formed Australian National Tourist Authority (Carroll 1991). Likewise the Canadian Bureau of Tourism was not established until 1934 (Go 1987; Jenkins 1995).

In Europe, the French NTO was established in 1910 (Sigaux 1966). By 1919, when the Italian NTO was established (Osti & Pechlaner 2001), the Alliance Internationale du Tourisme had been formed in Brussels, bringing together 30 European NTOs. In England, the government provided financial support for the 1929 establishment of the Travel Association of Great Britain and Ireland (Elliott 1997). However, the organisation was no more than embryonic until after World War Two when the publicly supported British Tourism and Holiday Board was formed in 1947 (Jeffries 1989). Predating this was the English Channel island of Jersey, where a tourism committee was empowered to promote the destination in 1937 (Cooper 1997). However, the first statutory legislation in Britain did not occur until The Development of Tourism Act of 1969 (English 2000). This legislation paved the way for the national tourist boards of Scotland, Wales and England, as well as the British Tourist Authority (BTA). Indeed it has been suggested that in Scotland, tourism was not seriously addressed until this time (Kerr & Wood 2000). Prior to this the Northern Ireland tourist board was established through the Development of Tourism Act of 1948 (Davidson & Maitland 1997). In a case of unfortunate timing, both the Irish Tourism Board and Belgium General Commission for Tourism were established in 1939 (WTO 1979).

Following World War II the International Union of Official Tourism Organizations (IUOTO), the predecessor of the WTO, had around 100 member NTOs in 1946 (Vellas & Bécherel 1995). In some countries no NTO existed until the 1950s, 1960s and 1970s. For example, in Asia the Hong Kong Tourism Association was established in 1957 (Gartrell 1994), with other NTO start-ups in the region including (Choy 1993): Japan and Thailand in 1959, and Singapore in 1964. In Africa the Ghana Tourist Board and Ivory Coast Ministry of Tourism were established in 1960, and the Nigerian Tourist Association was formed in 1962 (WTO 1979). Pearce (1996a) reported the first official NTO in Sweden was not established until 1976.

Interestingly, the government of one of the world's most popular destinations, the USA, did not become seriously involved in international tourism promotion until 1961 when the International Travel Act was passed by congress (Mill & Morrison 1985). This enabled the establishment of the United States Travel Service as a division of the Department of Commerce, which would later be changed to the U.S. Travel and Tourism Administration (USTTA). The main goal of the organisation was to help rectify the balance of international travel payments deficit. Edgell (1984) reported that while the United States National Tourism Policy Act (1981) created the USTTA as the NTO to develop increased international arrivals, the division had the smallest departmental budget with only US$8.1 million of a total departmental budget of almost US$2 billion, The USTTA also employed only 68 out of department's 35,000 employees. Morrison *et al.* (1998) observed CVBs such as Las Vegas had larger budgets. The USTTA folded in 1996 due to a lack of funding (Brewton &

Withiam 1998). Congress then established the National Tourism Organisation, a smaller organisation to encourage public/private sector cooperation, which was in turn scrapped (Blalock 2000). The USA became actively involved at a national level again in September 2003 with the formation of the new Tourism and Travel Promotion Advisory Board (Hoover 2003). Congress initially approved a budget of US$50 million for an international marketing campaign. The role of the new board would be to advise the Commerce Department on how the funds should be spent.

By 2004, WTO membership included 141 countries and seven territories (www.world-tourism.org/).

State Tourism Organisations

The Hawaii Visitors Bureau was established in 1903, following tourism promotional visits to the U.S. mainland in 1901 and 1902 by the Honolulu Chamber of Commerce and Merchants Association (Choy 1993). Most other American state tourism marketing did not occur until much later. Doering (1979) suggested that state tourism marketing offices were being established during the 1940s in anticipation of a post-war surge in domestic tourism. Of the then 48 states, 26 had become involved in tourism promotion by 1946. It would not be until the 1970s that all states had STOs. In Australia, the Queensland Tourist Development Board was established by the state government in 1946 to investigate and stimulate tourism development in the state (Craik 1991).

Regional Tourism Organisations

While Sheehan and Ritchie (1997) found respondent USA CVBS had been in existence only an average of 23 years, the reported history of regional tourism promotion significantly predates that for NTOs. For example, the first travel guidebook for Cambridge in England was published in 1758 (Davidson & Maitland 1997). In Switzerland, the first RTO was established at St. Moritz in 1864 (Lässer 2000). It has been suggested that the CVB format emanated from North America (Morrison *et al.* 1998), where the first was set up in Detroit in 1896 (Gartrell 1992). In 1920 the International Association of Convention Bureaus, later to become the International Association of Convention & Visitor Bureaus (IACVB — see www.iacvb.org) was formed with 28 CVB members (Gartrell 1992). Sheehan and Ritchie's (1997) survey of 134 North American CVBs identified 15 that had been in existence for over 50 years.

In the U.K., the Local Authorities (Publicity) Act (1931) permitted local government to engage in destination promotion (Lavery 1990). Following the establishment of the ETB in 1969, 12 English RTBs were created, jointly funded by the ETB, local government and private sector contributions (Davidson & Maitland 1997). Old industrial cities such as Bradford, Sheffield, Birmingham, and Manchester did not establish DMOs, either as units of council or RTOs, until the 1980s (Bramwell & Rawding 1994). Likewise, Davidson and Maitland reported the DMO for the remote rural North Pennines was not established until the 1980s, following identification of the region as a "tourism growth point" by the ETB.

Pearce (1996b) examined the emergence of regional tourism organisations in Spain, following the creation of 17 autonomous communities in the post-Franco era. Spain moved from a highly centralised state, with little regional public sector tourism involvement, to introduce the new tier of regional governments with responsibilities that included economic development and tourism. The new tier of government represented a new opportunity to develop regional tourism, although Pearce noted the move to establish regional tourism organisations had occurred only slowly since the 1980s.

In Australia, Dredge (2001) investigated aspects of the history of local government development in New South Wales to demonstrate that one of the key antecedents for local government involvement in tourism development in the state, had as much to do with the influence of "ideas, values, perceptions and beliefs developed over time, and which are deeply embedded in the institutions of local government" (357), as it was by legislative constraints. Dredge suggested councils were given legislative powers to develop leisure and recreation facilities as early as 1858, at a time when demand was increasing for such facilities by excursionists and holiday-makers, and by 1908 were given powers to stimulate tourism through advertising. However, for a number of reasons, including a legacy of paternalistic and centralised state government there has been, in general, a "timid approach" towards direct involvement in tourism development initiatives.

The Case for Government Intervention in Tourism

> Governments are a fact in tourism and in the modern world. The industry
> could not survive without them (Elliott 1997: 2).

While it has clearly been the private sector, led by entrepreneurs such as Thomas Cook, that has been responsible for the rapid growth of tourism, this would not have been possible without government support in the form of security, stimulation of increased affluence and leisure time, and infrastructure developments (Elliott 1997). Government intervention has since been necessary to guide the actions of both the private sector and the public sector (Mill & Morrison 1985). Mill & Morrison noted that in the USA during the 1980s there were over 150 government programmes across fifty departments that directly affected tourism. Such fragmentation clearly requires coordination. A 1982 report in the U.K. identified over seventy pieces of legislation that affected tourism (Jeffries 2001). However, it is not uncommon for those outside the tourism industry to question why taxpayers "subsidise" the tourism industry. A diverse range of groups can pose this challenge, from representatives of other industries such as horticultural/agricultural producer boards to retiree associations that have no vested interest in commerce. This issue has been a major hurdle for tourism interests in the USA, where a lack of Congress support for an NTO had been attributed to strong political views that this would represent "corporate welfare" (Gatty & Blalock 1997).

The globalisation of competition has impacted on the ability of democratic governments to provide traditional services, due to a resistance by residents to accept high tax levels (Wanhill 2000). Wanhill suggested there have been increasing calls for the public sector to focus on the core tasks required to operate in a market economy. These include the provision of essential services, assurance of macro environment stability and protection of the environment. Possible implications of this approach include a smaller state enterprise sector, the privatisation of infrastructure and a user-pays approach to the operation of museums and parks for example. Tourism would not usually be regarded as an essential government service such as health, education and security. However, at a local level at least, economic development initiatives are a key component of government attempts to adapt to changing conditions (Dredge 2001). From this perspective the stimulation of tourism, as a labour intensive industry, is a key economic development enabler. The industry can also be a source of increased tax revenue to help fund essential services. For example, the April 2003 newsletter of the Colorado Tourism Office reported the results of a study that estimated every advertising dollar spent by the STO generated US$12.74 in state taxes. In Florida, tourism generated US$51 billion in taxable sales during 2002, with the US$3.1 billion in tax representing 20% of the government's total sales tax take (Word 2003). Long's (1994) survey of over 100 British local authorities, which had an appointed tourist officer, regarded increased employment opportunities as the most important benefit of tourism for most councils. In addition to economic development opportunities, the case for government intervention in tourism may be made through the following:

- market failure
- provision of infrastructure
- fiscal revenue
- border controls
- spatial redistribution
- protection of resources
- regulatory safeguards
- exogenous events
- social benefits.

Tourism as an Enabler of Economic Growth

Opportunities exist even for the smallest communities to benefit from tourism as a vehicle for economical development. For example, Ioannides (2003) offered the examples of Pigeon Forge in Tennessee, Branson in Missouri, and Jackson in Wyoming, as places with populations of less than 5,000 that attract over five million tourists each year. Such economic growth opportunities have long been the prime motivation for government intervention in tourism. In the USA, almost every state offers economic incentives to attract industry investment (Hefner *et al.* 2001). In Australia, the enthusiastic endorsement of tourism in government policy documents has traditionally espoused the benefits of encouraging tourism solely on the grounds of economic benefits: "Other factors have been largely ignored or marginalised in the policy process (for example, environmental concerns)" (Craik 1991: 4).

In 1976, in a publication to mark the 75th anniversary of the establishment of the New Zealand Department of Tourist & Health Resorts, the then Minister of Tourism cited a pamphlet published 70 years previously by the *Herald* newspaper concerning the department:

> The whole colony shares in the benefits . . . accruing from the (department's) enterprise. For it is the instrument that is to bring us much wealth in the near future. And we must make the most of our priceless assets . . . our scenery, our spas, our climate. They are the richest and our most lasting gold-mine (NZTPD 1976: 1).

Following World War Two the U.S. Marshall programme to aid the economic development of Europe specifically referred to tourism as a dominant factor in economic revival (Elliott 1997). Indeed, the promotion of travel to Europe for Americans was designed to inject foreign exchange into Europe, which it was anticipated would in turn fund demand for USA products. The move did however lead to a travel receipts deficit for the USA. The creation of the USTTA was to offset the international travel deficit (Edgell 1984). Likewise, England's tourism balance of payments went from £3.2 billion in credit in 1990 to a £13.2 billion deficit in 2001 (TravelMole.com, 01/11/02). Interestingly however, the Japanese government, instigated a campaign encouraging more citizens to travel overseas in the early 1990s to counter a healthy international travel surplus.

Tourism has, in general, proved a stable investment vehicle, with overall global growth averaging 6% annually during the 1960s–1990s (Bull 1995). International tourism receipts grew faster than world trade during the 1980's, and by the 1990s constituted a higher proportion of the value of world exports than all sectors other than petroleum products and motor vehicles (WTO 1995). Also, for developing nations tourism has offered the advantage of being generally free of the artificial constraints of other export industries where import quotas and tariffs limit trade (Jenkins 1991).

One of the essential services for many governments is the stimulation of opportunities for the unemployed. Tourism as a service industry is labour intensive. For example, in the USA, tourism is the first, second or third largest employer in 32 states (Goeldner *et al.* 2000). Bradford became the first old industrial city to invest significant resources in destination marketing, when the city council's economic development unit initiated short break package promotion (Bramwell & Rawding 1994). During the mid-1980s the decline in traditional industries such as textiles had resulted in employment levels in parts of Bradford of up to 25% (Page 1986, in Davidson & Maitland 1997). Globally, tourism employment has been estimated at one in every 12 jobs, representing around 8% of all jobs (WTTC 2003). Table 1 highlights the ratio of full time equivalent jobs for a selection of macro regions, countries and communities.

Government recognition of the economic value of tourism activities to communities has to a large extent been responsible for the proliferation of DMOs world wide. As their title suggests, the focus of DMO operations is selling a place, with the desired end results being increases in visitor arrivals, length of stay and spending. The recognition that such increases lead to new job creation has seen tourism move from the shadows of fiscal policy to a place in centre stage (Hall 1998).

Table 1: The ratio of full time equivalent tourism jobs in the economy.

Destination	Ratio of Full Time Equivalent Tourism Jobs in the Economy (%)	Source
The World	8	WTTC (2003)
European Union	6	Akehurst, Bland & Nevin (1993), Jeffries (2001)
Central and Eastern Europe	12	WTTC/WEFA (1997, in Hall 2002)
Australia	6	Jenkins (1995)
England	7	Elliott (1997)
Scotland	8	Kerr & Wood (2000)
Wales	9	Shipton (1997, in Pritchard & Morgan 1998)
USA	6	Goeldner, Ritchie & McIntosh (2000)
Fiji	10	http://www.tcsp.com/invest/table_A2.shtml, viewed 25/3/04
New Zealand	9	Tourism Auckland (2002)
Cyprus	10	Ionnides & Apostolopoulos (1999)
Amsterdam, The Netherlands	6	Dahles (1998)
New Orleans, USA	16	Dimanche & Lepetic (1999)
Cambridge, England	6	Cambridge City Council (1995, in Davidson & Maitland 1997)
Isle of Thanet, England	15	Bishop Associates (1987, in Voase 2002)
Auckland, New Zealand	5	Tourism Auckland (2002)

Market Failure

The "one-industry" concept recognises that while businesses have individual goals, the success of the tourism industry relies on effective interrelationships between stakeholders to produce traveller satisfaction (Collier 1997). The assumption is that the traveller's perspective of a holiday, while made up of a composite of service encounters, is judged as a total experience (Medlik & Middleton 1973). At a destination level the implication is that poor service provision by one or more sectors of the community, which may or may not be directly involved in the tourism industry, may ultimately impact on the success of other suppliers. Clearly the need for a cooperative approach towards quality assurance, and stimulating a "cooperating to compete" philosophy/approach requires a champion with a holistic perspective. This is a challenge, since while there may be good vertical integration in tourism, there has been a general lack of horizontal co-ordination (Lickorish 1991). The argument that collaboration generates economic benefits for participants has been less accepted by tourism operators (Machiavelli 2001). Rather, Machiavelli suggests individual operators will tend to first consider the costs, rather than the benefits of collaboration. Poetschke (1995: 57–58) proposed the following benefits of a cooperative public-private sector cooperative tourist authority:

- reduced antagonism through representation of all stakeholders
- avoidance of duplication through enhanced communication channels between represented sectors
- combined areas of expertise, such as private sector efficiency and public sector holistic benefit seeking
- increased funding potential through the reduction in duplicated efforts as well as industry based taxes
- the creation of a win/win situation through an increase in industry profitability and ensuing increase in government tax revenue.

In New Zealand, Edlin (1999) cited a National Bank newsletter that presented a succinct argument for the government's financial support of the national tourist office. National Bank economists argued that offshore marketing was required to attract higher spending tourists, and suggested that an extra $10 million in offshore marketing spend could generate an extra 31,000 annual visitors spending $385 million a year. It was argued that without an NTO, market failure would result. In other words, if left to the tourism industry, the priority for individual businesses would to do what is best for their own operation.

What constitutes membership of the "tourism industry?" It is extremely difficult for tourism to adopt a cooperative producer board approach, such as is found in the horticulture and agriculture industries due to the difficulty in identifying those businesses that benefit from tourism spending. Since the vast majority tourism businesses are small businesses a vast pooling of resources would be required to achieve a reasonable destination marketing budget:

- In the U.K., over 75% of tourism businesses are small and medium sized enterprises (SMEs) with a turnover of less that £250,000 (Frisby 2002).
- In Europe, about 95% of tourism businesses employ less that 10 staff (Middleton 1998), and 96% of the 1.3 million hotels and restaurants have less that 9 employees (WTO 1997 in Jeffries 2001).
- The mean number of staff in Sweden's estimated 20,000 tourism businesses is 10 (Swedish Tourist Board 1990, in Pearce 1996a).
- An estimated 70% of accommodation houses in England have only 10 or fewer guest rooms (McIntyre 1995, in Davidson & Maitland 1997).
- Around 97% of USA travel businesses classified as small businesses (Jeffries 2001).

Would small tourism businesses survive against unfair competition from larger and better resourced operators without government intervention? Choy (1991) suggested the role of government intervention should be limited to focus on socially desirable outcomes that would not otherwise occur through market forces. From a case study analysis of tourism destination planning in the South Pacific, Choy found government planning was concerned primarily with economic issues. However, since so many tourism plans in the region had failed to meet expectations, Choy (328) questioned the very need for destination planning:

> In the final analysis, market forces still prevail in determining the actual level of tourism development. Government tourism planning may thus have served as a means of initiating development but it has limited effects in influencing the growth and pattern of development.

Stimulated by the decline in oil prices in the 1980s and a peace accord with Israel in the early 1990s, tourism was promoted in Jordan as the panacea to that country's economic woes (Hazbun 2000). Tourism would be "the oil of the Jordanian economy." However, Hazbun warned of the danger of false expectations created by unrealistic or overly optimistic projections by the Jordanian state. Jordan, which relied on Arab aid and remittances from expatriates abroad, announced ambitious plans to encourage private sector tourism developments. The strategy was to stimulate a rush of investment in mega projects, such as 30,000 new hotel beds in the Dead Sea area by 2010, to overcome the "low equilibrium trap" of low visitors arrivals generating little revenue for future tourism development. One of the results of this was a 68% increase in hotel beds during the period 1993–1996. However, by 1997 hotel occupancy rates had decreased to only 38%. Khouri (1998, in Hazbun 2000: 195) cited a Jordanian economist:

> Hotels, tourist buses and travel agencies are real and sad examples of how parts of the economy went on an investment binge in 1995, only to come down to earth with a thud a year later and then start to wallow in a depression which continues.

One of the problems with Jordan's "big push" in stimulating new tourism developments and infrastructure, was a failure to balance this with adequate initiatives to stimulate increased demand for the new products (Hazbun 2000). Part of the problem was a lack of public or private promotional organisations, resulting in a lack of information flow and cooperation between individual tourism businesses. The need for coordination applies to tourism more so than any other economic or social activity, and only governments can undertake such a coordinating role (WTO 1983a).

Torbay, an English seaside destination, is a useful example of the importance of government intervention in tourism. English's (2000) case study presented a snap shot of many of the issues discussed in this chapter. Torbay has been promoted as the English Riviera in reference to its picturesque bay and resort towns. The area suffered a decline in popularity from the 1970s due to the increased affordability and availability of European holiday packages. Tourism has a significant economic impact on the area with an estimated 16,000 people employed in the local tourism industry. English cited a leading local official to highlight the need for government intervention: "We all know the story of Torbay's decline but its trying to persuade Government that we suffer measurable deprivation that's the big challenge" (p. 91). There was a lack of direct involvement by central government, and poor communication between the regional tourism board and local operators. English's synopsis (96) provides sobering reading for one of Britain's leading resort areas, where tourism is the core industry, where standards are declining and where strong government leadership is lacking:

> Many tourism providers are trying to be all things to all people, and the result is often a lower standard of experience for the tourist. In Torbay the major problem is a lack of professionalism and the belief that they do not need help. Many come to the industry with no prior background or training and very little knowledge . . . Many providers only think short term, few have business plans or tourism development strategies and these are major failings that result in a lack of professionalism. Businesses also feel they are only in competition locally and do not see the broader U.K. or even European and world-wide perspectives and thus do not work together. On the whole few seem to be investing for long term benefits and standards vary considerably. This research has shown that many supporting the industry would like to see more Government involvement and feel that Government has an important leadership and co-ordination role to play.

Provision of Infrastructure

WTO's (1979) survey of NTAs found 41 that were directly responsible for investment funds for financing the development of tourism facilities. Such funds were used to provide loans to both public and private sector organisations for projects such as hotels and restaurants. Forty four NTAs were responsible for the development and operation of hotels, 28 were responsible for operating travel agencies, and 22 were responsible for transport companies. In countries where tourism is a fledgling industry, government support is required to help develop commercial viability (Akehurst *et al.* 1993). However, there are essentially two key arguments against public funding involvement in the support of commercial tourism development (Bull 1995). Firstly, such investments may distort markets. This may occur when a project would not ordinarily succeed in a free market, and the net welfare benefits such as employment creation are used to support commercial inefficiencies. Also, larger entities may receive a larger share of resources. Secondly, the subsidies may ultimately benefit visitors rather than suppliers through lower tariffs. Bull pointed out that this may not be an issue for domestic tourism, but that in such cases governments may in effect unintentionally subsidise international visitors.

Traditionally, governments have been responsible for the development of infrastructure to enable tourism, such as utilities, sewerage, cleaning, health and fixed communication and transport facilities (Bull 1995). In 2003 the first annual Africa tourism investment summit was announced by the Ugandan minister of tourism (TravelMole.com, 23/7/03). One of the principle aims of the forum was to promote infrastructure development, in a continent that was attracting only 2% of global tourism spending. Hazbun (2000) reported the difficulty faced by Jordan in attracting visitors prior to the 1990s, due in the main to a lack of infrastructure, accessibility and attractions. Poor quality infrastructure has also been one of the major challenges to overcome for destinations in Eastern Europe (Davidson 1992). Countries in Eastern Europe have relaxed foreign investment regulations since the 1980s in an effort to attract more capital from the west. As a result, many international hotel chains were able to establish joint venture operations with the state. During 2003 the Albanian government began an ambitious development tourism redevelopment programme in a bid to appeal to international visitors, according to a report in *The Guardian* (www.TravelMole.com, 23/6/03). The government organised the demolition of run down buildings along the best beaches, which would be replaced with 5-star accommodation developments. The country's minister of tourism acknowledged only Kosovans were willing to put up with the poor roads and other inconveniences of travelling within Albania: "To attract others, updating our coastline is an absolute priority." The report stated that of the country's 2002 international visitor arrivals, 230,000 were from Kosovo, and only 2,000 were from the rest of Europe. Apparently hundreds of illegally erected kiosks, shops and hotels did not have access to water and sewerage facilities (Brown 2003).

Fiscal Revenue

> As a government has no money of its own, the more it can collect in taxes from profitable businesses in tourism the more it can then afford to spend on creating the social, environmental and economic climate within which these businesses can flourish (Owen 1992: 358).

As well as the community benefits of increased employment, government also seeks a revenue tax base to fund essential services. Tourism provides significant tax opportunities for governments at all levels. For example, in 1995, total USA tourism related taxes at federal, state and local levels was estimated at US$64 billion (Brewton & Withiam 1998). Nevertheless, Kubiak (2002), a senior policy advisor to the Southern Governors' Association in the USA, suggested the potential of tourism as an economic enabler had been underestimated by state governments, and questioned why more had not been done to promote the benefits offered by tourism. Kubiak (19) referred to tourism as the "red-headed step-child" of state government policy makers. Wason (1998) also expressed surprise that the potential of tourism as a contributor to taxation income had been either unrecognised or ignored by many governments. Wason attributed this to the relatively recent emergence of tourism and the complexity of the tourism industry structure. However, there is a paradox in the balance between Government realisation of tourism's economic development potential vs. tourism as an easy target for taxes. While tourists are a valuable part of the tax base, they are not voters (Wanhill 2000).

Taxes on tourism may be used to provide funding for the industry and/or for general revenue. Most commonly, taxes are in the form of user-pays charges, as a percentage of price. In some cases the tax is levied across most goods and services, such as the Goods and Services Tax (GST) in Australia and New Zealand. In other cases there may be a special tax on specific services such as accommodation. Often this contribution from tourism goes into the government's consolidated fund rather than dedicated to tourism, much to the ire of the tourism industry. Links between the collection of taxation from the tourism industry and government spending in the sector are rare (Bull 1995). For example, the Hawaii state government introduced a 5% room tax in 1986, with all revenue allocated to the state general fund rather than to the HVB (Bonham & Mak 1996). In other cases a bed tax is used as a dedicated destination marketing fundraiser. For example, the Tokyo metropolitan government collected a bed tax that provides revenue solely for tourism promotion (*The Daily Yomiuri*, viewed online at www.yomiuri.co.jp, 11/8/03). While it could be argued that these are a levy on consumers, the tax is collected by tourism operators who must decide whether it is feasible to pass it on to the consumer (Bull 1995).

Taxes also commonly target international travellers at gateways, such as airport departure fees. Bull (1995) estimated that by 1994 for example, 110 of the world's 180 countries applied a departure tax. Bull also offered the cases of Paraguay and Venezuela as countries that apply an arrivals tax. In other cases revenue may be raised through visa application fees. Other examples include admission to national and forest parks and marine reserves. Such "tourist taxes" to help pay for their use of public amenities (Wanhill 2000).

Another form of tourism tax is a levy on businesses. This can be used as an effective means of raising revenue for RTOs, as an alternative to funding through the general household tax or rates base, or through industry subscriptions. The efficacy of this approach has been demonstrated in smaller resort areas where tourism has a high profile. Examples include the New Zealand resort destinations of Lake Taupo and Queenstown. The local authority charges a levy to all local businesses, thereby avoiding the challenge of defining "tourism businesses," at a percentage rate of the business' capital value. The mechanism provides the main source of funds for the RTOs in both areas. Another example is Monaco, which with no income taxes relies to a large extent on levy fees of casinos for example (Bull 1995).

Not surprisingly, tourism taxes are often controversial. Internet news wire service TravelMole.com (10/6/03) reported news from Spain and England about a controversial eco-tax, introduced in May 2003 in Spain's Balearic Islands, which was in danger of being scrapped one year later. The purpose of the tax was to offset environmental damage caused by tourism. At the same time as the levy was imposed however, visitor numbers declined significantly, The report cited the spokespersons from the Federation of Tour Operators and the *Majorca Daily News* who suggested strongly that the tax had made a significant negative impact on the affordability of the islands.

Border Controls

One of the most obvious aspects of tourism is that so much travel crosses national borders. As a result, governments have been forced to develop policies for entry and exit by residents and visitors. At the 2003 IACVB convention chairman Rick Antonson lamented the USA's new visa programme was putting off travel to that country (Travelwire News, 4/8/03). Security issues aside, in many cases coordination between tourism policy and immigration policy has resulted in visa regulations that are designed to enhance international visitor arrivals. For example, a new visa regulation introduced by Oman in 2003 was promoted by officials as a measure to boost tourism to the Gulf nation (Rahman 2003). Also, many countries have been lobbying emerging outbound giant China for Approved Destination Status (ADS).

For example, Cuba became the first Western Hemisphere to gain ADS during 2003 (Xinhua News Agency 2003). At the time of writing, 28 countries had achieved ADS (*Inside Tourism*, IT484, 4/2/04).

Spatial Redistribution

Using a combination of taxation and spending, it is possible for governments to use redistribution policies that spread economic benefits throughout the economy (Bull 1995). For example Malaysia, Italy, Thailand and the U.K. have used regionally-variable taxation and developments grants. The stimulation of domestic tourism also represents an opportunity to redistribute economic benefits. This might be particularly necessary in developing countries where the private sector does not invest in domestic markets due to the low incomes of the host population (WTO 1983b). However, WTO also suggested that the government will usually be more interested in attracting the "hard cash" of currency from overseas visitors. The imbalance of the London-centric nature of British inbound tourism has long been controversial in Britain for example (Jeffries 1989). Around two thirds of all holiday visitors to Britain arrive in London (Bowes 1990). The government did establish a grant scheme to stimulate new tourism projects in 1969 and provide assistance to poorer regions (Elliott 1997). While the grants were ceased in England in 1989 they were continued in Wales and Scotland to assist deprived areas. Other notable examples of spatial redistribution policies to improve regional economic opportunities by government are the Languedoc Roussillon development in France (see de Haan *et al.* 1990; Jeffries 2001), Cancun in Mexico (Jeffries 2001) and Korea's Cheju Island (Jeffries 2001).

Protection of Resources

A successful destination is one that: (i) provides a satisfactory visitor experience; (ii) maintains or improves local residents' quality of life; (iii) protects the environment; and (iv) generates profits for commercial operations (Davidson & Maitland 1997: 2). The rationale for sustainable development planning is that the tourist experience is the central element in the tourism market (Hall 1998). The experiences of tourists influence future travel:

> Therefore it becomes imperative that the tourist experience and the tourism industry is sustainable and does not damage the capacity of the physical, social and economic environment to absorb tourism (Hall 1998: 18).

There has been increasing conflict between the tourism industry and the conservation movement (Carroll 1991). Importantly, a completely free market environment may not be congruent with a nation or community's wider interests such as the protection of the environment and public goods (Jeffries 2001). For example, would an unfettered tourism industry ensure all members of the host and visiting community retained access to natural features such as beaches and rivers? Would unrestricted access to such assets by private sector developers place an undue strain on public sector infrastructure responsibilities?

Could we rely on all entrepreneurs to adopt sustainable resource practises without government intervention? This conflict has played a role in stimulating government policies relating to the protection of natural resources for sustainable use.

In recent years there has been increasing realisation that tourism depends on the protection of environmental and community resources. The concept of "sustainable tourism," albeit a term that is regarded as an oxymoron, has undeniably emerged as one of the hottest topics in tourism planning. There has been increasing criticism about the negative impacts of tourism on societies and environments (Elliott 1997). Problems include the pressure of mass tourism on communities, natural and built environments and infrastructure; lack of control over tourist developments; and lack of controls over sex tourism. Government intervention is required to identify solutions that are in the public interest. Examples of government leadership in environmental protection have included:

- the 1887 establishment of the Rocky Mountains Park by the Canadian federal government, to protect Banff National Park (Go 1987).
- the establishment of the world's first national parks in the USA in 1872 (Elliott 1997) and New Zealand in 1903.
- Hawaii's Land Use Law of 1961 in the face of rapid tourism developments (National Tourism Resources Review Commission 1973, in Doering 1979).

Regulatory Safeguards

Key reasons for government policies relating to regulatory safeguards are concerned with economic controls, consumer protection and orderly markets (Bull 1995). Economic controls impact on international travel where a generating country might impose restrictions on the export of the local currency or regulations concerning tax deductibility for business travel. Bull also suggested that in 1994 there were at least 17 countries where compulsory currency exchange regulations were used. In such cases international visitors are forced to exchange a minimum daily quota of currency. Consumer protection areas include the licensing and bonding of goods and services providers and accommodation classification systems and the fulfilment of contracts. As temporary residents of a community, travellers also have a right to expect protection from unfair practises and to safe passage.

Exogenous Events

An emerging area of interest in the tourism literature is the issue of disasters and their impacts on the tourism industry, both at a global and local level. Swift decisions must be made in times of crisis (Elliott 1997). Such decision making and resultant responses should also be of a cooperative nature and therefore coordinated. Individual businesses are at the mercy of exogenous events, but few have the resources individually to engage in strategic planning for crises, particularly at a destination level. The government therefore has a vested interest in ensuring adequate leadership.

Social Benefits

> The Manila Declaration, recognizing that "world tourism can be a vital
> force for world peace" and "can contribute to the establishment of a
> new international economic order", drew the attention of the international
> community to the fact that tourism can flourish only if is based on equity,
> sovereign equality and cooperation among states (WTO 1983b: 2).

A key factor in the rise of tourism during the 1950s and 1960s was the introduction of
the social policy of leave with pay from work (WTO 1983b: 3). The ensuing growth in,
and diversity of, the demand for tourism led to increased industry calls for government
policies and funding: "Tourism was crying out for policies and ever-increasing funds,
and so state participation became a necessity." Jeffries (2001) referred to research by
Cadieu (1999), which recorded French government initiatives in the 1930s to promote
social tourism through publicly subsidised holiday for low income earners as part of a
welfare programme. Cooper *et al.* (1993) reported on Welsh plans to develop tourism in
ways that would optimise the social and economic benefits. Long's (1994) survey of British
local authorities found that, after increased employment opportunities, the social benefits of
an increase in the range and quality of facilities, services and events designed for the visitor
industry, was the next most cited benefit of tourism development in their community. Long
also found tourism was a source of enhancing local pride in the community. Likewise,
Bramwell and Rawding (1994: 430) cited the head of the Manchester City Council
tourism section:

> Tourism can make the city a better place to live, visit, work and invest in and
> so the standard of living goes up, and the quality of life improves and the
> profile of the city is raised, and (this process) goes round in a circle.

The Manila Declaration at the 1980 World Tourism Conference promoted social tourism,
in the interests of the least privileged in society, as a key objective in guaranteeing a more
widespread access to rest and tourism:

> The State should take a series of measures to channel tourism investment
> towards the development of low-cost plant that is more accessible to low
> income groups (WTO 1993: 13).

Tourism can bring a number of social benefits to a community. WTO (1983b) analysed the
social effects of domestic tourism, on the basis that 80% of the world's tourism movements
were domestic at that time. The study broke new ground in terms of addressing the social
costs and benefits of tourism. The following socio-cultural benefits from domestic tourism
at a national level were proposed (7–8):

- contact among people from different regions stimulates socio-cultural integration at a
  national level
- socio-cultural integration foster national identity and pride

- stimulation of educational diversification, in terms of learning national values
- travel stimulates progress and modernity
- increased travel opportunities lead to quality of life enhancement.

WTO (1983b) suggested the following socio-cultural benefits of domestic tourism at a local level (9–10):

- rural areas develop urban infrastructure facilities, medical care and education
- tourism income leads to the development of a middle class
- family relations change as a result of increased employment opportunities and therefore economic independence for the younger generation
- local cultural values, customs, arts and monuments can be revitalised
- increased contact with visitors broadens the mind of locals.

The Case Against Government Funding of Tourism

> Typically, with many other calls on the government's budget, treasury officials are naturally parsimonious with regard to expenditure on marketing because of difficulties in measuring effectiveness and they like to encourage co-operative ventures with the private sector (Wanhill 2000: 231).

Not all governments have a vested interest in tourism. For example, Long's (1994) survey of over 100 British local authorities that had a tourist officer, found 5% viewed tourism as unimportant, and therefore did not have a specific tourism strategy. One local authority respondent stated: "It is viewed as a non-essential service. This is a Green Belt area and no tourism development is permitted" (18). Even though few countries are self sufficient, and therefore require foreign exchange earnings to purchase necessary imports, not all have embraced the idea of an international tourism trade. Historically, authoritarian regimes have either banned tourism or tightly controlled it (Gartner 1996). While a full discussion on the negative impacts of tourism is beyond the scope of the text, it is important to acknowledge there are often strong arguments by members of society against tourism. Students of destination marketing should be aware of the nature of these points of view to develop a balanced perspective. In this regard, readers are referred to Roper (2001) for a comprehensive discussion on the arguments against tourism. Roper summarised these points of view as primarily falling into the following six categories:

- *A dislike of strangers and xenophobia.* While such views are probably in the minority, there are many closed societies where outsiders are not welcome. Roper cited the Hawaiian island of Ni'ihau as an example of a destination virtually off limits to tourists. Other examples include towns and rural communities that are the base for religious sects such the Jews of Mea Sharim in Israel and the Amish of Ohio.
- *Changes to the character of the destination.* The character of a destination and it's people can be negatively affected by the very people who come to experience it. The number,

characteristics, morality and behaviour of visitors can spoilt the very nature of what attracted interest in the first place.

- *Negative social and cultural impacts.* New visitors not only bring money into a destination, but they can also bring crime, ideas that create disharmony and envy among the host community. To cater to the entertainment tastes of mass tourists, traditional cultures have been replaced with ersatz rituals.
- *Economic damage.* Critics of tourism argue the majority of jobs are low paid and servile in nature, and that most of the profits flow out of the community to outside investors.
- *Negative environmental impacts.* Tourism developments have been the cause of damage to the environment. Also, ironically, increasing numbers of "eco-tourists" are spoiling the very serenity of the nature they seek to enjoy.
- *Colonialism or external control.* It has been argued that tourism is the new form of colonialism, and is even more powerful than any imperial power.

One of the problems with destination marketing is that it has been difficult to actually quantify the contribution of DMO efforts to the overall success of the destination. The lack of such data rightly leaves the industry open to attack from politicians and other industries seeking justification for funding from the public purse. For example, in the late 1980s, a British government review of the BTA examined the extent to which the private sector should be responsible for overseas marketing. Jeffries (1989: 75) cited the then minister responsible as stating the government's wish was "to see such activities carried out in the private sector wherever possible."

As discussed, the USA has traditionally adopted a non-interventionist approach to tourism destination marketing at a national level. However, it has been suggested that any criticism of the devolvement of NTO activities to the states should first consider the significant federal resources committed to the protection of recreation resources such as the National Park Service, the Fish and Wildlife Service, the Forest Service and the Bureau of Land Management (Jeffries 2001). In a few cases state governments have adopted a similar stance to the federal government, such as in Colorado, California and Maine. In 1976, California and Maine closed their tourism marketing offices, although California had reinstated the office in 1978, albeit with almost the lowest budget in the USA (Doering 1979: 312):

> Apparently the prevailing sentiment in California is that since the state is already the nation's leading trip destination, there is little reason for additional state travel marketing, especially when attractions such as Yosemite National Park are already overcrowded.

California, the world's fifth largest economy, and home to such globally recognised tourism icons as Disneyland and Hollywood, is not clear of the problem. In 2003 the then governor of California had proposed the state tourism office be closed as a cost saving measure. The STO had a $7.5 million budget and at the time California faced a $35 billion shortfall (*Inbound*, 13 January 2003: 1). When Colorado abolished the state's DMO in 1993, the state became the only one that did not have a travel office (Bonham & Mak 1996). Bonham and Mak cited a *Wall Street Journal* article entitled "Paying for Tourism," which promoted the view that the private sector was better equipped for tourism promotion. Interestingly, at the time tourism was the state's second largest industry, worth an estimated $6.4 billion annually (La Page *et al*. 1995). Donnelly & Vaske (1997) suggested the effects in the market place were significant, citing estimates that Colorado slipped from 3rd to 17th in terms of traveller recognition of state destinations, and pleasure travellers decreasing by up to 10%.

Chapter Key Point Summary

Key Point 1— Proliferation of DMOs

DMOs have been around for over a century. The first RTO was established in the 19th century and the first NTO at the beginning of the 20th century. Most, however, have been established relatively recently. Recognition of the positive impacts of tourism, and the need for a coordinated destination promotion effort, has led to a proliferation of DMOs world wide.

Key Point 2 — Government Intervention in Tourism

Governments generally interact with tourism in the following ways: stimulating economic growth, provision of infrastructure, fiscal revenue, border controls, spatial redistribution, protection of resources, regulatory safeguards, managing of exogenous events, stimulating social benefits, and minimising market failure. Effectively attaining these benefits requires significant levels of cooperation and coordination. Coordination is required within and between government departments, within industry and between government and industry. Only governments can provide such coordination through their access to taxation revenue and ability to legislate. Many DMOs, at national, state and local levels, would simply not be able to function in their current form without the resources of government.

Additional Reading

Bull, A. (1995). *The economics of travel and tourism* (2nd ed). Melbourne: Longman.
Elliott, J. (1997). *Tourism: Politics and public sector management*. London: Routledge.
Hall, C. M. (1994). *Tourism and politics: Policy, power and place*. Chichester: Wiley.
Jeffries, D. (2001). *Governments and tourism*. Oxford: Butterworth-Heinemann.
Wason, G. (1998). Taxation and tourism. *Travel & Tourism Analyst, 2,* 77–95.

Chapter 3

DMO Roles and Structure

> The continual stream of great products and services from highly visionary companies stems from them being outstanding organizations, not the other way around (Collins & Porras 1997: 31).

Chapter Perspective

Ultimately, the role of a DMO must be to enhance the long term competitiveness of the destination. In terms of being organised for this quest it is worthwhile considering whether good strategy emerges from an effective organisational structure, or whether organisations should be structured to implement an innovative strategy. After all, being organised will increasingly be the basis for gaining competitive advantage in the future (Galbraith & Lawler 1993). The management literature is divided on the issue on the relationship between structure and strategy. On one hand there is the view (e.g. Treacy & Wiersema 1995) that strategy is paramount, and therefore structure, processes and culture should be designed to enable it. On the other hand is the view that a value oriented organisation is first required to underpin the development of an effective strategy (e.g. Collins & Porras 1997). There are two organisation routes for existing DMOs. The first option is to make changes to the existing structure to enable a new strategic direction. However, restructuring is challenging for any organisation, and DMOs have the added dimensions of the local tourism industry and the local political environment to contend with. A second and more pragmatic course is to ensure the strategy realistically fits the existing structure. However there has been little research into the relationships between organisation, strategy and effectiveness of DMOs to guide destination marketers on effective organisation. Indeed there has been little published at all about the structure and roles of NTOs (Choy 1993; Morrison *et al.* 1995). What is apparent is that no universally accepted model for NTO structure currently exists. This is evidenced by the great variety in existence:

> This variety is reflected in different organizational names (eg authorities, commissions, boards, tourist organizations, bureaux, tourist offices, corporations, departments, councils, ministries, etc), relationships to national governments, budget levels, tourism policies, goals, objectives, responsibilities and foreign office locations. It is clear that no typical 'model' for and NTO can be suggested because of the great diversity that there is in existing organizational types (Morrison *et al.* 1995: 606).

At the RTO level, different models exist in different countries. In some cases a system is imposed from the national or state level, such as in England and in Queensland, Australia. The incentive for regions to participate is usually access to government funding. In other cases, such as in Sweden (see Pearce 1996a) and in New Zealand, regions are free to establish, or not establish, any RTO structure desired. Little or no financial support is available from central government, and RTOs will be at the mercy of their local government for contributions. A hybrid of these approaches is also evident. For example, in Scotland the Area Tourist Boards are statutory bodies, coming under the control of the Scottish Tourism Board (Kerr & Wood 2000). However they do not receive statutory funding, relying instead on grants from the STB and local government. Some RTOs have been based on a single county, such as in Sweden, while others based on macro regions such in Wales. What emerges from an analysis of DMO evolution is a general shift that has taken place, with DMOs' moving from bureaucratic government departments to more entrepreneurial and accountable private-public partnerships (PPPs). Such PPPs represent a maturing in attitudes of both the public and private sectors.

Destination Competitiveness

The purpose of any DMO is to foster sustained destination competitiveness. For many destinations maintaining competitiveness is now a major challenge (WTTC 2001, in Australian Department of Industry, Tourism & Resources 2001). While destination competitiveness has been described as "tourism's holy grail" (Ritchie & Crouch 2000a), this field of research has only emerged since the 1990s. Leading academic journal *Tourism Management* devoted a special issue to "The Competitive Destination" (see Vol. 21, Issue 1 2000). The range of topics covered in this issue demonstrate the complexity associated with the analysis of destination competitiveness:

- sustainable competitiveness (Ritchie & Crouch 2000b)
- price competitiveness (Dwyer *et al.* 2000)
- managed destinations (d'Hauteserre 2000)
- responding to competition (Kim *et al.* 2000)
- the destination product and its impact on traveller perceptions (Murphy *et al.* 2000)
- the role of public transport in destination development (Prideaux 2000)
- environmental management (Mihali 2000)
- integrated quality management (Go & Govers 2000)
- regional positioning (Uysal *et al.* 2000)
- marketing the competitive destination of the future (Buhalis 2000).

Also, an issue on tourism and travel competitiveness in *Tourism* (see Vol. 47, Issue 4 1999) featured three papers at the destination level: Price competitiveness (Dwyer *et al.* 1999), the role of Spanish public administrations (Pedro Bueno 1999) and the competitiveness of alpine destinations (Pechlaner 1999).

In the pursuit of destination competitiveness it has only been relatively recently that DMOs have begun to develop coordinated tourism strategies. For example the need for an industry-wide tourism strategy has been called for in many countries in recent years, including Scandinavia (Flagestad & Hope 2001), Canada (Go 1987), New Zealand (NZTP 1989; OTSP 2001), USA (Ahmed & Krohn 1990), Central and Eastern Europe (Hall 1999) and Australia in the federal government's 2004 white paper (see http://www.atc.net.au/aboutus.asp?sub=1twp, accessed 24/4/04). Leslie (1999: 40) criticised the then Northern Ireland Tourist Board for a lack of long term strategic planning, which had resulted in the destination losing touch with changing patterns of demand:

> For those involved, to consider publicly that the troubles have masked attention to significant underlying trends counteracting demand for the province would not only bring into question their personal role and job but also that of the value of the organization.

The WTTC recently developed a destination competitiveness index, in conjunction with the Christel de Haan Tourism and Travel Research Institute at the University of Nottingham (see www.wttc.org). The purpose is to track the extent that each of over 200 countries provides a competitive environment for travel and tourism development. The data is summarised through a traffic light colour coded system for each country across eight indices. These are intended to provide a measure out of 100 that is relative to the other countries rather than one that is absolute. Green, amber and red lights indicate above average, average and below average performance. For example, the assessments for Australia and China are compared in Table 1. It can be seen that Australia is judged a world leader in terms of infrastructure, technology, human resources and social, but lags in a number of areas such as price competitiveness and openness. China on the other hand is regarded as a leader in price competitiveness but falls short in areas such as environment, openness and human tourism.

An important question raised by Ritchie & Crouch (2000a) was whether destination "stars" were made or born. They offered the example of Russia, well endowed with natural resources but lacking in deployment, in comparison to destinations such as Singapore, Las Vegas, Branson and San Antonio, all of which had developed successful tourism

Table 1: WTTC competitive indices for Australia and China.

Index	Australia Index Value	China Index Value	Australia Rank	China Rank
Price competitiveness	35 (red)	89 (green)	95	3
Human tourism	32 (red)	9 (red)	68	107
Infrastructure	100 (green)	34 (red)	1	93
Environment	60 (orange)	38 (orange)	42	133
Technology	100 (green)	51 (orange)	24	93
Human resources	100 (green)	50 (orange)	1	82
Openness	56 (orange)	35 (red)	89	127
Social	96 (green)	53 (green)	6	93

strategies with limited endowed resources. Ritchie & Crouch suggested an understanding of success drivers was of fundamental importance, and categorised these into resources that would represent sources of either comparative or competitive advantage. Endowed resources inherited by a destination, such as climate and scenery, are categorised as sources of *comparative advantage*. However, resources created by the destination, which may be the way in which endowed resources are deployed in the market, represent sources of *competitive advantage*. An example of this was provided by Dascalu (1997), who cited comments from a former Romanian Minister of Tourism concerned that his country had enormous tourism resources but that the tourism industry was under-performing. These resources may represent sources of comparative advantage but were not being used to achieve a competitive advantage.

Competitive advantage is expressed in terms of competitors and customers. Porter (1980) suggested a competitive strategy was one that positioned a business to make the most of strengths that differentiated the organisation from competitors. A firm's success is ultimately achieved through "attaining a competitive position or a series of competitive positions that lead to superior and sustainable financial performance" (Porter 1991: 96). A sustainable competitive advantage (SCA) is gained when consumers perceive a performance capability gap that endures over time (Coyne 1986). Coyne suggested that to gain an advantage the gap must be through a product attribute that represents a key buying criterion, which was not offset by a negative performance on another attribute. Barney (1991, 1996) developed the VRIO model as a tool for determining the competitive status of resources controlled by a firm. The model was based on the assumption that resources are heterogeneous and immobile across firms. Heterogeneity means organisations are not created equal and will vary in terms of the resources they control. Immobility refers to the difficulty of buying resources from the market place. To achieve SCA, the VRIO model firstly requires a resource to be "valuable" to the firm for either increasing revenue or decreasing costs. Secondly, the resource should be "rare" among competitors. Thirdly, it should be costly for competitors to "imitate" the resource. Finally, the firm must be "organised" in such a way that it is able to exploit the resource in the market. An example of the VRIO model is provided in Table 2.

A tourism resource may be viewed as anything that plays a major role in attracting visitors to a destination (Spotts 1997). Sources of competitive advantage are essentially assets and skills (Aaker 1991). An asset is a resource that is superior to those possessed by the competition, and a skill is an activity undertaken more effectively than competitors. A resource audit is therefore be a key component of marketing planning. However, Ferrario

Table 2: Barney's resource model.

Strength	Valuable?	Rare?	Unduplicable?	Organised?	Status
Resource A	Yes	Yes	Yes	Yes	SCA
Resource B	Yes	Yes	Yes	No	TCA
Resource C	Yes	No			CP

Notes: CP = competitive parity, TCA = temporary competitive advantage, SCA = sustainable competitive advantage.

Table 3: DMO resources representing competitive advantage.

Sources of Comparative Advantage	Sources of Competitive Advantage
Natural resources Location, landscape features and climate *Cultural resources* History, language, cuisine, music, arts & crafts, traditions and customs *Human resources* Skills and availability of the region's labour force; industrial relations; industry service standards; and attitudes of locals *Goodwill resources* Travellers' ancestral links to the destination; friends and/or relatives; novelty or fashionability of the destination; ToMA levels; levels of previous visitation and satisfaction; and perceived value	*Developed resources* Accessibility, infrastructure, and the scale, range and capacity of man-made attractions and other superstructure *Financial resources* Size and certainty of the DMO budget; private sector marketing resources; influence on government fiscal policy such as taxation, investment incentives and capital expenditure on infrastructure developments; size of the local economy; access to capital for product developments and ability to attract new investment *Legal resources* Brand trademarks, licenses and visa policies *Organisation resources* Governance structure and policies; staffing levels, training, experience, skills and retention; organisational culture; innovation; technology; and flexibility *Information resources* Marketing information system *Relationship resources* Internal/external industry integration and alliances; distribution; stakeholder co-operation; and political influence *Implementation resources* Sustainable tourism development planning; brand development, positioning and promotion; ease of making reservations; consistency of stakeholders' delivery

(1979a, b) suggested the availability of tourism resources was often taken for granted by both practitioners and academics. More recently the process of auditing a destination's resources has received increased attention in the literature (e.g. Faulkner *et al.* 1999; Pearce 1997; Ritchie & Crouch 2000a; Spotts 1997). A categorisation of DMO resources representing sources of comparative and competitive advantage is suggested in Table 3.

Vision, Values, Mission, Goals and Objectives

The corporate vision of the Western Australian Tourism Commission is to make Western Australia the world's natural choice (Western Australia

Table 4:   DMO vision statements.

Organisation	Vision
Canadian Tourism Commission	Canada will be the premier four-season destination to connect with nature and to experience diverse cultures and communities (Smith 2003: 131)
Australian Tourist Commission	To be respected by our stakeholders for the value we add to inbound tourism (ATC 2004: 2)
Tourism New Zealand	New Zealand is known as the ultimate destination for interactive travellers (TNZ 2004: 5)

Tourism Commission Marketing and Communication Strategy 2003–2006
— accessed at http://www.tourism.wa.gov.au/media/, 22/10/03).

Much of marketing planning is about considering opportunities to meet unmet consumer needs. In this regard marketing is a forward thinking discipline, and it is often useful from DMOs to articulate an envisioned future as a way of rallying and motivating stakeholders. Following Collins & Porras (1997), it is important to preface this section with the understanding such statements should essentially be verbalising what the organisation already stands for, rather than an attempt to calculate what would the most pragmatic or popular. A destination vision has been described as an "inspirational portrait of an ideal future that the destination hopes to bring about at some defined future" (Goeldner *et al.* 2000: 445). Table 4 highlights a number of articulated DMO vision statements. An important element in the vision design is an understanding of the organisation's values, which are a small set of deeply held and enduring beliefs. Collins & Porras (1997: 87) found visionary organisations tended to have between three and simply stated six core values, but that there was no single common ideology:

> Our research indicates that the authenticity of the ideology and the extent
> to which a company attains consistent alignment with that ideology counts
> more than the content of the ideology.

An organisation's mission statement is a declaration of the overall purpose of the organisation. While mission statements are often criticised as being bland, it is important to clearly articulate to stakeholders the organisation's reason for being (Johnson & Scholes 2002). Given the political dynamics of tourism destination marketing, a succinct and clear mission is important for DMOs. The structure of mission statements varies, and may include the vision, values, activities and target market. Examples of DMO mission statements are listed in Table 5.

Organisations are established to achieve goals. Goals are general statements of intent, related to the mission, and are usually qualitative (Johnson & Scholes 2002). Collins & Porras (1997: 94) articulated the concept of a big hairy audacious goal (BHAG) as a way of capturing the attention of stakeholders.

Table 5: DMO mission statements.

Organisation	Mission Statement
Canadian Tourism Commission	Canada's tourism industry will deliver world-class cultural and leisure experiences year-round, while preserving and sharing Canada's clean, safe, and natural environments. The industry will be guided by the values of respect, integrity, and empathy (Smith 2003: 130).
Australian Tourist Commission	We market Australia internationally to create a sustainable advantage for our tourism industry and the benefits of all Australians (ATC 2004: 2).
Tourism New Zealand	To motivate interactive travellers to come now, to do more, and to come back (TNZ 2004: 5).

A BHAG engages people — it reaches out and grabs them in the gut. It is tangible, energizing, highly focused. People "get it" right away; it takes little or no explanation (Collins & Porras 1997: 94).

Key DMO goals can be summarised as relating to the following four themes:

• enhancing destination image
• increasing industry profitability
• reducing seasonality
• ensuring long term funding.

From a survey of 49 NTOs Baum (1994) found the highest rating goal was to generate foreign exchange earnings. Likewise, in a survey of USA CVBs, Sheehan & Ritchie (1997) found 85% indicated their primary goal was to maximise the economic contribution of tourism to the region; 5% of CVBs indicated their main goal was to increase membership revenue, and 5% indicated the main goal was to generate a nominated ROI. In an investigation of tourism policy in member nations of the European Community, Akehurst, Bland & Nevin (1993) found the most important goals were related to attracting higher yield visitors. Hawes, Taylor & Hampe's (1991) analysis of the marketing plans of USA STOs found the most common goals were to enhance the image of the state, encourage residents to see their state first, and to develop tourism as a year round industry. The six goals of the Australian Tourist Commission are shown in Table 6.

One of the most practical, and least academic, aspects to tourism marketing is the setting of objectives (Wahab *et al.* 1976). Objectives are the quantifiable targets of the goals, and should clearly describe specific outcomes. Ideally objectives should be SMART (Tribe 1997: 32):

• specific
• measurable

Table 6: Australian tourist commission goals.

Theme	Goal
Industry — strategic leadership	Improve the tourism industry's ability to act on market/consumer opportunities
Industry — supply	Improve the ability to identify and lead to market products and experiences that best meet identified consumer segment opportunities
Industry — international distribution	Improve the performance of existing and new international distribution channels linked to identified consumer opportunities
Consumer — demand creation	Increase international consumers' desire to visit Australia
Sustainability	Enhance adoption of ecotourism and sustainability agendas in overall tourism promotion
Key stakeholders	Continuously improve internal and external stakeholder engagement and performance delivery

Source: Adapted from ATC (2004: 3).

- agreed with those who must attain them
- realistic
- time-constrained.

From a survey of local government in Australia's state of Victoria, Carson, Beattie & Gove (2003) suggested up to one third of Councils lacked clear tourism objectives. Likewise, an earlier survey in the USA by Hawes *et al.* (1991) found only 7 of 37 STOs used measurable objectives.

The general roles of DMOs are similar around the world. This is highlighted in the role of RTBs in the U.K. (Pattinson 1990: 210) and the roles of CVBs in North America (Morrison *et al.* 1998: 5) as shown in Table 7, and in the responsibilities of Tourism Auckland (Tourism Auckland 2002) in Figure 1.

The most important role of DMOs at all levels is marketing, which is the focus of Chapter 8. Other important responsibilities of a DMO include:

- *Industry coordination.* Since destinations are multi-attributed, a common challenge faced by DMOs is the number of suppliers who make up the destination product. At the state level, Pennsylvania has more RTOs than any other in the USA, with 59 agencies in 67 counties (Goeldner *et al.* 2000). In the U.K., the North West Tourist Board conceded the product range was too diverse to market effectively as a single entity (Alford 1998). In New Zealand, Pike (1998) found seven RTOs that identified over four hundred local tourism businesses within their territory, while eight RTOs indicated a range of two hundred to four hundred. One of the major roles of the DMO is to develop a cohesive approach among stakeholders to enhance destination competitiveness. It makes sense

Table 7: Roles of RTBs and CVBs.

Roles of RTBs	Roles of CVBs
• To produce a coordinated regional tourism strategy in liaison with local authorities and consistent with the broad aims of the English Tourist Board • To offer advice to both commercial tourism businesses and local authorities on tourism planning • To encourage the development of tourist amenities and facilities which meet the needs of a changing market • To administer the national financial aid scheme for assisting tourism development • To represent the interests of the region at the national level and the interests of the tourism industry within the region • To market the region by providing reception and information services, producing and supplying suitable literature, and undertaking promotional activities	• An economic driver of new income, employment and taxes to create a more diversified local economy • A community marketer, communicating the most appropriate destination image, attractions and facilities to selected markets • An industry coordinator, providing a clear focus and encouraging less industry fragmentation so as to share in the benefits • A quasi-public representative adding legitimacy for the industry and protection to visitors • A builder of community pride by enhancing quality of life and acting as the flag carrier for locals and visitors

Sources: Pattinson (1990: 210), Morrison *et al.* (1998: 5).

to share resources in an effort to create a bigger impact in the market, a philosophy referred to as "cooperating to compete" or "flying in formation." One of the leadership challenges for DMOs is to identify destination images of mutual value to stakeholders and travellers, and then foster a consistency of message. However, it cannot be assumed that all individual businesses will accept a holistic and focused approach to generic destination imagery. Instead, DMO stakeholders will usually seek a profile for their product, which may not necessarily meet consumer needs. For example, Curtis (2001: 77) reported the resistance of regional tourism organisations to a recommendation by the Oregon Tourism Commission to use a central advertising agency in a major repositioning campaign: "Ultimately the coordinated regional Brand Oregon marketing efforts began to fail."

• *Monitoring service and quality standards*. The very nature of tourism as a service industry demands a fixation with quality standards: "The tourist is buying an illusion. He will be embittered by anything or anybody who shatters it" (Wahab *et al.* 1976: 74). In the early 1990s, a consultancy commissioned to investigate the state of Northern Ireland's tourism industry reported a "considerable disparity" between visitor expectations and the actual experience (O'Neill & McKenna 1994: 33). The Tourism (Northern Ireland) Order 1992 incorporated the recommendations of the review, which included the

Developing Marketing Plans: developing comprehensive plans and strategies for marketing the Auckland Region as a tourist destination, and developing the means of implementing, monitoring and reviewing those plans and strategies;

Marketing Region: marketing, in New Zealand and overseas, the advantages of the Auckland Region for visitors and tourists, including promoting and co-ordinating the development of parks, holiday resorts, scenic reserves and recreational, business and tourist facilities and activities.

Convention Location: establishing, maintaining and marketing the Auckland Region as a premier convention location.

Visitor Information Services: operating visitor information and entertainment services to ensure visitors and tourists to the Auckland Region are welcomed and given information and assistance;

Reservation Services: providing a reservation service for accommodation, travel and tour services within the Auckland Region;

Information on Resources: researching, publishing and disseminating information on the resources of the Auckland Region in order to encourage and promote the development, co-ordination and marketing of commercial, industrial, communication, transportation, recreational, and education interests, services and facilities conducive to tourism;

Coordinating Marketing: coordinating joint venture marketing campaigns with the private sector and publicly funded regional tourism organisations in order to raise the profile of the Auckland Region and to contribute to sustained tourism growth in the Auckland Region.

Statistical Information: researching and recording statistical information on tourism and monitoring visitor numbers in order to provide forecasts of visitor numbers and visitor research information for the Auckland Region.

Promoting Events and Conventions: promoting, supporting and bidding for events and conventions that bring economic benefit to, or increase the profile of, the Auckland Region in a cost effective manner;

General: all such things as are incidental or conducive to the attainment of the charitable objects and purposes;

No limitation: The objects and purposes of the Trust shall not, except where the context specifically or expressly requires it, be in any way limited or restricted by reference or inference from the terms of any other clause or sub-clause or from the name of the Trust and none of the objects or purposes of the Trust shall be deemed subsidiary or ancillary to any other object or purpose of the Trust;

Objects and Purposes Independent: The Trustees shall be empowered to carry out any one or more of the objects or purposes of the Trust independently of any other object or purpose of the Trust . . . Trust Deed.

Figure 1: Responsibilities of Tourism Auckland.

introduction of an accommodation classification registry, to which providers could only be included upon an inspection assessment. Similarly, in 1999 a report tabled in the British parliament criticised the state of the Scottish tourism product, including poor quality accommodation, unwelcoming hosts, uncompetitive and unattractive prices, poor standards at visitor attractions and poor accessibility (Kerr & Wood 2000: 287). In New Zealand, Tan *et al.*'s (1995) survey of tourism businesses from six sectors found 78% had no formal quality system, with 65% having no intention of introducing one. Plog (2000) predicted managed destinations, such as resorts and cruise ships, would become increasingly popular in the future due to their ability to manage capacity and maintain consistency of quality. Likewise d'Hauteserre's (2000) analysis of Foxwoods Casino Resort suggested the success factors would be much more problematic for destinations than managed resorts. These included for example staff empowerment and the reinvestment of earnings into product development.

• *Enhancing community relations.* The underlying purpose of the DMO is not always obvious to some members of the host community, including some local tourism operators. Many have been surprised to learn that the purpose, from the government funder perspective at least, is to enhance the economic prosperity of the district, usually with a focus on direct, indirect and induced job creation. Rather, many have assumed the DMO was there only to serve local tourism operators, which is the case in a minority of member-based associations that do not receive government funding. Clearly, there is a difference, but if the community hasn't been informed, it is dangerous to assume they should automatically understand. The DMO should therefore initiate regular measures to identify the extent to which the community understands the organisation's purpose and role. To enhance credibility in the community, Gartrell (1994: 281) recommended a strategy of consistently using messages that repeat key terms: "Telling the bureau's story may seem mundane or repetitious, but the message must be stated again and again." Examples of key repetitive terms include those related to "economic development" and "tax benefits."

Funding

Positioning multiple brands in a dynamic environment requires significant financial and management resources (Moutinho 1994). However, destination marketing is undertaken by organisations that have no direct financial interest in the visitor industry. Also, many DMOs have limited budgets. For example, relative to RTOs in other major cities, the London Tourist Board (LTB) is poorly funded by government (Hopper 2002). The LTB received £1.85 million from central government and £241,000 from local authorities. The remainder of the £6 million annual budget was contributed by the private sector through subscriptions, partnership marketing and sponsorship. Non-business organisations usually cannot cover costs through sales, and often devote ongoing efforts to generating new tax revenues, sponsorships and/or contributions from members.

Funding is a critical issue for DMOs. In fact for any marketing organisation without products or services of its own to gain sales revenue it is arguably the most important consideration. In particular, the high reliance on government funding leaves many DMOs at the mercy of political masters. For example, a state government referendum in 1993 resulted in the abolishment of a tax to fund the Colorado Tourism Board (CTB). Without such government funding the CTB was closed (Bonham & Mak 1996). A survey of USA CVBs identified the main impediment to financial management was future funding security (Sheehan & Ritchie 1997). RTO budgets in Australia have generally been modest, and in New South Wales, many have struggled to survive (Jenkins 2000). In Scotland, Kerr & Wood (2000) reported on the financial difficulty, including near bankruptcy, for some ATBs due to reduced levels of local government funding. They cited the example of the Dumfries and Galloway Tourist Board, which was £1.2 million in debt in 1998. One of the problems was that the ATB areas did not match local government boundaries, and so ATBs were forced to lobby several councils for funding support. The challenge of spending scarce resources lobbying several local authorities in an RTO's "regional" catchment area is common elsewhere, including for example:

- Manchester's CVB, in the U.K., with 10 local authorities (Bramwell & Rawding 1994).
- Bundaberg Region Ltd, in Australia, with 10 local authorities (www. bundabergregion.info).
- Tourism Auckland, in New Zealand, with 7 local authorities (www.aucklandnz.com).
- The former West Country Tourist Board in the U.K. was responsible to six and a half counties (Meethan 2002).

The structure of local government can make a regional approach to regional problems extremely difficult. Tourism Auckland CEO Graeme Osborne strongly lamented the impact of the resultant "multiple accountability" and "multiple governance," where the RTO reports to the committees of each council as well as to the tourism industry (personal communication 2004):

> It prevents truly visionary leadership being exercised at a regional level, which of course is the correct approach for destination marketing. The fundamental flaw then is the structure and (ridiculously excessive) scale of local government, the ensuing lack of regional vision, the 'sovereignty driven', duplicative, parochial leadership offered by generally low-average-quality local government politicians.

Tourism Auckland received NZ$2.1 million in local authority funding for the 2003/2004 financial year. As can be seen in Table 8 most of this was from one local authority. However, it has been estimated that while the Auckland City Council contributes 79% of the RTO's funding, the city area receives only 55% of the economic contribution of tourism to the Auckland region (Tourism Auckland 2002).

Table 8: Local authority funding for tourism Auckland.

Local Authority	Population Base	2003/2004 Contribution	Per Capita
Auckland City Council	377,382	$1,645,000	$4.36
Manukau City Council	281,604	$300,000	$1.07
Waitakere City Council	167,172	$0	$0.00
North Shore City Council	184,287	$90,000	$0.49
Rodney District Council	77,001	$10,000	$0.13
Papakura District Council	40,035	$5,000	$0.12
Franklin District Council	51,450	$20,000	$0.39

Table 9: Comparison of local authority contributions to major New Zealand RTOs.

RTO	Population Base	Local Authority Contribution	Per Capita
Auckland	1,178,931	$2,000,000	$1.70
Christchurch	316,224	$2,600,000	$8.22
Wellington	163,827	$4,600,000	$28.08
Rotorua	64,473	$1,212,000	$18.08
Queenstown	17,040	$1,600,000	$93.90
Mean	581,895		$18.24

Auckland is New Zealand's largest population centre, and most visited destination. Auckland International Airport facilitates 71% of all visitor arrivals to New Zealand. Given the prominent status of the region, Tourism Auckland's budget might be considered low relative to other New Zealand RTOs, as shown in Table 9. A recent Tourism Auckland (2002) funding presentation to the Auckland City Council suggested a more realistic budget would be $9.6 million from local authorities.

Security of long term government funding is not only a challenge faced by STOs and RTOs. WTO (1999a) estimated collective worldwide NTA budgets declined during the 1993–1997 period, from US$2,224 million to US$1,791 million. There is no common model for determining the appropriate level of funding for a DMO. In an examination of government policy of EC member countries, Akehurst *et al.* (1993) found little correlation between central government tourism expenditure and international receipts on a per capita basis. For example, Greece, which had the highest government spend per capita was at the lower end of international tourism receipts per capita. However, if countries with the smallest populations were excluded from the analysis the correlation for the seven large states was stronger.

Comparisons can be made between DMO budgets from different regions using all manner of different measures, including:

• host population
• visitor numbers
• as a ratio of visitor spend
• number of commercial accommodation beds/rooms
• number of taxpayers/ratepayers.

Ultimately the funding decision process will depend on the local situation, with influences including:

• local politics
• destination life-cycle stage and industry maturity

Table 10: The World's top 10 NTA budgets in 1997.

Country	Budget (US$ Millions)
Spain	$147
Mexico	$103
Thailand	$94
Brazil	$92
Australia	$88
Singapore	$87
Puerto Rico	$79
China/HK	$68
South Korea	$63
France	$58

Source: Adapted from WTO (1999a).

- economic importance of tourism relative to other industries
- DMO history and current structure.

The world average for NTA budgets was estimated at US$19 million in 1997, which, as discussed in Chapter 1, pales into insignificance in the global market place in comparison to leading consumer goods brands such as Sony and Philips. DMOs compete with such brands for a share of voice in discretionary spending categories. The top ten NTA budgets in 1997 are shown in Table 10.

A key management challenge for DMOs is finding the optimal balance between fixed costs and promotional spend (WTO 1999a). The average marketing allocation was 74% for those with budgets over US$50 million and for those with budgets between US$10 and $20 million. For NTOs with budgets between US$20 and US$50 million, the average was 64%. In the USA, Morrison *et al.*'s (1998) 1992/93 survey of 254 CVBs found budgets ranged from US$250,000 to over US$10 million. IACVB (1993, in Morrison *et al.* 1998) estimated that of all room taxes collected, approximately 27% is used for the convention centre construction, debt servicing and operations, 25% for CVB marketing and 48% for "non-visitor uses." Getz *et al.*'s (1997) survey of CVBs in Canada found budgets ranged from less that C$100,000 to over C$7.5 million. Ranging from 1 to 100%, the average level of funding from government was 46%. McKercher & Ritchie's (1997) study of local government tourism units in New South Wales and Victoria identified a median operating budget of A$215,000. Over half of average budgets were allocated to staffing, with the median marketing allocation only A$70,000, after overheads. Carson *et al.* (2003) found local authority budget contributions to tourism in the state of Victoria ranged from A$2,000 to A$6.5 million, with a median of $232,000. They found 40% of councils surveyed indicated a tourism budget of less than A$150,000. Within the tourism budget, 44% of local authorities provided contributions to a RTO.

Sheehan & Ritchie's (1997) survey of USA CVBs found the largest source of revenue was hotel room taxes, generating a mean 72% of revenue. The next level of funding sources were modest by comparison: membership fees (7% — highest was 58%), government grants (6% — highest 90%), local authority taxes (2.6% — highest 100%), cooperative programmes (2% — highest 41%), restaurant taxes (2% — highest 60%). Other sources, representing an average of 8% included: convention centre grants, merchandise, advertising sales, county tax, events, admissions, in-kind services, and a provincial or state tax. Key funding trends identified by respondents included:

- the establishment of private funding sources, such as increased membership and dedicated tourism taxes
- the raiding of tourism tax funds
- cooperative programmes with industry
- increased advertising support from members
- increased fee-based services
- increased revenue from merchandise sales.

Likewise, Morrison *et al.*'s analysis of CVBs (1998: 6) identified the following future funding trends:

- increasing levels of local room taxes used for non-visitor expenses
- investigation and application of other types of user fees
- declining levels of government grants
- increased emphasis on industry-member support
- more importance placed on partnership and buy-in programmes
- any increases in room tax rates will result in a consumer backlash.

Key advantages of the room tax are that it directly targets the visitor industry, and can generate large amounts of revenue for a relatively low cost. Room taxes, which are additional to any other local, state or national general sales taxes, have existed in the USA since at least the 1940s (Migdal 1991 in Morrison *et al.* 1998). However, the hotel room tax is far from universally lauded. The repeal of the 5% bed tax in the state of New York was hailed by some in the tourism industry as the removal of an inhibitor to destination marketing (Cahn 1994: 19). The tax, which was introduced in 1990, was the subject of strong criticism from industry, with one executive likening it to "economic suicide" for the meetings sector. In a survey of delegates attending the 1999 Scottish Hospitality Industry Congress, Kerr & Wood (2000) found a resounding 93% of respondents against the concept of a bed tax, although 35% did indicate possible support if all the revenues were devoted to the tourism industry. A variation of this, reported by the *The News Mail* (31/503: 3) was used in Queensland's Wide Bay region. Around A$80,000 was collected from a visitor levy during the 2002 whale watch season, which was being used on an advertising campaign to promote the 2003 season.

An alternative tax, which may become more common in the future, is one that is levied on business turnover or capital value. Bonham & Mak (1996) reported the Oklahoma

Tourism Promotion Act (1991) levied a tourism promotion tax of 0.1% of gross turnover of accommodation, rental car, restaurant and bar operations. The intent was for the state government to collect the tax from the tourism industry, to be used solely by the industry, for which the state would charge a 3% collection fee. Prior to its demise in 1993 Colorado STO had a similar tax of 0.2% (Bonham & Mak 1996). A downside of this approach is a reduction in funding during periods of crisis when visitation levels have fallen, even though such periods demand more marketing funds. For example, in Canada, the *Calgary Herald* (13/1/03: B4) reported that a fall in the Banff/Lake Louise Tourism Bureau's 2003 revenue was likely to result in a reduction in marketing spend of C$168,000, which would directly impair the organisation's ability to promote Banff in their traditional secondary markets such as New Zealand and Australia.

The IACVB (1993, in Morrison *et al.* 1998) found that while half of their member CVBs received membership subscription fees, for those responding to a survey, the level of subscriptions was only 5% of their collective budgets. Bonham & Mak (1996) found only Alaska, Hawaii and Washington DC received significant private sector contributions such as through membership subscriptions. The HVB, which has one of the longest histories of private membership, has offered a range of incentives to financial members, including: monthly newsletters, HVB posters and brochures, reduced fees for HVB meetings, participation in trade promotion and cooperative advertising, listings in information guides, and a copy of the annual report. In its early years the organisation received more in private sector contributions than from government. However, by 1988 only an estimated 7% of all businesses were financial members of the HVB, and by 1994 private sector contributions represented less than 10% of the annual budget. One of the reasons offered by Bonham & Mak was extensive "free riding" by tourism operators. They cited Mok's (1986) PhD thesis, which estimated HVB memberships representing 78% of airlines, 66% of hotels, 32% of banks, 24% of restaurants and only 4% of retail outlets. Since membership is voluntary the organisation was forced to spend up to $500,000 to generate $2 million in membership dues (Rees 1995, in Bonham & Mak 1996). This is a common problem for RTOs, many of which have abandoned attempts to generate subscriptions due to low returns relative to costs incurred in the process. Therefore it is more cost effective to lobby for government funds. For example, two decades ago, as a direct result of the STO lobbying state political candidates in the 1978, the elected governor tripled the destination marketing budget between 1979 and 1982 (Pritchard 1982). Bonham and Mak reported the HVB employed three political lobbyists.

Membership fees may be based on tiered sponsor categories, a standard arbitrary amount, tiered based on organisation turnover level or number of employees or per room for accommodation establishments. Donnelly & Vaske (1997) investigated the factors influencing membership of the voluntary organisation established to replace the previously state funded, the Colorado Travel and Tourism Authority (CTTA). The CTTA targeted businesses that directly benefited from tourism, such as hotels, restaurants and attractions. Their review of the literature relating to voluntary organisations identified two participative incentive themes; instrumental and expressive. Instrumental incentives are those public goods, such as promotion of the destination, that are obtained by both members and non-members. Expressive incentives are resultant benefits that will only be obtained by membership, such as access to a database of consumers who have requested tourism information from the DMO. Donnelly & Vaske (51) suggested the value placed on expressive incentives to join a DMO will depend on an individual's:

- financial ability to pay membership dues
- beliefs about tourism and destination marketing
- level of perceived importance about the costs and benefits of membership.

Some RTOs have developed an income stream from their own activities to fund destination marketing. For example, Pritchard (1982) reported an innovative approach used by Alaska to stimulate industry contributions to the STO budget. For every dollar contributed by an individual business, the STO would provide one name and address from the consumer database for direct marketing. The database was tailored to provide contacts from segments of interest to the contributing tourism business. *Marketing News* (29/9/97) reported the new logo developed by Florida's FTIMC in 1997, would be used to generate royalties of 6% of the wholesale price of items featuring the logo. The report claimed universities such as Florida State and Notre Dame earned millions of dollars annually from such royalties. In some cases however legal issues can prevent some types of DMOs from maximising their earning potential. In the USA, most CVBs have been structured as non-profit associations, qualifying for tax-exempt status. These organisations promote the business interests of their members but are not permitted to engage in regular profit making business activities. In New Zealand, local government regulations prohibited many local authority-owned VICs to trade commercially, other than sales of sightseeing tickets and postcards. However the greater empowering provisions of the Local Government Act (2002) have enabled enhanced trading opportunities. It is also not uncommon for RTOs to earn commission from their member hotels for conference bookings. However this approach can lead to the DMO focusing on conference promotion, business travel and short break hotel packages to the exclusion of other destination products (Bramwell & Rawding 1994).

Other RTOs earn commissions through subsidiary visitor information centre (VIC) sales. However, net returns are often modest, even with a substantial turnover, if there is an absence of big ticket items. VICs are labour intensive, and as their title suggests, a large component of visitors are there seeking "information." They make seek advice, collect brochures, make a decision and then book direct with the tourism provider, from the comfort of their accommodation. It is difficult for VICs to generate a profit when relying on sightseeing sales paying on average 10% commission. Many of these VICs could be profitable if they adopted private sector practises used by travel agencies such as "preferred supplier" agreements. This might involve, for example, one operator per service category, receiving preferential treatment and in return providing commissions up to 25–30%. A tiered system of commissions might be used to rank providers in terms of preference levels and prominence of brochures on display. For example, in Canada, travel agents represent on average only four tour wholesalers (Statistics Canada 1999, in Hashimoto & Telfer 2001). However, it would be hypocritical for an RTO that receives government funding for the purpose of developing tourism in the region to then preclude the majority of suppliers from receiving VIC bookings in a preferential system. Many local authorities understand the need for a trade-off and provide an operating grant for the VIC on the basis that the contribution is for the public good.

DMO Names

As with so many aspects related to DMOs there is no consistency in names used. There currently exists a myriad of DMO names, including:

* agencies (Latvian Tourism Development Agency)
* authorities (The Gambia Tourism Authority)
* boards (British Virgin Islands Tourist Board)
* bureaux (Hawaii Visitors Bureau)
* centres (Le Centre Gabonais de Promotion Touristique)
* commissions (Australian Tourist Commission)
* companies (NYC and Company)
* corporations (Virginia Tourism Corporation)
* councils (Swedish Travel & Tourism Council)
* departments (Dubai Department of Tourism and Commerce Marketing)
* destinations (Destination Northland)
* directorates (Crete Tourism Directorate)
* institutes (Nicaraguan Institute of Tourism)
* ministries (Israel Ministry of Tourism)
* offices (China National Tourism Office)
* organisations (Cypress Tourism Organisation).
* regions (Bundaberg Region Limited).

Recently, new types of names have emerged, such as those incorporating "tourism" (Falkland Islands Tourism), "destination" (Destination Lake Taupo), and "visit" (Visit Heart of England), and then others that are difficult to categorise such as Maison de la France, Fáilte Ireland, Latitude Nelson, and Positively Wellington Tourism. While there is no one naming theme common to DMOs, there has been a shift in recent years away from the more bureaucratic sounding names representative of government divisions, such as the examples in Table 11, which compare the current name to one used in the past.

When Visit Britain (see www.visitbritain.com) was chosen as the name for the UK's new DMO, it had to be purchased from a company that had owned it for 25 years (TravelMole.com, 16/4/03). The chairman of Visit Britain discussed some of the difficulties associated with selecting an appropriate name:

Table 11: DMO name changes.

Current Name	A Previous Name
Tourism New Zealand	New Zealand Tourist and Publicity Department
Tourism Queensland	Queensland Tourist and Travel Corporation
Visit Britain	British Tourist Authority

> You have no idea how much trouble goes into creating a new name. It
> has to be legal, we have to make sure it means the same thing in different
> languages, and that it sounds good over the phone, and works in different
> media (TravelMole.com, 26/3/03).

Intuitively it is perhaps more likely that organisational names that either begin with the
destination name and include a reference to tourism, and names that begin with the word
destination, are likely to resonate with more meaning among consumers. This may or may
not be an important issue, unless for example, a consumer is searching for the DMO as
an impartial source of information. However, there has been little if any research into the
effectiveness of DMO brand names, in relation to traveller information searches.

Entity

In terms of geographic scale, the largest DMOs are those that have been established to
market the tourism interests of a group of countries. In this regard there have been calls for
increased cooperation between countries in many parts of the world, including for example:
Scandinavia (Flagestad & Hope 2001), central and eastern Europe (Davidson & Maitland
1997; Hall 1998), East Africa (Beirman 2003b) and Australasia (Tourelle 2003).

The Caribbean Tourism Organisation (CTO, see www.onecaribbean.org) is a cooperative
approach to marketing the region's small island nations. Formed over 50 years ago,
the CTO comprises 32 member governments. In 2003, the secretary of the Caribbean
Tourism Organisation (CTO) called for even greater cooperation between private and public
sector organisations, by suggesting a merger between the CTO and the Caribbean Hotel
Association:

> It is clear that the demarcation of public and private sector roles that existed
> formerly in tourism no longer applies. In this world of globalisation and
> consolidation, fragmentation and duplication is the surest recipe for disaster
> for the Caribbean (Travel Mole, 21/7/03).

Similar organisations in other parts of the world include:

- The European Travel Commission (ETC, see www.etc-europe-travel.org) is the Brussels-
  based headquarters for Europe's 33 NTOs. The roles of the ETC are to market Europe
  as a tourism destination, and to provide advice to member NTOs. A key aspect of the
  organisation's structure has been the formation of "Operations Groups" of member NTOs
  in North America, Japan and Latin America.
- The South Pacific Tourism Organisation (SPTO, see www.tcsp.com), which was formed
  in the 1980s to promote tourism to the region. SPTO represents 13 member NTOs.
- The Confederación de Organizaciones Turísticas de la America Latina (see www.cotal.
  org.ar)
- The ASEAN tourism association (see www.aseanta.org)
- The Indian Ocean Tourism Organisation (see www.cowan.edu.au)

- During 2003 the Irish government established a new national tourism development authority, Fáilte Ireland (see www.failteireland.ie), to replace Bord Fáilte and CERT. Previously the countries of Ireland and Northern Ireland operated separate NTOs.

Visit Britain was also established in 2003, to replace the British Tourist Authority (BTA) and English Tourism Commission (ETC). The move came only four years after the ETB was restructured to create the ETC.

> The very existence of several national tourist boards (BTA, ETB, STB, WTB) has been a source of confusion for consumers and for those operating in the tourism industry in the U.K. and overseas, who have often been unclear as to which organisation should be addressed on what issues (Davidson & Maitland 1997: 148).

TravelMole.com (14/2/03) reported that a parliamentary committee expressed doubts about the effectiveness of the merger of the BTA and ETC. The committee, which consulted with the BTA, ETC, Visit Scotland, Wales Tourism Board and other tourism organisations, felt the merger world encourage competition between U.K. countries rather than cooperation. The report suggested a particular fear from Scottish interests that the new organisation would be biased towards English products:

> We feel it would make better sense for England to have a distinct national tourist board with a marketing function, and for each national tourist board in Britain to relate to the BTA in the same way.

However, an earlier report (TravelMole.com, 1/11/02) cited representatives of the BTA and ETC as welcoming the move. Under the new structure, the new organisation would be responsible for developing inbound tourism to Britain as well as the domestic marketing of England within Britain, whereas Scotland and Wales would retain their DMOs.

At an NTO level, DMOs have historically been government departments. By the 1970s however it was evident a shift was emerging away from direct government involvement in DMO operations. From a survey of 95 NTOs in 1975 the WTO (1975) found only 6 that were non-governmental. However, within a few years the WTO (1979) found that of 100 recognised NTAs, 68 were part of the country's government administration, which the WTO suggested provided the advantage of being able to directly influence government tourism policy in addition to undertaking promotional work. The remaining 32 NTAs were operating outside the central administration. Although still linked to, and funded by, central government, these organisations had a separate legal identity. A benefit of this structure was greater financial and administrative independence:

> The proper solution for each country can only be found within the framework of the national situation, but the main point is that the NTA should be able to work closely with, and obtain the active support and cooperation of, all government authorities whose responsibilities affect various aspects

of tourism, as well as the private sector, if it is to help develop balanced travel plant and an effective tourism development programme (WTO 1979: 3).

This is representative of a public-private partnership (PPP), which, has become the most common form of DMO at all levels. The WTO adopted the theme of "Public-private sector partnership: the key to tourism development and promotion" for world tourism day in 1998. Poetschke (1995) suggested a typology of public-private partnership models, depending of the level of industry involvement, ranging from "lobby group," to "advisory group" to "general commission" to "tourist authority." Lobby groups provide input to the government, which is responsible for designing and implementing tourism policies. However, such lobbying efforts are often antagonistic. An advisory group provides input through a formal council. However government remains in full control of setting and implementing policy. In a general commission, the tourism industry plays a formal role in policy decision making at a strategic level. A tourist authority is commonly a separate entity controlled by a board of directors comprising members from industry and government. The board of an authority is involved in more detailed planning than a commission. Advantages for the private sector include larger budgets and increased access to government policy makers. In the U.K., private-public partnerships (PPPs) became a means towards generating larger budgets for local destination marketing during the 1980s and 1990s when tight spending restrictions on local governments were applied by central government (Bramwell & Rawding 1994). For example, in 1993 Leicester Promotions Ltd was established as a non-profit RTO with a £1.1 million grant from the local council (Miller 2003). A decade later and partnerships with the private sector have led to the council funding representing less than 50% of the annual budget. Smith (2003) described the evolution of Canada's NTO to a new public-private partnership, the Canadian Tourism Commission (CTC) in 1995. A major impetus for change was complaints by industry that the previous administration was under funded and not market driven. In Australia, STOs have commonly been formed as statutory authorities, which are established by an Act of Parliament. However they are not required to be as accountable as government departments on a regular basis (Craik 1991: 1):

> Some may be required to submit an annual report, while others are not even obliged to do this. Statutory authorities which are engaged in profit-making activities (including government business enterprises) require flexible personnel policies, and generally have considerable autonomy from public scrutiny.

This can create a dilemma in balancing powers of authority with public accountability. With the assertion that governments provide a range of business interventionist assistance and incentives without attention to actual outcomes, Craik (1991) undertook an evaluation of the Queensland Tourist and Travel Corporation (QTTC), which was a statutory body established by the Queensland government to replace the Queensland Government Tourist Bureau in 1979. The new organisational form was chosen to forge closer links between the public sector and private sector, but at the same time to avoid the restrictions that apply to a government department. The aim was to provide increased flexibility and capacity to act (Queensland Parliament, RLA 1978–1989: 119, in Craik 1991: 7):

Although the QTTC was established as a statutory authority, amendments to its Act gave it enormous freedom to pursue tourist promotion and development as it saw fit. Within a few years it exemplified the problem of controlling statutory authorities, although the previous government showed little inclination to curb its activities significantly. Over time, the corporation channelled its energies into high profile and commercial activities which realized a financial return for the corporation, corporation members and potentially for some staff members. Many of these activities were difficult to justify in terms of the interests of the state or the public, and were indistinguishable from those of a private company engaged in tourist development. The QTTC exceeded the functions of usually associated with and industry policy body and of a statutory authority. Charges of clientelism and conflict of interest accompanied its history. Despite growing public antipathy to the corporation, the QTTC paid scant attention to public interest (Craik 1991: 23).

In North America, CVBs are usually one of four types (Morrison *et al.* 1998: 3): independent, non-profit associations/business leagues; chambers of commerce as non-profit associations or non-independent subsidiaries; local government agency, department or public authority; or a special legal entity/authority. Sheehan & Ritchie's (1997) survey of 134 North American CVBs found 75% of the sample were independent organisations, with the remainder being part of a chamber of commerce, economic development agency or city department. In other parts of the world RTOs have commonly been formed as statutory bodies, trusts, local authority departments and more recently as private companies. For example the latter applies to England's 12 RTBs (Greenwood 1993) and in Wales where the original RTBs were rationalised into three private companies (Davidson & Maitland 1997).

There have been moves in recent years towards rationalising the number of RTOs, in order to improve the efficiency of resources. In Scotland the 32 area tourist boards (ATB) established during the 1980s were amalgamated into 14 in 1996, following a 1993 government review of tourism (Davidson & Maitland 1997; Kerr & Wood 2000). A reduced number of RTOs was called for in the New Zealand Tourism Strategy released in 2001 (see Tourism Strategy Group 2001). One of the strategy goals was for a smaller number of "NewRTOs" to be established from the existing 25 RTOs. Through sharing common back office functions, it was suggested the reduced number of RTOs would make significant savings in overhead costs, which could then be more effectively used in promotion. The "NewRTOs" would take an enhanced role in overseas and domestic marketing. However, the strategy did not discuss how the proposal would be implemented, and in particular how the political implications would be addressed. Three years later the issue remained problematic despite the efforts of an RTONZ taskforce: "Obviously it's a delicate one with lots of political overtones, but it has to be addressed" (Paul Yeo, RTONZ Chair, personal communication 2004). A similar restructuring strategy was announced in Western Australia during 2004 (www.tourism.wa.gov.au/media/discussion_03.asp, 22/2/04). As part of the "New Concept for State Tourism Strategy," the number of official RTOs in the state would be reduced from ten to five. A commitment of A$3.25 million annual funding for the five RTOs was announced by the Western Australian state government: "These measure will increase economies of scale, and empower the regions."

Governance

> In the actual practise of management there is always a danger of politicians, public and private organisations and managers becoming self-serving and failing in their official responsibilities. Public organisations and resources can be used for private purposes. There can be financial corruption but more insidious is organisational corruption, where public objectives and principles are displaced by private objectives (Elliott 1997: 7).

Governance of DMOs of globally competitive destinations features four critical success factors (Poetschke 1995: 62–63):

- a significant level of private sector control over authority spending
- understanding of the need to incorporate public sector objectives to achieve a balance between marketing and new product development
- a dedicated revenue stream that is not subject to annual government control
- a broad, integrated, mandate encompassing al function critical to developing a strong tourism industry, such as marketing, education, research and infrastructure development.

Politics in decision-making is a significant aspect of DMO decision-making, and may even be unavoidable. From one perspective politics may be viewed as the art of getting things done. From another perspective, politics has been described as "the striving for power, and power is about who gets what, when and how in the political and administrative system and in the tourism sector" (Elliott 1997: 10). The political environment in tourism at national and local levels includes governments and ministers, bureaucratic cultures, competing entrepreneurs, the media, the host community, and special interest groups. The industry is made up of a diverse range of organisations and individuals involved in a complex array of relationships, and it is the challenge of the manager to understand this and work within the system to achieve objectives (Elliott 1997). However, the discussion of tourism politics in the academic literature has been rare (Hall 1994), and there have been calls for increased coverage of the study of the politics in tertiary tourism education (see Dredge 2001; Hollingshead 2001).

When the British Travel Association was replaced by the BTA, a key difference was in the selection of the governance structure (Jeffries 1989). The former had a large board of predominantly tourism industry representatives elected from member organisations with a government appointed chair, whereas the new organisation comprised a small group appointed by the government. An excellent discussion topic for students is how a DMO should structure its board. For example, key questions include:

- How many directors are appropriate?
- Who would be most effective, and should directors be appointed on merit or democratically elected?
- Who should make the appointment decisions?
- What length of term should directors serve?

Some boards can be quite large. For example, Bramwell & Rawding (1994) reported Birmingham's board comprised 25 directors, with seven representatives from the local authority and 18 from industry. The first CTC board contained 26 members, of which 16 were from the private sector and the remainder from the public sector (Smith 2003). The large size of the board reflected the effort to ensure all regions of Canada were represented.

The danger in any board election system there is a danger of appointing those who are popular, or even articulate incompetents, rather than those best qualified. An articulate incompetent is someone who is great at expressing issues and explaining solutions, but fails to act on them (Wintermans 1994). Bramwell & Rawding (1994: 431) suggested that when appointments are made to public funded RTOs by selection, the organisation is "less democratic and less accountable to the local electorate." However, local authority representatives on the board can serve this purpose. If government representatives are not included on the board, the issue of accountability needs to be carefully addressed in the funding contract and government reporting process. In 2003, the USA Commerce Department secretary appointed 15 travel and tourism executives to the new Travel and Tourism Promotion Advisory Board (Hoover 2003). Tourism New Zealand has a board of 9 members appointed by the Minister of Tourism for a term of three years. Directors receive an annual fee of NZ$15,000. Qualities sought in directors, and expectations of Tourism New Zealand by the government, as listed in a 2003 position description, are highlighted in Table 12. The broad member position description is detailed in Appendix 1.

There has been little research attention towards the influence exerted by special interest groups on DMO governance. Greenwood (1993) suggested interest groups are usually more successful the less they use public channels of communication. Media is only used as a last resort. In tourism, groups with an active interest in DMO governance at all levels include sector associations and local/national tourism umbrella associations, In some cases there are organised lobby groups such as the Tour Operators Study Group in the U.K. An interest group has been defined as:

> Domain based in economic fields of operation, operating with a degree of permanence, where membership is restricted to organizations such as firms and pressure is exerted through developing permanent relations with government, often in 'behind closed doors' environments (Greenwood 1993: 336).

Gee & Makens (1985) provided a candid explanation of the opportunities, challenges and conflicts that face members of tourism boards:

> Tourism boards can be an effective force for a community's hospitality industry, and the hotel manager is a crucial part of such a board. But to

Table 12: Government expectations of tourism New Zealand directors and operations.

Expectations of Tourism New Zealand Operations	Skills and Experience of Directors
• Integrity • Frugality and due care in the use of taxpayer money • Advancing activities beneficial to the tourism sector and wider community rather than to any individual business • Focusing on medium to long term strategies rather than short term gains • Showing openness and having good communication with the Minister, the Ministry of Tourism and other government agencies • Partnering with the private sector to add value rather than displace or duplicate private businesses	• A wide perspective on issues • Good oral and written communication • Understanding of public sector governance and accountability • Previous experience as a company director • Ability to work in a team and work collaboratively • Strategic skills • Experience in developing and maintaining partnerships with other organizations and companies • Experience with financial statements • Understanding of and/or experience in the tourism sector at a senior level • Understanding the importance of value creation, innovation and international best practise comparisons • Experience of marketing issues

do its job, the board may have to resist the influences of politics, unrealistic community "cheerleading," and intra-industry competition (Gee & Makens 1985: 25).

While Gee & Makens were writing specifically for hotel managers, their paper is a worthwhile read for any prospective RTO board member. An account of DMO governance issues likely to be faced was provided in Kelly and Nankervis (2001) observations of the challenges faced by one of Victoria's RTOs, the Yarra Valley, Dandenong and the Ranges Tourism Board:

• diversity of features
• board representatives not focused on the "big picture"
• operator's suspicions of others' sectoral interests
• cumbersome organisational name to reflect all areas covered
• a regional community not fully informed on the advantages of tourism
• lack of reliable visitor statistics.

Palmer's (1998) literature review of the governance literature identified a loose-tight or informal-formal continuum of managing organisational relationships. Loose styles are likely to be more suited to creative tasks, and important considerations are trust and levels of access to resources. Informal relationship controls are self control, based on financial or psychological incentives, socio-cultural control, based on group norms. Tight styles are governed by more formal legal controls. The former might signal unclear objectives and strategy, but more flexible, creative and fast moving. The tight style, on the other hand, is more likely to generate clear and formal goals, contractual rights and obligations, but also be more bureaucratic, particularly in terms of decision making. This approach can be frustrating to entrepreneurial tourism operators. Palmer's review identified a number of antecedent factors that might influence the type of DMO governance. These include:

- the local socio-cultural environment
- the organisation's purpose, level of financial, human and operational resources
- the age of the organisation and destination life-cycle stage
- the scale of membership.

Palmer (1998) hypothesised that while a loose style might suit a local tourism association because of the dynamic nature of tourism markets, a tight governance style would be more effective in terms of maintaining a strategic focus. In a survey of 172 members of 13 English local tourism associations, there was evidence to suggest a strong link between a tight governance style and organisation effectiveness (196):

> The most effective local tourism associations were ones characterized by formal rules and conditions which governed relationships between members, the presence of an efficient and effective secretariat, and a lack of opportunities for discussing the management of the association.

Career Opportunities

In the post industrial era, the success of a corporation lies more in it's intellectual and systems capabilities than in it's physical assets (Quinn *et al.* 1996: 71). As with any organisation, staff are an important asset for any DMO. This is important at all levels, from the front liners at VICs to the CEO. DMOs usually enjoy a high profile within the destination community, and this carries political implications beyond "normal" customer services skills. Increasingly, DMOs are being recognised as providing serious career opportunities. However, there is a dearth of literature relating to human resource management in DMOs.

In Australia, McKercher & Ritchie's (1997) study of local government tourism officers raised questions about levels of professionalism in the field. They found, for example, a lack of formal tourism qualifications, little prior tourism industry experience and turnover of up to 50% of staff each year. Given the nature of the challenges discussed and the high turnover, McKercher and Ritchie questioned whether local government tourism management is seen as a valid career in its own right or merely a stepping stone to other opportunities? Some of the difficulties faced by local government tourism officials that were identified included:

- working in small organisations with no internal promotion opportunities
- isolation from counterparts

- understaffing
- under funding
- unrealistic expectations from elected council representatives.

McKercher & Ritchie identified three primary reasons for this mobility. First, many local authority tourism staff aspire to higher positions within the tourism industry and use the LTA as a stepping stone to other organisations such as STOs. Such moves offer higher salaries as well as greater status within the tourism hierarchy. Second, LTA roles are generally very high profile within the community, and managers are likely to become "public property." As a result the role is forced to become involved in a broader range of activities than tourism promotion, which can be seen as being invasive. Third, LTA roles require constant innovation as well as ongoing lobbying of local politicians. Therefore it can be easier to move and transfer existing ideas to a new community. Ultimately the impact of a high turnover is disruption to what are predominantly small teams.

Morrison *et al.*'s (1998) 1992/1993 survey of 254 member CVBs of the IACVB found executives of the highest funded CVBs were more likely to be males over 55 years with a university degree and an average of 16 years experience:

- *Gender*. The executives of 59% of CVBs were male and 41% were female. Female executives tended to work with smaller budgets than male executives, with only 8% of females managing budgets over US$2 million compared to 39% of males.
- *Education*. Two thirds of executives had university degrees, with three holding doctorates. 80% of male executives had degrees but only 49% of females.
- *College major*. Less than 2% indicated a tourism major. Of the 66 majors listed the most common were business administration (18%), marketing (10%), and education (8%).
- *Tourism work experience*. Two thirds of executives indicated prior tourism industry experience, while 45% had previously worked in a CVB.
- *Income*. Two thirds of executives had salaries of US$50,000 or more. Incomes tended to rise in relation to age and education. Males averaged US$70,000-$74,999, while females averaged US$45,000-$49,999. Fourteen percent of males earned over US$110,000 compared to 1% of females.
- *Job titles*. A total of 19 different titles were reported, with the most common being Executive Director (50%) and President (15%). Forty one percent of males were listed as President/CEO, in comparison to only 12% of females.
- *Period of tenure*. The average period of tenure for the current executives was 5.6 years, from a range of 1 to 25 years.

Given the noticeable gender differences, Morrison *et al.* proposed a worthwhile project being to identify the characteristics of successful female executives. Likewise McKercher & Ritchie (1997) found a gender imbalance among LTAs in the Australian states of Victoria and New South Wales. Women tended to be relegated to lower status positions of managing VIC units, while the management of larger local authority tourism departments were more likely to be male. There was also a significant gender salary gap, even though males were generally no better qualified than women.

Sims' (1990) survey of 79 CVBs identified a mean of seven professional staff, of which five were male and two female. The paper listed respondents' views on desirable attributes for service level, sales, and administration positions. Frequently mentioned personal qualities were: creativity, flexibility, friendliness, honesty, motivation, outgoing personality, and honesty. The majority of respondents felt a university degree was a prerequisite for employment. In a survey of STO and CVB management, O'Halloran (1992) found 76 and 80% respectively held university degrees. Both groups considered people as the most important DMO resource. The most important DMO management skills were leadership and employee relations, followed by marketing and other technical skills. From the responses, the paper summarised the following essential characteristics of a successful DMO manager:

- At least six years *experience* with a DMO, with additional prior business experience
- A minimum of a bachelor's *degree*, preferably in tourism or business
- Excellent *communication* skills
- The ability to *work well with people* at all levels
- *Knowledge of the tourism system* and its potential impacts on the community
- *Leadership* and strategic planning
- *Political savvy*, in terms of the political system and the relationship between the public and private sectors.

It is one of the great business myths that visionary organisations are great places to work (Collins & Porras 1997). Rather, they are great places to work for those who fit the culture of the organisation. Prospective DMO staff should do their homework to find out everything they can about the culture of the organisation. In return candidates should expect a rigorous screening process. In many communities the DMO is a high profile organisation, and so there can be high levels of competition for advertised positions. Students seeking a career in destination marketing, and considering what courses will be most suitable, might be interested to note the O'Halloran's (1992: 90) curriculum recommendations for DMO management training:

> Subject areas for study should be communication (persuasion and negotiation, advertising, business writing, oral communication, and inter-personal communication), business (tourism systems, management skills, policy, services management, economics, planning and development, marketing, finance and accounting), social sciences (geography, anthropology, psychology, sociology, and political science). Other critical skills include research methods and management, information systems, transportation and international studies.

In terms of professional development training for DMO staff, the IACVB offers a Certified Destination Management Executive Programme (CDME):

> Recognised by the CVB industry as its highest educational achievement, CDME is an advanced educational programme for veteran and career-minded CVB executives looking for senior-level professional

development courses. The focus of the programme is on vision, leadership, productivity and the implementation of business strategies (www.iacvb.org/iacvb/view_page.asp?mkey=&mid=100, 23/4/04).

The CDME features three core courses, listed below, as well as a number of electives:

* Strategic issues in destination management
* Destination marketing planning
* Destination leadership.

Chapter Key Point Summary

Key point 1 — Destination Competitiveness

The core purpose of DMOs is enhancing sustained destination competitiveness. While maintaining competitiveness represents a significant challenge for many destinations, there has been little research on the topic published in the tourism literature. A major element in striving for competitive advantage in the crowded tourism markets is the development and implementation of tourism strategies, since destinations endowed with natural attractions have been forced into competition with places that have developed attractive built environments. To achieve competitiveness the four main goals are enhancing destination image, increasing industry profitability, reducing seasonality, and ensuring long term funding. The primary responsibility of DMOs is destination marketing, which is the focus of Chapter 8. In general, the three other important responsibilities are industry coordination, monitoring service and quality standards, and fostering community relations.

Key point 2 — Structure

There is a plethora of DMO structures, with no widely accepted model. Historically, DMOs emerged either as government departments or as industry association collectives. More recently there has been a shift towards the establishment of public-private partnerships (PPPs), as a way of ensuring destination marketing programmes are industry driven but also accountable to public funders. PPPs, at both a national and local level, are generally governed by a private sector board that is appointed by, and reports to, a government representative.

Key point 3 — Funding Sources

The majority of DMOs, at all levels, and regardless of how they are structured, rely to a large extent on government support. Government funding is commonly provided through annual grants or through some form of levy on visitors or businesses. The over reliance of government funding has been a concern to many DMOs, given the long term uncertainty of political commitment towards tourism. The withdrawal of state government funding in

Colorado serves as a warning to all DMOs. More research into alternative forms of funding is required.

Additional Reading

Collins, J. C., & Porras, J. I. (1997). *Built to last — Successful habits of visionary companies.* New York: HarperCollins.

Pearce, D. (1992). *Tourist organizations.* New York: Wiley.

Ritchie, J. R. B., & Crouch, G. I. (2003). *The competitive destination: A sustainable tourism perspective.* Oxon: CABI Publishing.

WTO (1996). *Towards new forms of public-private sector partnership: The changing role, structure and activities of national tourism administrations.* Madrid: World Tourism Organization.

WTO (1999). *Budgets of national tourism administrations.* Madrid: World Tourism Organization.

Chapter 4

Destination Branding

> One industry after another has discovered that brand awareness, perceived
> quality, customer loyalty, and strong brand associations and personality are
> necessary to compete in the marketplace (Aaker & Joachimsthaler 2000: ix).

Chapter Perspective

Today's consumers have more product choice but less decision making time than ever before. Consequently, a brand that can help simplify decisions, reduce purchase risk, create and deliver expectations is invaluable (Keller 2003). The topic of product branding first appeared in the literature fifty years ago (see Gardner & Levy 1955). However, most of the work relating to brand theory and practise has only been published since 1991 (e.g. Aaker 1991, 1996; Aaker & Joachimsthaler 2000; Keller 1993, 2000, 2003; McEnally & de Chernatony 1999; Morgan 2003; Urde 1999). While works such as these provide a valuable resource for consumer goods marketers, research related to the branding of tourism destinations has been sparse. This is a significant gap in the tourism and travel research fields, particularly given a number of leading brand authors have cited the prediction that the future of marketing will be a "battle of brands, a competition for brand dominance" (see Aaker 1991: ix; de Chernatony 1993: 173), and that within the tourism industry destinations are emerging as the biggest brands (Morgan *et al.* 2002). However, in many competitive markets it is likely that most destinations will become increasingly substitutable, if not already so, and therefore commodities rather than brands. This chapter explores the reasons behind these assertions, with the discussion underpinned by four themes. First, the understanding that promoting product features is not sufficient to differentiate against competitors is fundamental to brand theory. Second, the already complex process of product brand development and management is intensified for destination marketers, who exert no control over the actual delivery of the brand promise. Third, and following the previous point, there has been little published research to date to guide DMOs on the long term effectiveness of destination branding. Fourth, the view has been adopted that branding is at the very heart of marketing strategy, and so the purpose of all destination marketing activity must be to enhance the value of the brand.

The Importance of Brands

> Brands incite beliefs, evoke emotions and prompt behaviours . . . they speed
> up consumers' information processing and learning . . . Brands have the

ability to add or subtract from the perceived value of a product (Kotler & Gertner 2002: 249).

The first branding paper to appear in the literature was Gardner & Levy's (1955) discussion on the stereotypes that had emerged in advertising, which failed to differentiate competitive products. They espoused the importance of considering a brand as representing a personality (35):

> ... a brand name is more than the label employed to differentiate among the manufacturers of a product. It is a complex symbol that represents a variety of ideas and attributes. It tells the consumers many things, not only by the way it sounds (and its literal meaning if it has one) but, more important, via the body of associations it has built up and acquired as a public object over a period of time ... The net result is a public image, a character or personality that may be more important for the over-all status (and sales) of the brand than many technical facts about the product.

Brand practise however was around centuries before it became an academic field. Keller (2003) for example cited reports about identification marks of craftsmen being found on pottery in China, Europe and India dating as far back as 1300 BC. The evolution of brand development since the 1870s was examined by King (1970), who suggested the driving force was the cyclical balance of power in the manufacturer-distributor relationship. Branding of manufactured goods emerged during the late 19th century to counter the dominating force of wholesalers who controlled what were essentially commodity markets. Retailers purchased what was available in stock from wholesalers, who in turn dictated what manufacturers should produce. From the 1900s to the 1960s the role of the wholesaler was reduced to that of distributor, as manufacturer numbers declined to the level of oligopolies. Brands were then used to build demand for a smaller line of goods, with economies of scale leading to increased profits for manufacturers. This occurred at the expense of retailers' margins since manufacturers controlled consumer prices. By 1970, the balance of power had shifted towards large scale retailers, where economies of scale and their own brand labels enhanced profit levels: "After all, many retail chains are bigger businesses than most consumer goods manufacturers; and on the whole there are more manufacturers still in most fields than the retailer really needs" (pp. 7–8). The new role for product marketers was to improve the value of their brands to the consumer as well as the mega-retailer. King also used the term "brand personality" to suggest brands held "values" beyond their physical and functional attributes (p. 11):

> People choose their brands as they choose their friends. You choose your friends not usually because of specific skills or physical attributes (though of course these come into it) but simply because you like them as people. It is the total person you choose, not a compendium of virtues and vices.

Following Aaker (1991: x), de Chernatony (1993: 173), and Keller (2003: 39–41), there are a number of compelling reasons why branding is generating increasing awareness of the importance of brands among product and service providers.

Brand Equity

One of the most important impacts of branding for commercial organisations has been the increasing awareness of the balance sheet value of brands, referred to as brand equity. That is, a brand can be an asset or a liability to the firm, and as such can affect the valuation of the firm. Given the difficulty in developing new brands, there is a willingness by firms to pay a premium for the purchase of well known brands. Of the different methods available to measure intangible brand equity, *Business Week* (August 2003) selected that used by brand consultancy Interbrand (www.interbrand.com) to calculate the value of the world's 100 top brands. Interbrand valued brand equity based on the net present value of future earning potential. The top ten brand values are shown in Table 1, where it can be seen that the intangible Coca-Cola brand was valued at US$70 billion. The tourism related Disney brand was ranked seventh, at US$28 billion. Strong brand equity can enable a competitive advantage by generating greater sales or higher margins than would otherwise be achieved without the brand name (Belch & Belch 2004). In this regard the power of branding is now also recognised by sports administrators. For example, at the 2003 Rugby World Cup the New Zealand Rugby Union's CEO lamented the prospect of the All Black "brand" being damaged by defeats: "Clearly, winning the Rugby World Cup underpins the brand, it leverages it" (Harvey 2003: 21).

The marketing budget should be regarded as an investment in consumers' associations of the brand (Keller 2000). There is a growing view that branding lies at the core of marketing strategy, and that the purpose of the marketing programme should be to focus on developing favourable brand associations, linking the brand's attributes to consumer needs. The other motive for measuring brand equity, other than financial asset valuation, therefore is marketing effectiveness. It is the latter, consumer-based brand equity, which may be the most critical for organisations, since financial valuation is irrelevant if no underlying

Table 1: The World's top 10 brands in 2003.

Rank	2003 Brand Value US$ Billions
1. Coca-cola	70.45
2. Microsoft	65.17
3. IBM	51.77
4. GE	42.34
5. Intel	31.11
6. Nokia	29.44
7. Disney	28.04
8. McDonalds	24.70
9. Marlboro	22.18
10. Mercedes	21.37

Source: Adapted from Business Week, Aug 2003: viewed 22/10/03 at: www.interbrand. ca/pdf/Best_Global_Brands.2003.pdf.

consumer-based value of the brand has been established (Keller 1993). For destinations the concept of consumer-based destination brand equity is clearly more relevant than balance sheet values.

Increasing Global Competition

Competition is intensifying through the breaking down of trading barriers between nations. This and other impacts of globalisation, such as the internet, has led to a greater awareness of global competitors by both producers and consumers. Since 70% of international travellers visit only 10 countries, over 90 NTOs compete for 30% of total international arrivals (Morgan *et al.* 2002). The new competition phenomenon does not discriminate against famous destinations. For example, Dahles (1998: 56) claimed that while once competing with London and Paris to be Europe's most popular destination, Amsterdam was "fighting for survival." Increasing competition between traditional and emerging destinations has significant consequences for most places:

> The great majority will need to review and adapt their traditional organisational and marketing methods to survive and prosper in the next millennium. One can only speculate that some will be unable to make the change and will not survive as holiday destinations beyond the next decade or so (Middleton 1998: 153).

Commodification

Commodification of products is increasing, due to the difficulty of differentiating like-products in crowded markets. As the craftsmen of a century ago would have been only too aware, product features can be quickly imitated and so do not provide a lasting source of advantage. The effect of continued commodification in markets is ultimately competition based on price:

> Too many brands drift aimlessly and appear to stand for nothing in particular. They always seem to be shouting price, on sale, attached to some deal, or engaging in promiscuous channel expansion — symptoms of a lack of integrity (Aaker & Joachimsthaler 2000: 40).

Dolnicar & Mazanec (1998) cited research in Germany that found the number of travel agency customers who asked for information on travel activities outweighed the number who asked for information about a destination. An effective brand strategy can provide a means for successful differentiation. After all, in commodity categories "something" must make a greater difference to a consumer's thinking about the competing products offer features of a similar quality, and that something is the symbol a brand represents to the consumer (Gardner & Levy 1955). Keller (2003) pointed to successful branding within a number of commodity categories, where product differentiation is difficult to achieve, such as water (Perrier), beer (Budweiser), cigarettes (Marlboro), soap (Ivory), pineapples (Dole), oatmeal (Quaker) and bananas (Chiquita).

The Power of Retailers

The power of mega retailers is increasing. The development of their own labels, access to customers, combined with their control of high profile shelf space can be a significant barrier for small product suppliers. The trend has been of concern to marketers since at least 1970 when the topic was the hot issue at the Advertising Association conference (see King 1970). This power of retailers not only applies to fast moving consumer goods in supermarkets, but equally to the distribution of tourism services through retail travel, both traditional and on-line.

Sophisticated Consumers

Today's consumers are the most sophisticated ever to be faced by marketers. We are experienced, having been exposed to unprecedented levels of media communications, and have access to increasing sources of product information and consumer advice. In so many cases we are spoilt for choice, and we know it.

Brand Extensions and Portfolios of Products

Many major brands have capitalised on brand equity by extending their range of offerings across categories and segments. For example, what is a Ford, or a Cadbury or a Nike? Both managing and competing against an extensive brand portfolio hierarchy are now major challenges.

Media Cost Effectiveness

Marketers are now faced with escalating media costs, often in tandem with declining advertising budgets. Also, the proliferation of new and niche media is resulting in a relative decline in the effectiveness of traditional advertising. This is resulting in increased interest in below the line promotional opportunities.

Short Term Performance Orientation

Marketing planning has long been driven by short term measures of accountability. Such pressures, which may be exerted by shareholders, management and/or economic analysts, place emphasis on tactical initiatives for short term gain rather than longer term strategies.

Branding Tourism Destinations

> ... we have "somehow" failed to recognize the significance of the Branding function in our efforts to increase awareness of destinations and to create the positive attitudes that are so essential to the final choice of a travel destination (Ritchie & Ritchie 1998: 89).

How often do we hear in everyday conversation "... yes, (product x) is a good brand" in response to someone discussing their options for the purchase of a new car, fridge, TV or other important item? What is meant by such a claim; what exactly is a "brand?" Are they simply "collective hallucinations" as suggested by John Urry in the key note address to the 2003 *Taking Tourism to the Limits* conference at the University of Waikato? When considering definitions of the brand construct, it is important to consider the perspectives of both the organisation and the market. From the market perspective the commonly cited definition provided by Aaker (1991: 7) is pertinent to the ensuing discussion on the branding of destinations, which effectively represent "groups of sellers":

> A brand is a distinguishing name and/or symbol (such as a logo, trademark, or package design) intended to identify the goods or services of either one seller or a group of sellers, and to differentiate those goods from those of competitors.

Importantly, a brand is more than simple symbols presented to the public. A brand must stand for something, a promise to the consumer, and is therefore more than a logo. A brand also involves an "image or type of association that comes to mind when consumers think about a brand" (Belch & Belch 2004: 14). Therefore it is useful to consider a brand as representing an identity for the producer and an image for the consumer. Aaker (1996) distinguished these separate components of a brand as the *brand identity* (internal organisation orientation), representing self-image and aspired market image, and the *brand image* (external market orientation) of the actual image held by consumers. Aaker strongly cautioned against falling into the brand image trap where the image held by consumers dictates the brand identity. In this scenario the soul and vision of the brand is overshadowed by the changing whims of the consumer. The model in Figure 1 highlights these two distinctive components, along with a third overlapping element, which is *brand positioning*. It is proposed brand positioning is the interface between brand identity and brand image, over which the DMO has some control. This chapter focuses on the development of a destination brand identity. The components of destination brand image are outlined in Chapter 5, and destination positioning is the focus of Chapter 6.

There is a lack of published research relating to tourism destination branding. This is in spite of general agreement in academia and industry that the concept of branding can be applied to destinations (Pritchard & Morgan 1998). In fact the topic of destination branding did not appear in the tourism literature until the late 1990s (see also Gnoth 1998; Ritchie & Ritchie 1998). Gnoth (1998: 758–760) suggested the special track on "Branding Tourism Destinations" he convened at the 1997 American Marketing Science conference, represented

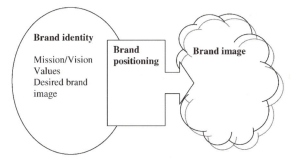

Figure 1: Brand identity, brand positioning and brand image.

the first meeting of practitioners and academics on the topic. The track attracted four other paper presenters from the U.K., Australia and the USA, and common issues discussed included:

- the magnitude of product types and attributes involved in a destination brand
- the social and managerial problems when developing a brand for generically different partners with the tourism system supplying the tourism experience
- the fledgling domain of developing an attribute taxonomy and measurement instruments evaluating and monitoring success and impact of a destination brand.

Since then there have been relatively few published case studies applying theory to destination branding, particularly at the RTO level. However, this should be tempered by the understanding that in the general marketing and strategy literature and practise, branding has received much less attention than the product and its functional attributes (Urde 1999). The application of brand theory to practise is a complex and challenging process, magnified for destinations by the constraints faced by most DMOs. A worthwhile starting point in considering how brand theory might apply to destinations is to consider Aaker's (1991) model of consumer-based brand equity. The model proposed brand equity comprised four major assets: brand loyalty, brand awareness, perceived quality and brand associations.

Brand Loyalty

Brand loyalty is ultimately measured by repeat and referral custom. Given the increasing substitutability of destinations, the key advantages of brand loyalty for destinations include lower marketing costs, increased travel trade leverage, and word of mouth referrals. While a number of studies in other fields have identified correlations between customer retention and increased profits (see Aaker 1996: 22), there is a dearth of literature relating to destination loyalty and switching costs (Grabler 1997a). In an early study of repeat visitation, Gitelson & Crompton (1984) found five factors that contributed to a return to a familiar destination:

- reduced risk of an unsatisfactory experience
- knowledge that they would find their own kind of people there
- emotional or childhood attachment, to experience
- opportunities to visit aspects of the destination not previously experienced
- to expose others to a previously satisfying experience.

Destination loyalty is an important avenue of research given suggestions that in many cases travellers are initially selecting a holiday type before considering the destination choice. The ability to create customer loyalty is the main benefit of branding (Gilmore 2002), since consumers have favourites, and they perceive these more favourably than lesser known rivals (Simon 1970). Simon's experiments using blind tests of advertising found brand leaders scored higher than the advertising content warranted, such was the power of the name. Similar consumer goods brand recall results have also been reported (e.g. Allison & Uhl 1964).

Brand Awareness

Brand awareness is the foundation of all sales activity. Consider for example the hierarchical AIDA advertising axiom, which aims to *attract* attention, stimulate *interest*, create *desire*, and ultimately result in consumer *action*. Awareness represents the strength of the brand's presence in the mind of the target, with the goal not being to achieve general awareness, but to be remembered for the reasons intended (Aaker 1996). In other words the aim should be to increase familiarity with the brand through repeated exposure and strong associations with the product category (Keller 2003).

Perceived Quality

Perceived quality is the perception of superiority in a product class, and is a significant contributor to financial performance due to the ability to set higher prices. Market perceptions of quality may be quite different to actual quality for a number of reasons, including: the experience of previous poor quality, quality being achieved on attributes not deemed important, or a lack of information processing by the consumer. However, whether an individual's perceived images are correct is not as important as what the consumer actually believes to be true (Hunt 1975; Mayo 1973).

Brand Associations

Brand associations held in the mind about a product aid consumer information processing: "A brand association is anything 'linked' in memory to a brand" (Aaker 1991: 109). For destinations, associations are a combination of functional and affective attributes, of which some will represent key buying criteria. The traditional view has been that brand positioning should focus on only one or a few associations as the focus of the reason to buy (see for example Ries 1996). What is most critical is that brand associations are strong, favourable and unique, in that order (Keller 2003).

In moving towards a structure for destination brand strategy it is useful to consider potential critical success factors. In this regard Keller (2000) identified ten characteristics of the world's strongest brands, which could be used by marketers to identify strengths and weaknesses of a brand and its competitors. Unfortunately no destination brands were included in the analysis. However, Keller's brand report card does warrant consideration by destination marketers, albeit with a caveat that the level of control or influence able to be exerted by DMOs makes implementation problematic:

- The brand excels at delivering the benefits customers truly desire. Two implications of this for DMOs are firstly a market research system that identifies these benefits and unmet needs, other than functional attributes, and secondly stimulating the consistency of service delivery in a myriad of service encounters over which the DMO has no control. Complicating this is the challenge of dealing with differing market needs and seasonal variations in the visitor experience.
- The brand stays relevant to customers. This is a key challenge for all destinations, which evolve over time through a life cycle. As well as staying in tune with changing consumer and travel trends, two other aspects of this are important, but over which the DMO has little if any control. First is the necessary (re)investment in product improvements to maintain and enhance the destination experience. Second is the influence of the development of new attractions and facilities by entrepreneurs, which may or may not fit the original character of the destination. For example, SnowWorld at Australia's Surfer's Paradise seems incongruent with the image of a sub-tropical beach resort, and yet fits the Gold Coast's "Coast with the most" brand theme that implies the benefit of lots to see and do.
- The pricing strategy is based on consumers' perceptions of value. While DMOs usually have no control over product pricing, it is possible for the DMO to institute measures to monitor perceptions of value held by customers and non-customers in target markets. Clearly this is an important issue for DMOs, with increasing commodification of destinations, and the importance placed on "value for money" as an important destination attribute by travellers (e.g. Baloglu & Mangaloglu 2001).
- The brand is properly positioned in the market by offering a distinctive value proposition. This is particularly challenging for DMOs for three main reasons. First, the sheer number of destinations with similar offerings crowding the market place. Second, the issue of intangibility and risk, and the resultant reliance on perceptions rather than concrete experience, in travel decision making. Third, the multi-attributed nature of the destination. Destination brand positioning, which is one area where the DMO is able to exert influence, is another area lacking a depth of academic research. This topic is discussed in more detail in Chapter 6.
- The brand is consistent. DMOs should ensure the delivery of all communications consistently reflects the brand's values. Politics can be problematic for destinations, with no control over politicians, intermediaries, product suppliers and host community. At the level of government politics, many DMOs are obligated to political masters. For example, in the case of Valencia in Spain the public funded DMO is required to issue

new advertising contacts every year (Pritchard & Morgan 1998, 2002). In the state of Louisiana, the Department of Culture, Recreation and Tourism (DCRT) is legislated to review its advertising agency account every three years (Slater 2002). At another level is the politics of intermediaries such as airlines, travel agents and wholesalers. Vial (1997, in Morgan & Pritchard 1998) cited the example of the "Feast for the senses" brand developed by Publicis for the Morocco Tourist Board. This was an attempt to develop an umbrella brand for use in all markets. Previously, different campaigns had been used in different markets, which had resulted in a confused image. The proposed campaign did gain the support of the tourism industry in Morocco. However it was derailed by resistance from travel agents and tour wholesalers who viewed the campaign as promoting cultural tourism when they were in the business of catering to the need for sun and sea packages. At the level of DMO governance and decision making, politics arises through inequality between tourism organisations. For example, Ritchie & Ritchie (1998) referred to the heavy influence of the Disney Corporation on the "Orlando Magic" destination brand. Furthermore, a long term and consistent brand strategy might be subject to tampering with the appointment of new marketing managers wanting to leave their personal stamp on strategies. For example, McKercher & Ritchie (1997) cited the example of an LTA in Australia, which had four managers in six years. This led in the development of four different marketing plans, with each having a different positioning statement, resulting in marketplace confusion.

• The brand portfolio and hierarchy make sense. Hopper (2002) reported how the plethora of brands used by tourism businesses to promote London had led to a dilution of the brand designed by the London Tourist Board. In tourism there may be up to six or more levels in the destination brand hierarchy, as shown in Table 2, ranging from the country brand to local tourism businesses. The issue becomes complex when considering that a major product supplier, such as Stonehenge in south England, Legoland in California, Seaworld on the Gold Coast, Disneyland Resort Paris for example, might have different destination umbrella brands at the LTA, RTO, STO, and NTO levels with which they work with. A destination may be viewed as the umbrella brand, with individual products as sub-brands. Flagestad & Hope (2001) suggested an umbrella brand for Scandinavian tourism suppliers could prove an efficient means of addressing image problems in non-Nordic markets. Such an umbrella brand can be used to endorse the credibility

Table 2: Destination brand hierarchy.

Level	Entity
1	Country brand
2	Country tourism brand
3	State tourism brands
4	Regional/macro regional brands
5	Local community brands
6	Individual tourism business brands

of the tourism sub-brands. The Australian Tourism Commission has assisted STOs such as the Western Australia Tourism Commission with brand development. Another example is the proactive role played by Tourism Queensland in developing regional brands within the state. The incentive for the RTOs is funding by Tourism Queensland, to a level that can exceed the contributions of local shire councils. The concept of destination umbrella branding is related to the consumer goods strategy of applying the name of a brand to a broad range of products. The purpose of which is to spread positive elements of a brand's value over multiple products, through transfer phenomena such as "semantic generalisation" (e.g. Mazanec & Schweiger 1981). Potentially, the marketing efforts of each product within the brand hierarchy can flow across to other partners. Extending this concept further than creating synergies for tourism suppliers, Gnoth (2002) offered a model for leveraging local export brands through a country destination tourism brand.

- The brand makes use of, and coordinates, a full repertoire of marketing activities. If it is accepted that the focus of marketing activity is to enhance consumer based brand equity, this is a critical issue for DMOs, and one which the organisation exerts control. However, this area is not fully addressed in the destination branding literature.
- The brand's managers understand what the brand means to consumers. This emphasises the importance of establishing and monitoring a focused brand positioning strategy for the destination, to stimulate congruence between the brand identity and the brand image.
- The brand is given proper support, and that support is sustained over the long run. Senior management must genuinely share the belief that brand building results in a profitable competitive advantage (Aaker & Joachimsthaler 2000). More case studies examining the long-term effectiveness of destination brands are required, particularly in terms of monitoring the long-term nature of the investment. This is particularly important given the relatively limited budgets of most, if not all, DMOs. Morgan & Pritchard (2001) compared Sony's annual advertising budget of US$300 million with a WTO estimate that the total tourism advertising spend of all governments in the world to be US$350 million.
- The organisation monitors the sources of brand equity. Keller (2000) offered the example of a brand audit undertaken by Disney during the 1980s, to highlight how such sources could be diluted in value. The audit found the Disney characters, which were the main source of brand equity, were overexposed in the market through a myriad of product endorsements and licensing agreements. The serious impact of this commercialism resulted in strong negative perceptions of the brand by consumers. The Disney example highlights the value of developing a system of brand-equity management. This begins with a brand charter, detailing the philosophy of the brand and the value of branding, details of brand audits, tracking and research, and guidelines for strategies, tactics and treatment of the brand's visual components. Within this system, there must be effective communication between key stakeholders and marketing decision makers.

Undoubtedly, studies similar to Keller's (2000) that analyse leading destination brands to identify CSFs for DMOs would be invaluable. However, as has been stated, the number of published destination brand case studies has been limited, and there a need for more case study-based research into destination brand management.

Destination Branding Case Studies

Relative to the number of papers published on destination image, there have been few reported destination branding case studies. Given the recent emergence of the destination branding literature it is not surprising that the focus of cases published to date has been on brand development. With the exception of Curtis' (2001) analysis of Brand Oregon, there has been a lack of case studies examining the long term management and effectiveness of destination brands. The case studies published to date do however provide valuable insights to the practical challenges of applying brand theory to destination brand development, particularly since most have been written by practitioners involved in the brand campaigns. This section briefly summarises the contribution of six such cases.

Case 1 — Brand Oregon

> *Oregon. Things look different here.* In conjunction with the world-famous advertising agency, Wieden + Kennedy, the Oregon Tourism Commission has worked for 15 years to differentiate Oregon's travel product from its neighbours and attract visitors with this creative tagline that supports what the commission calls "Brand Oregon" (Oregon Tourism Commission 2003–2005 Strategic Marketing Plan).

One of the most cited destination branding cases has been Curtis' (2001) candid evaluation of the evolution of Brand Oregon. Curtis wrote from the perspective of a senior research executive with the Oregon Tourism Commission (OTC). The paper provided a balanced discussion on the strengths and weaknesses of the "Oregon — things look different here" brand campaign during the 1980s and 1990s. Impetus for the brand's development was an ailing state economy, and the approach of the campaign was to develop and umbrella brand for both tourism and economic development. Curtis observed that this proved a difficult fit and that the strength of the tourism/economic development connection fluctuated over time.

To achieve brand consistency, the tourism component of the strategy required all RTOs that received state funding to use the OTC's advertising agency. While the rationale for this approach was to achieve a consistency of promotional material, ultimately the top-down approach met resistance from the regions. However, the initiative did result in an increased awareness of the potential for cooperative marketing efforts.

Initially, the brand campaign resulted in a dramatic increase in the level of visitor enquiries, which, combined with a number of marketing awards, were regarded as positive performance indicators. More comprehensive measures were later developed to measure consumer perceptions, which ultimately are a more effective indicator of a brand's success than award ceremonies. The case provided a brief but insightful glimpse at the challenges involved in the development, implementation and management of a state destination brand over time. The paper concluded with a summary of four key lessons learned. First, avoid a top down approach of imposing a branding system on tourism business. Second, build on the destination's strengths and integrate newer images. Third, continually evaluate the effectiveness of the brand. Fourth, develop a long term commitment to the strategy.

Regarding the final point, at the time of writing the brand theme was still in use by the OTC, with the organisation calling for more support by other state agencies in its *2003–2005 Strategic Marketing Plan*:

> Much more could be accomplished with a cohesive branding effort being adopted by all state agencies involved in promoting Oregon and state products (www.traveloregon.com/OTC.cfm, 9/10/03).

Case 2 — Ohio's Identity Crisis

At the 2001 TTRA conference, May (2001) presented the process used to develop a new tourism brand for the state of Ohio. Previously the Ohio Division of Travel and Tourism had been successfully leveraging the advertising budget by using cooperative campaigns with industry partners. However the partners were dominating the messages, and as a result, Ohio suffered from a lack of a distinctive image in the market. As a tourism destination, Ohio had an identity crisis. The STO recognised the potential benefits of effective branding, and so a commitment was made to develop a new tourism brand that would feature in all communications.

The new brand development involved two initial research phases. Stage 1 used open-ended questions in interviews with 375 callers to the STO's free consumer enquiry line 1–800 Buckeye, as well as a series of focus groups in three out-of-state markets. A key question posed in the telephone interviews was: "How would you describe Ohio to someone who has never been here before?" The four most common responses were: "variety of things to see/do," "beautiful country, scenery and natural places," "theme parks" and "friendly people." The purpose of the focus groups was to identify positive and negative perceptions of the state. The three key positive perceptions identified were "amusement parks," "a place for children," and "shopping," while two key negative perceptions were "rustbelt" and "congested." The focus groups also suggested a lack of awareness of major destination features, such as: nature, history, scenery, lots to see/do, and culture.

The second research stage involved a structured questionnaire containing a battery of 75 image attributes. This was distributed to 3,800 consumers in different markets. The results identified the "hot button" attributes desired in a holiday destination by the target audience. For these attributes, survey participants rated their perceptions of Ohio and key competitors, which were: Michigan, Pennsylvania, Indiana, Illinois, Kentucky and West Virginia. This competitive analysis identified Ohio's key strengths and weaknesses, which are listed in Table 3.

From the results, the STO identified the core challenge as being the creation of an emotive message that would overcome the weaknesses and change perceptions. A number of brand slogans, along with associated music and imagery, were developed and tested in key markets. These included:

- Ohio . . . Oh!
- Ohio . . . Where America comes to play
- Ohio, the thrill of it all

Table 3: Ohio's competitive analysis.

Ohio's Strengths	Ohio's Weaknesses
Affordable	Scenery
Theme parks	Nature
Children enjoy	History
Close distance	

- Ohio . . . Where the fun never sets
- Ohio Oh WOW
- Ohio, Let Yourself Go!

The selected brand slogan, "Ohio — so much to discover," was introduced and tested in 2000, with full implementation during 2001. The Ohio Division of Travel and Tourism claims the most frequently called state tourism free phone hotline in the country. The call system responds to approximately 1.5 million inquiries annually (http://www.odod.state.oh.us/Travel.htm, 13/11/03). The presentation by Colleen May (May 2001), research manager for the Ohio Division of Travel and Tourism, provided TTRA conference delegates with an insider's perspective of the steps involved in destination branding, and as such represented a much needed interaction between a tourism practitioner and tourism academics.

Case 3 — Wales' Natural Revival

> For many years that venerable and respected British oracle of information and explanation, the Encyclopaedia Britannica, essentially denied Wales' existence. Under the entry for Wales it simply stated 'for Wales please see England' (Pride 2002: 109).

Another insightful practitioner perspective on destination branding was provided by Pride (2002), director of marketing for the Wales Tourist Board (WTB). Pride discussed the problems associated with a lack of national identity for a country that has historically been seen by the world as a suffix to England. For example, the nation has often been referred to as "And Wales." During the 1990s, research undertaken by the WTB and other organisations was consistently pointing to negative perceptions as a primary hindrance to the country's economic development. Tourism was one of a number of export industries affected by either negative or distorted images. Pride described the process and challenges of developing a brand strategy aimed at turning Wales' "identity deficit" into an "identity premium."

Travellers from Wales' traditional markets of England's northern industrial cities had become more experienced and sophisticated in their holiday needs and expectations. They had also been increasingly drawn away to Europe's cheap sunshine destinations. These trends have forced significant structural changes in the Welsh tourism industry.

Pride reported that while the tourism industry had responded with necessary high quality accommodation and recreation facilities, the negative image remained a significant barrier to growth:

> We recognised that if we going to enhance Wales' reputation as a leisure destination, we needed a single-minded, consistent, integrated and innovative communication strategy (Pride 2002: 112).

A framework was designed to subsume a new tourism destination brand development and communication strategy under the umbrella of a new nation brand. Pride reported that the development of the country brand was the most difficult part of the entire process, primarily due to a lack of government leadership and responsibility. The intent for the tourism brand was to develop one key positioning theme, which could be adapted to suit individual markets. This was complicated by the results of extensive research by the WTB that identified significant differences in both the perceptions of Wales, and the holiday needs of international and domestic travellers. Ultimately, "natural revival" was selected as the brand positioning, based on the following qualities: unspoiled, down to earth, traditional values, back in time, genuine, beautiful, physical, spiritual and hidden on England's doorstep.

   A summary of the brand's implementation in the domestic and international markets, key results and an impressive list of marketing awards are included in the paper. Pride concluded with a candid acknowledgement that the brand was still in its infancy and discussed future challenges, central to which was the real need to ensure the brand promise is actually delivered at the destination. The case provided a rare insight into a DMO's approach to one of the core questions of this text, that is, is one position for a multi-attributed destination suitable for all markets?

Case 4 — Brand Western Australia

The Western Australian Tourism Commission's (WATC) approach to branding the state was reported by the STO's CEO and brand manager (see Crockett & Wood 1999). The authors advised the development of a new brand strategy in the 1990s not only resulted in a successful global repositioning but also an "entire organisational shift" (276). Western Australia's landmass represents one-third of the Australian continent, a rich tourism resource with significant variations in geography and climate between different regions. In the early 1990s, WATC research found the state lacked a meaningful identity, particularly in international travel markets. Crockett & Wood reported the development of Brand Western Australia (Brand WA), which would drive all marketing activities. The new brand was launched in 1996 and went beyond being a market repositioning campaign:

> Brand WA provided the catalyst for an entire organisational restructure within the WATC. This reflects a new corporate culture, new direction, increased accountability, performance measurement, partnerships with industry and a clear customer focus (Crockett & Wood 1999: 278).

The budget for developing and implementing an international brand strategy was limited to AUD\$8.8 million over five years. The process began with the formation of a representative "brand strategy group," to oversee the project. Significantly Brand WA was to be a state brand, rather than only a tourism brand. Furthermore the brand would attempt to maximise synergies with the ATC's Brand Australia. ATC representatives were therefore involved in the development of Brand WA. Other tourism partnerships established during the development phase extended to the formation of ten regional tourism organisations within the state.

The market research programme focused on consultation with end users of the brand, as well as qualitative studies in domestic and international markets. The key questions raised were (280):

- What are the attributes tourists rank as high motivators for their travel?
- What are the consumers' perceptions of Western Australia and Perth as a holiday destination?
- What do travellers imagine when they think of Western Australia and Perth?
- What are the state's major strengths and weaknesses as a holiday destination in the eyes of consumers?

While the research revealed positive perceptions of nature based attractions, the lack of a distinctive image was also apparent. Due to limited financial resources available to address the lack of identity on a global scale, a "Market Potential Assessment Formula" was then developed to prioritise target markets. The formula was based on the criteria of access, growth rate, market share and synergy with ATC activity. Crockett & Wood reported the formula was used twice a year to monitor market shifts.

The market research enabled the development of a brand identity and a five year strategy for increasing market exposure, industry partnerships and developing new infrastructure and tourism products. The paper described many elements of the marketing mix, media campaign, regional brand extensions and performance measures. For example, it was estimated that an initial six-week campaign in the U.K. resulted in 5,886 visitors who spent AUD\$7.3 million within the state.

Case 5 — War Torn Central and Eastern Europe

Hall (1999) provided a rare analysis of the branding opportunities and challenges faced by what are predominantly fledgling destinations in post-communist Central and Eastern Europe (CEE). Tourism earnings in the region had lagged behind the rest of Europe for a number of reasons, including a short length of stay and low spending tourists from other CEE countries. Destination branding by CEE countries was constrained by lack of finance, lack of international marketing experience and public pressure for short-term results. To illustrate the destination branding challenges faced in the region Hall focused on Slovenia and Croatia. As new states, which were part of the former Yugoslavia, both have needed to establish national identities untainted by the conflict in the Balkans. For example, despite a long history of tourism promotion as part of Yugoslavia, post-war Slovenia faced the challenge of re-attracting previously established markets. Although Slovenia gained independence in 1991, an NTO was not established until 1996. The Slovenia Tourism Board's brand strategy was to position the destination as a western civilised country with contiguity to Austria and Italy, and away from the Balkan association. However, the destination found it difficult to achieve the numbers of visitor arrivals generated when part of the pre-war Yugoslavia federation. Hall suggested the promotional material used to support the brand did not adequately and clearly convey a unique position for the country.

Containing most of the former Yugoslavia's coastline, Croatia was a major benefactor of tourism in the region. Following the war years it was important therefore for Croatia to establish a national tourism brand strategy that would "convey a distinct image to clearly differentiate the country from its neighbours and reassure former markets that quality and value had been restored" (Hall 1999: 234). However, Hall observed that initial branding attempts failed to differentiate the destination from others in the region. The cases demonstrate the challenges faced by war-torn countries attempting re-branding away from the former negative associations of communism and conflict. Hall concluded destination branding was poorly developed in CEE countries, and called for a more collaborative approach between private and public sectors. Although Hall found little evidence of coordination between local, regional and national tourism interests, he admitted the issue was politically complicated (235):

> This is understandable given that over much of the region there has been a desire to reduce any form of centralised planning as a reaction to the previous half-century of state socialist impositions.

The development of national brands in the "re-imaging" of former Yugoslavia has also since been discussed by Hall (2002) and Martinovic (2002).

Case 6 — New Zealand's Global Niche

> Global competition in the world of destination marketing has never been more intense. September 11 2001 focussed the spotlight on the travel and tourism industry around the world with troubled airlines and nervous passengers creating unprecedented uncertainty . . . In such a competitive environment, it is more vital than ever that those marketing a destination can make their voice heard. The 100% Pure New Zealand global marketing campaign was instigated in 1999, with the purpose of achieving this cut-through (Tourism New Zealand 2003 — www.tourisminfo.co.nz, 22/10/03).

Morgan *et al.* (2002) promote a critical exploration of Tourism New Zealand's (TNZ) development of the 100% Pure New Zealand as a powerful niche travel brand. With one of the authors acknowledged as a TNZ staff member responsible for promoting the brand internationally, the case represents a much needed destination practitioner/academic collaboration. Launched in 1999, "100% Pure New Zealand" was the country's first global tourism brand. Prior to this, different campaigns had been used in different markets. New Zealand is a small, geographically disadvantaged player in the international travel market, with a relatively small NTO budget. TNZ recognised that to be more competitive on the international stage, particularly against larger neighbour Australia, required the development of a single niche brand across all markets. The vision was to position New Zealand as the world's ultimate travel destination, with a key output being to double international tourism receipts by 2005.

The focus of Morgan *et al.*'s paper is the U.K. phase of the brand research and positioning implementation. Within New Zealand, significant research was undertaken in the development of the brand strategy, including surveys of local businesses, regional economists and previous visitors. The U.K. research stage, which was one of a number of overseas market analyses, involved a series of 28 in-depth interviews and four focus groups. These were used primarily to identify long haul travel motivations/needs/barriers, perceptions of New Zealand and effective communication propositions. The paper provided a summary of U.K. traveller types and their needs and motivations. New Zealand was seen to appeal to a number of distinctive segments, particularly those motivated to travel for reasons of special interest or "real travel," which was described as "serious, adventure travel and a trip of a lifetime" (Morgan *et al.* 2002: 344). The key perceptions held of New Zealand were: "sense of achievement and prestige in visiting," "adventure," "landscape of contrasts," "good quality wine reputation," "friendly and welcoming," "space and freedom," "nature/outdoors," and "fresh pure air." However, major barriers to travel included: long travel distance and costs, concern that New Zealand only offered an outdoor experience, the weather, lack of things to do, and the country's conservative and serious image (345):

> The branding consultants' research concluded that the outside world sees New Zealand as being full of green hills, sheep and aggressive Maori warriors, and that it is somewhat boring.

The mixed findings motivated TNZ to develop a position that focused on "energising the traveller." The process resulted in the brand being "New Zealand," the brand essence "landscape," the positioning "New Pacific Freedom," and the global campaign slogan "100% Pure New Zealand."

During the first year the global brand campaign attracted financial support from 102 industry partners in 13 countries. This was seen as a critical success factor for an NTO with limited funding. The authors might also have added that TNZ's limited international advertising budget is also in New Zealand dollars, which is significantly discounted to all major currencies. The contribution of this case for destination marketers is the emphasis on the importance of extensive research, the need for a collaborative approach to implementation, the value of public relations and the WWW as brand promotion vehicles, and the need for a long-term commitment to the brand. In New Zealand's case the most significant long term challenge lay in combining the brand essence "landscape" with a globally unique point of difference.

Destination Brand Identity Development

As presented in Figure 1 three inter-related components of the destination brand construct are *brand identity, brand position* and *brand image*. Brand identity has an internal focus on issues such as self image and a vision for motivating stakeholders, while brand image represents the actual image held in the market. Brand positioning is the interface between the two. Destination brand identity development essentially involves four stages: (i) the appointment of a brand champion; (ii) identification of the brand community; (iii) a destination audit; and (iv) production of a brand charter.

Brand Champion

> You create passion for brands first of all by example. It depends on the attitude of top management. If you are totally convinced, you become a missionary salesperson, so to speak within the company.

This comment from a former head of marketing for Nestlé was cited by Urde (1999: 124), whose analysis of brand oriented companies identified a characteristic passion for the brand. The appointment of a brand manager is an important precursor to the destination brand development. As evidenced in the case of Wales (see Pride 2002), a lack of leadership can inhibit the brand's development, particularly in the initial phase. Such a role will vary depending on the size of the DMO, but will nevertheless be driven by the same principles. Branding is a complex and challenging process, and leadership, responsibility and accountability is required. At the NTO level there have been a growing number of brand manager appointments made since the mid-1990s, such as by the Scottish Tourist Board and British Tourist Authority for example, reported by Pritchard & Morgan (1998). Clearly, the case studies written by those intimately involved with destination brand development show a passion for the cause. Such brand managers must in effect be brand champions, since "many practitioners currently responsible for marketing destinations also regard the branding process with suspicion" (Pride 2002: 110).

If the bottom up philosophy to brand development is to be adopted it is doubtful an outsider, such as a brand consultant, will be successful in championing the process over the longer term. The author is aware of the problems encountered by one RTO which delegated too much responsibility, not to mention finance, to a high profile and articulate brand consultant, who was also commissioned by competing destinations. The brand champion must be seen to be part of the community. In this regard, there is in some cases a fine line walked by Brisbane-based Tourism Queensland staff who play a key role in brand development for the state's RTOs.

Brand Community

> Issue 33 — WTB Branding
> How can we influence the trade and local authorities to support the WTB brand and the values that have been developed?
> (Wales Tourism Board Policy Framework Review — Competitiveness and Quality. Accessed at http://capture.wtb.lon.world.net/ 22/10/03).

The effective development and nurturing of the destination brand will depend on the identification of a brand community. Ultimately, the destination brand community will be as important a brand communications medium as any advertising campaign, since it is they who must deliver the brand promise. Therefore it is critical the brand identity encapsulates the values of the community, the essence of the visitor experience, as well as provide a vision to guide and motivate active stakeholders. The Oregon case (see Curtis 2001) demonstrated the importance of avoiding a top-down approach by involving the local tourism industry. Research in Singapore (Henderson 2000) suggested the views of the host community must be taken into account, while the Morocco experience (Vial 1997, in Morgan & Pritchard 1998) demonstrated the influence of travel intermediaries. Also important are members of the wider business community, who may not view tourism as being their core business, but who may nevertheless be indirectly involved in providing goods or services. For example, these include such diverse groups as local produce suppliers, architects, real estate agents, hairdressers and employment agencies. A destination brand community consists therefore not only of local tourism providers but also the host population, local business community and key travel distribution intermediaries. After all, tourism, as Gnoth (1998) reminded us, is user-defined, and the product is not controlled by any one channel power structure. This issue was acknowledged by the Singapore Tourism Board:

> In essence, the New Asia-Singapore brand is not a product one consciously creates. It presents a total picture of the way we live, work and think. Its dynamic feature is reflected in the STB's marketing collaterals. They prompt us for example to reflect on Singapore as a "City with its Head in the Future and a Soul in the Past" (Singapore Tourism Board: http://www.stb.com.sg/services/des/index.stm, 22/10/03).

Research into the perceptions of "New Asia — Singapore" by Henderson (2000), however, highlighted the real world challenges involved in gaining acceptance of the brand. While the development of the brand, which was launched in 1996, has been well documented (e.g. STPB 1996), Henderson argued that the actual impact of the branding efforts was uncertain. A small exploratory survey of local residents and English speaking visitors revealed gaps between actual perceptions (brand image) and the intended brand values (brand identity). Concerns about place commodification were also evident. Sample limitations aside, Henderson's study insightfully highlighted the importance of consultation with the host community to ensure what is being communicated in brand strategies is both realistic and appropriate (215):

> When residents are called on to live the values of the brand in pursuit of tourism goals, it would seem that marketers are in danger of assuming too much influence and a sense of balance needs to be restored. Societies cannot be engineered or places manufactured for tourist consumption without a loss of authenticity which is ultimately recognised by the visitor who will move on to seek it elsewhere.

There may also be a view within the community that branding of the place is not appropriate, and this needs to be ascertained. It has been asked whether selling a city to tourists is a Faustian bargain:

> Packaging and promoting the city to tourists can destroy its soul. The city is commodified, its form and spirit remade to conform to market demand, not residents' dreams. The local state and business elites collude to remake a city in which their special interests are paramount; meanwhile, resources are diverted away from needy neighbourhoods and social services (Holcolm 1999: 69).

This view is not often reported in the literature, perhaps due to the lack of research into the host community's views on branding "their place." Brand consultant Wally Olins (Olins 2002) commented on the "visceral animosity" of some people toward the concept of a nation as a brand. As an example Olins cited Girard's (1999: 241) view of the inappropriateness of a brand for France:

> In France the idea of re-branding the country would be widely unacceptable because the popular feeling is that France is something that has a nature and a substance other than that of a corporation . . . A country carries specific dignity unlike a marketed product . . . In France it is unimaginable for Chirac to attempt to re-brand.

A strong brand can be a unifying force for increased co-operation by all stakeholders, as observed by Curtis (2001) in the case of Oregon. Likewise, Hawes *et al.* (1991) found a number of USA STOs that employed a state-wide slogan as a unification mechanism. The formation of a project group that is representative of the brand community can act as a conduit between the DMO and the community, help identify stakeholder groups warranting involvement in qualitative discussions on place meaning, assist the brand manager with the development of recommendations for the DMO board, and help develop means of briefing the community on the purpose and role of the brand. Admittedly the selection of such a representative group will always be problematic, in terms of achieving a political balance and a manageable size.

The primary role of a working group will be to develop the means for investigating: (i) the host community's values and sense of place; (ii) the tourism community's view of the essence of the visitor experience; and (iii) the destination's tourism resources. The purpose of this stage is to identify the core values of the destination, to work towards the development of a destination brand identity. As with people, a brand's personality can be a powerful source of differentiation (Aaker & Joachimsthaler 2000). Also, the personality of the brand may represent a symbol of the consumer's own identity: "The brands we select as consumers can be used to express something about ourselves and our roles" (Urde 1999: 128). While there has been little reported on the concept of destination personalities, there have been studies of residents' community values (e.g. Page & Lawton 1997).

Brand Charter

It has been suggested in the chapter that the brand should be the foundation for all marketing planning. Indeed, the idea of thinking about the destination as a brand might represent a new way of thinking to many stakeholders. A brand charter can serve to motivate, remind and guide stakeholders. Like any formal planning document, the key to readability and application is succinctness rather than the production of an overly detailed and weighty tome. Essential elements include, but are not limited to: a brand mission, vision, brand identity/essence statement, brand values, and guidelines for implementation and auditing. The brand mission summarises the reason for the brand's existence. For example, the following statement of the ATC leaves the reader with no doubts about the importance of the brand to the organisation:

> Brand Australia is the essence of all ATC activities. It guides the tone, design and imagery used in all ATC communications to consumers, the travel trade and tourism industry. It forms the basis of all television, cinema, print and online advertising as well as PR, direct mail, travel guides, Internet and trade marketing activities (ATC 2003).

Urde (1999: 126) suggested a brand vision is also required to answer the following questions: What do we want to achieve with our brand? How will the organisation realise this vision? The brand essence statement is the articulation of the brand identity. This has also been described as a brand mantra by Keller (2003), who suggested a three to five word statement that clearly defines the focus and boundary of the brand category, such as "authentic athletic performance" (Nike) and "fun family entertainment" (Disney). Aaker & Joachimsthaler (2000) suggested a brand identity will usually have two to four dimensions, as well as a focused brand essence statement. They offered the example of Virgin's core identity dimensions being service quality, innovation, fun and entertainment, and value for money, while the brand essence statement is "iconoclasm." The purpose of the brand essence statement and core values is to guide and motivate those within the organisation, and will not necessarily be explicit in all promotional communications. In the case of Rotorua (Tourism Rotorua 1996: 2) the purpose of the brand identity was fourfold:

(1) To reflect reality by making a compelling and believable statement about the unique qualities of the district.
(2) To encompass all aspects of the destination by developing a theme to fit with all community and commercial applications.
(3) To be meaningful and motivational by avoiding empty clichés and creating an idea to inspire both interest and action.
(4) To have lasting value by remaining relevant to the aspirations of the destination for many years to come.

Examples of destination brand identities and core values from a selection of NTOs, STOs and RTOs are shown in Table 4.

Table 4: Destination brand core values.

Destination	Brand Identity	Core Brand Values
Wales (Pride 2002)	In Wales you will find a passion for life – Hwyl	Lyrical, sincere, confident, inviting, down to earth, warm
Australia (ATC 1997 in Morgan 2000)	Brand Australia	Youthful, energetic, optimistic, stylish, unpretentious, genuine, open, fun
New Zealand (Morgan *et al.* 2002)	New Pacific freedom	Contemporary and sophisticated, innovative and creative, spirited and free
Western Australia (Crockett & Wood 1999)	Brand Western Australia	Fresh, natural, free, spirited
Rotorua (Tourism Rotorua 1996)	Feel the spirit Manaakitanga	Cultural diversity, stunning natural environment, awe-inspiring earth forces, sense of adventure, people, progressive community

An important document for DMOs responsible for co-ordinating the efforts of a multiplicity of stakeholders is a brand policy manual that provides guidelines for use of symbols by the local tourism industry and intermediaries. The purpose is to ensure a consistency in application. While guidelines can be distributed in brochure form, a more cost effective approach is the internet. For example South West England maintains a dedicated destination brand web site (see http://southwestbrand.info). Registered users have access to a comprehensive range of resources including: image library, guidelines for the correct use of logos, typeface and tone of voice, and examples of brand use.

Chapter Key Point Summary

Key Point 1 — Emergence of the Brand Literature

It has been suggested that the future of marketing will be a battle of the brands, and that in tourism, destinations are emerging as the world biggest brands. The concept of branding consumer goods has attracted research interest in the marketing literature since the 1950s. In the time since, a rich resource of information has been developed to guide product marketers. However, in the tourism literature, the issue of branding destinations was not reported until the late 1990s. While interest in the field is increasing, there remains a dearth of published information to guide destination marketers. This represents a significant gap in the literature given the acknowledged importance of brands in competitive markets and the emergence of destinations as the tourism industry's biggest brands. While many aspects of brand theory have applications for DMOs, the process of branding destinations is a more complex undertaking than that for most consumer goods and services.

Key Point 2 — Destination Brand Identity

The purpose of a brand is to establish a distinctive and memorable identity in the market place that represents a source of value for the consumer. For DMOs, the value of strong consumer based brand equity lies in the opportunity to minimise destination switching through a differentiated value proposition and increased loyalty. The fundamental challenge for DMOs is to somehow develop a brand identity that encapsulates the essence or spirit of a multi-attributed destination representative of a group of sellers as well as a host community. Such a brand identity should serve as a guiding focus for the marketing activities of the DMO and stakeholders.

Additional Reading

Aaker, D. A. (1991). *Managing brand equity*. New York: Free Press.

Aaker, D. A. (1996). *Building strong brands*. New York: Free Press.

Aaker, D. A., & Joachimsthaler, E. (2000). *Brand leadership*. New York: Free Press.

Keller, K. L. (2003). *Strategic brand management* (2nd ed.). Upper Saddle River, NJ: Prentice-Hall.

Morgan, A. (1999). *Eating the big fish — How challenger brands can compete against brand leaders*. New York: Wiley.

Morgan, N., Pritchard., A., & Pride, R. (2002). *Destination branding: Creating the unique destination proposition*. Oxford: Butterworth-Heinemann.

Chapter 5

Destination Image

Sometimes the notions people have about a brand do not even seem very sensible or relevant to those who know what the product is "really" like. But they all contribute to the customer's deciding whether or not the brand is the one for me (Gardner & Levy 1955: 35).

Chapter Perspective

Ultimately a destination brand manifests as an image (or lack of) in the mind of the consumer, which may be quite different to the self-image intended in the brand identity. In this regard there has been a lack of research into the relationship between projected and perceived destination images (Ashworth & Goodall 1990b). The images held by consumers play a significant role in travel purchase decisions. Therefore, an understanding of the images held of the destination by consumers is important, to determine whether there is congruence between the desired brand image and that which resides in the minds of consumers. The previous chapter introduced the concepts of *brand identity, brand positioning* and *brand image* as distinctive components of the brand construct. These are graphically presented in Figure 1. *Brand identity* represents the values and essence of the destination community, is the self-image aspired in the market place, and has an internal focus on motivating and guiding stakeholders. The concept of consumer-based brand equity was highlighted as the real measure of a brand's success. This chapter discusses *brand image*, which is representative of consumer-based brand equity. Major objectives of any marketing strategy will usually be to either create a new image, or to reinforce positive images already established in the minds of the target audience. Unfortunately for some destinations there may not be any image held, or the image held might bear little resemblance to that intended in the brand identity.

The Importance of Image in Tourism Marketing

At the 2000 TTRA conference in Hollywood, John Hunt used the example of three peasants breaking in a new field, to describe the 1970s destination image research undertaken by himself, Edward Mayo & Clare Gunn. In the thirty years since their pioneering work, destination image has been one of the most prevalent topics in the tourism literature. For example, Pike (2002a) categorised 142 destination image studies published in the literature

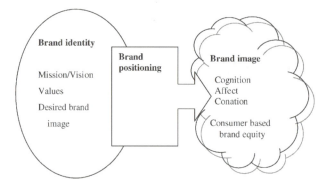

Figure 1: Brand identity, brand positioning and brand image.

between 1973 and 2000. Chon's (1990) review of 23 of the most frequently cited destination image studies found the most popular themes were the role and influence of destination image in buyer behaviour and satisfaction. Indeed Hunt's (1975) view, that images held by potential travellers are so important in the destination selection process that they can affect the viability of the destination, has become axiomatic. After all, most tourism products are services rather than physical goods, and can often only compete via images. Key implications of this for destinations are the issues of intangibility and risk, substitutability, heterogeneity, inseparability, and perishability.

Intangibility and Risk

Prior to purchase, a guitar may be played in the store, shoes can be fitted, and a car taken for a test drive. Products are tangible "things" that can generally be inspected, touched, trailed, and exchanged. All of our senses are available to us as we shop for products at the mall. However, the only physical evidence of a holiday destination may be in brochures, web pages, holiday snapshots or in the media. Thus, expectations of the holiday are realisable only after purchase and actual travel (Goodall *et al.* 1988). It follows then that a consequence of intangibility is an increased risk in the travel purchase decision. Several types of risk may be of concern to travellers and suppliers:

- Performance risk — will the service perform as expected? Tourism destination performance risks include a diverse range of factors, such as poor weather, labour strikes, substandard service encounters, civil unrest, grumpy travellers, theft and other crimes, volcanic eruptions and earthquakes, fluctuating exchange rates, traffic delays, airport congestion, and terrorism.
- Social risk — to what extent will the travel experience enhance well being or self-concept (Mayo & Jarvis 1981). Is there potential for embarrassment? There may also be a risk of stress involved when travelling in unfamiliar environments. Mansfield (1992) referred to the social stress of tourism, when motivated to travel by membership of a social reference group. For example, social risk may occur when joining a coach tour of strangers, since

holidays represent interplay between merging into a group and affirming individuality (Mollo-Bouvier 1990).

- Physical risk — is there potential for harm? Travellers not only assess the risk of harm at a destination, but will also consider the transport facilities and transit environments en route (e.g. Page *et al.* 1994; Page & Wilks 2004).
- Financial risk — does the financial investment represent value? The annual holiday is often regarded as a high involvement decision with significant household expenditure (Driscoll *et al.* 1994). The higher the level of involvement in the decision the higher the perceived risk will likely be.

Inseparability and Variability

Customers are actively involved in the delivery of a service, since production and consumption occur simultaneously. Increasingly, travellers have been seeking greater involvement in tourism products, as participants rather than passive observers (Crouch 2000). Since satisfaction with a destination will result from a series of numerous service interactions, over which the DMO has no control, the potential for dissatisfaction is considerable. Also, perceptions of the same destination experience may be quite different among different travellers, leading to different perceptions of value (Kotler *et al.* 1999).

Perishability

Destination services are perishable, since they cannot be stored for sale later during high demand periods (Goodall *et al.* 1988). Individual businesses attempt to match capacity with projected levels of demand though measures such as yield management and sales promotions. For DMOs, this presents challenges in forecasting the impacts of seasonality, periodicity, special events and exogenous events.

Substitutability

As has been suggested, destinations are close substitutes for others in crowded markets, since travellers have available to them a myriad of destinations that will satisfy their needs. Even taking into account price incentives, what influences a traveller to select a destination they have not previously visited? In such cases images can provide a pre-taste (Crompton 1979a). Influencing these images by DMOs requires insights into the image formation process.

Image Formation

While it is agreed that destination images can play an important role in travel decisions, defining destination image and understanding image formation are not so clear. A number of authors have been critical of attempts to conceptualise the construct. Certainly the range of definitions used in the tourism literature has been so great that "image" is becoming marketing jargon (Cossens 1994a). It has been proposed that most destination image studies have lacked any conceptual framework (Echtner & Ritchie 1991; Fakeye & Crompton 1991). From a review of 15 studies between 1975 and 1990, Echtner & Ritchie suggested most definitions were vague, such as "perceptions of an area." Jenkins (1999) found the term destination image had been used in a number of different contexts, including for example perceptions held by individuals, stereotypes held by groups and images projected by DMOs. Questions have been raised as to whether researchers were actually certain of the unique properties of destination image, and whether it could be accurately measured. However, this not a problem faced by destination image researchers in isolation since, in the wider marketing literature, Dobni & Zinkhan's (1990) review of brand image studies found little agreement on either the definition of the construct or on how it should be operationalised. Poiesz (1989) also pointed out the consumer behaviour literature did not provide any generally accepted definition of image.

Our minds struggle to cope with the daily flood of advertising and other media (Ries & Trout 1981). In this regard the explosion in destination choice and destination publicity material has only served to increase confusion among potential travellers (Gunn 1988). A central theme within the marketing literature has been the difficulty in which the mind has in dealing with this increasingly busy world. However, Jacoby (1984) argued that while consumers could become overloaded with information, they would not generally allow this to occur. Instead, coping mechanisms are developed. The need for simplified processing by the mind was implicit in the definition of image proposed by Reynolds (1965: 69):

> The mental construct developed by the consumer on the basis of a few selected impressions among the flood of total impressions.

This viewpoint holds that we develop simplified images through some sort of creative process. For example, we are selective about which messages attract our attention; we are selective about how we interpret and even distort information; and we are selective about which information we will retain in memory. This selective filtering is a form of "perceptual defence" (Moutinho 1987).

Reynolds (1965) used the term "indifundibular" to describe the funnel shaped process of image building, where elaborated images are creatively developed from impressions selected out of the message milieu. However, the "black box" of how this filtering of cognitive information occurs in the internal brain processes to produce a composite image is not yet fully understood (Stern & Krakover 1993). The same may be said of the process of destination image formation by individuals (Baloglu & McCleary 1999a). A number of extensive literature reviews on the topic of memory structure (e.g. Cai 2002; Cossens 1994b; Keller 1993) have found the most commonly accepted conceptualisation has been by a spreading action. This has been referred to as the associative network memory model, which sees memory as consisting as nodes and links (see Anderson 1983). A node represents stored information about a particular concept, and is part of a network of links to other nodes. Activation between nodes occurs either through the action of processing external information or when information is retrieved from memory. When a node concept is recalled, the strength of association will dictate the range of other nodes that will be activated from memory. A destination brand is conceptualised as representing a node, with which a number of associations with other node concepts are linked. Key implications of this are the level of awareness of the destination and the strength and favourability of associations with important attributes and benefits.

Unfortunately for the marketer, images may only have a tenuous and indirect relationship to fact (Reynolds 1965). However, whether an individual's perceived images are correct is not as important as what the consumer actually believes to be true (Hunt 1975; Mayo 1973). This proposition continues to underpin consumer behaviour research today, often referred to as "perception is reality." Also, given a single fact, a consumer can create a detailed image of a product through simple inferences (Reynolds 1965). One way this occurs is through plot value where certain attributes are seen by an individual to go together. In this way we construct a plot from a small amount of knowledge. Knowledge of a destination's location may enable the construction of an image including likely climate and geography. For example, New Zealand's location in the South Pacific may incorrectly stimulate an image of a tropical climate. A similar phenomenon may occur through the halo effect where a product that is rated highly on one attribute is then also assumed to rate highly on others. The reverse may also apply. Wilkie & Pessemier's (1973) literature review found sufficient evidence of the halo effect in marketing studies to suggest that it may impair analysis of a brand's strengths and weaknesses. Pizam *et al.* (1978) suggested a halo effect may occur at a destination where satisfaction, or dissatisfaction, of the total product is the result of an experience of one of its components.

Another important concept for multi-attributed entities such as destinations is that of an overall or composite image (see Baloglu & McCleary 1999a; Dichter 1985; Gartner 1986; MacInnis & Price 1987; Mayo 1973; Stern & Krakover 1993). MacInnis & Price described imagery as a process of the representation of multi-sensory information in a gestalt. Discursive processing on the other hand is the cognitive elaboration of individual attributes. Echtner (1991) proposed a key issue for destination image research was whether imagery or discursive processing is used to evaluate destinations. A parallel issue exists in the evaluation of the holiday experience — is there a holistic experience as proposed by Medlik & Middleton (1973), a sequence of separate experiences or a mixture of both? For example, from an analysis of travellers' diaries, Laws & Ryan (1992: 68) concluded an overseas flight was "experienced as a series of events which have varying influences on passenger satisfaction." In the view of Echtner & Ritchie (1991), the definitions of image used by destination researchers did not explicitly identify whether the interest was in a holistic image or in the individual attributes. Pike's (2002a) review of 142 destination image studies found most were using lists of attributes. Studies interested in measuring holistic impressions included Pearce (1988), Um & Crompton (1990), and Reilly (1990).

A further dimension of destination image introduced by Echtner & Ritchie (1991) was the issue of common functional attributes vs. unique and psychological features. Since most of the studies they reviewed required respondents to compare destinations across a range of common attributes, there was little opportunity to identify any attributes that may be unique to a destination. They proposed a continuum between those common functional and psychological attributes on which destinations are commonly rated and compared, and more unique features, events or auras. However, it should also be recognised that unique features may not necessarily explain a destination's competitive position if they do not offer benefits in a specified travel context.

Crompton (1979a) suggested two schools of thought concerning destination image formation. Firstly, images are person-dominated. Variance will always exist as individuals have different experiences and process communications differently. On the other hand images can be destination determined, where people form images based on experience at the destination. This implied that a destination cannot do much to create an image that is different to what it actually is. Phelps (1986) proposed destination images were either primary or secondary. A primary image is developed from an individual's experience of a place, whereas secondary images are those held prior to a first visit. Geographers have commonly referred to images held of environments being either designative or appraisive (Stern & Krakover 1993). The former use a cognitive categorisation of the landscape, while the latter are concerned with attitudes towards the place. These ideas are consistent with Gunn's (1988) organic/induced images, which, along with cognition, affect and conation, have been the most cited destination image formation concepts.

Organic and Induced Images

Gunn (1988) suggested images were formed at two levels, organic and induced. The organic image is developed through an individual's everyday assimilation of information, which may include a wide range of mediums, from school geography readings to mass media to actual visitation. In the case of Ireland, Ehemann (1977) found an overwhelmingly negative image portrayed in both the hard news and general media. Ehemann was interested in the evaluative vocabulary used in the media about a destination, and the nature of the image that might be developed by an individual with no direct experience of a destination. It was suggested this would become important to the DMO when the individual was in holiday decision-making mode. The induced image on the other hand is formed through the influence of tourism promotions directed by marketers. This usually occurs when an individual begins sourcing information for a holiday. The distinction between organic and induced images is the level of influence held by destination marketers. Gunn suggested destination marketers should focus on modifying the induced image since they can do little to change the organic image.

Gartner (1993) proposed a typology of image formation agents, with practical implications. These ranged in a continuum from overt induced advertising through to organic sources such as visitation, as shown in Table 1. Marketers could use such agents independently, or in some combination, depending on the marketing objectives. Due to increasing use of public relations (PR), organic and induced images may not necessarily be mutually exclusive (Selby & Morgan 1996), since news is more volumous than advertising and has higher credibility (Crompton 1979a).

Images held of a destination may be either positive or negative, although in reality will usually consist of both positive and negative images. Effective corrective marketing is difficult, and it has been suggested that once a negative image has become established, marketing activities will not be able to reverse it (Ahmed 1991a). A number of case studies concerning this issue have been reported in the tourism literature. For example,

Table 1: Image change agents.

Image change agent	Examples
Overt induced 1	Traditional advertising
Overt induced 2	Information received from tour operators
Covert induced 1	Second party endorsement through traditional advertising
Covert induced 2	Second party endorsement through seemingly unbiased reports, such as newspaper articles
Autonomous	News and popular culture
Unsolicited organic	Unsolicited information received from friends
Solicited organic	Solicited information from friends
Organic	Actual visitation

Bramwell & Rawding (1996) reported on the challenges involved in attempting to change the negative image of Bradford, an English industrial city. In Wales, Selby & Morgan (1996) found that even after considerable redevelopments, Barry Island still had an image of being dirty and tatty. This may have reflected the organic perceptions held prior to the redevelopment. Similarly, Amor, Calabug, Abellan & Montfort (1994) reported the image held of Benidorm remained negative, despite consumer and trade awareness of attempts to change it. Meler & Ruzic (1999), discussing the negative image of post-war Croatia, suggested one or a few negative attributes could stimulate the creation of a negative image of a destination. While individual components of a destination image may fluctuate greatly over time, their effect on overall image may not be important (Crompton 1979a; Gartner 1986). Gartner & Hunt (1987) found evidence of positive destination image change, but concluded any change only occurs slowly. Likewise a study by the English Tourist Board (1983, in Jeffries 2001), which analysed the impact of an advertising campaign to modify Londoners perceptions of England's North Country over a three year period, found only minor changes in destination image. Gartner (1993) proposed the larger the entity the slower the image change. This supports the proposition that it is difficult to change peoples' minds, with the easier marketing communication route being to reinforce positively held images (Ries & Trout 1981). However, repositioning is not necessarily impossible. Spain, Las Vegas, Torbay as the 'English Riviera, and the Calvia Municipality in Mallorca are all examples of destinations that have been successful in repositioning (see Buhalis 2000; Gilmore 2002; Pritchard & Morgan 1998).

Since tourism demand is heterogeneous, it is important to recognise the difference between those images held by an individual, and stereotypes. Gunn (1988) proposed we all have images of destinations, whether or not we have visited them. Such images are indicative of our own likes and dislikes, and are therefore highly personal. However, stereotypes can also occur when there is a consistently uniform account of a destination by a group of people. Lynch (1960) proposed common images of a city environment would be held by large numbers of people. The number of people holding this particular image will be, therefore, a calculable percentage of the total population (Reynolds 1965). Pearce (1988) suggested a stereotype could be said to exist when more than 20% of respondents offer similar descriptions of a place. The wider body of work on stereotyping was beyond the scope of the chapter. However, it is acknowledged that stereotyping points towards a simplification of the complex, and implies a decreased willingness to change perceptions. Since stereotypes are easily accessed from memory, the encouragement of positive stereotyping, and avoidance of negative stereotypes, will therefore be key goals of DMOs. In this regard, Gronhaug & Heide (1992) suggested advertising may produce stereotype images in receivers who had little knowledge of a destination. Reynolds (1965) argued that word associations generally tended to be consistent among consumers. Therefore, transmitting the right code words could stimulate the desired associations.

Unlike the majority of products, where information sources are mostly commercial, destination images appear to be derived from a wider range of sources (Echtner & Ritchie 1991). They suggested therefore Gunn's concept of organic and induced images was unique to destinations. There are two important implications of this. First, it is possible for individuals to have images of destinations that they have not previously visited. Second, since image may change after visitation (Chon 1991; Hu & Ritchie 1993; Hunt 1975; Pearce 1982a; Wee *et al.* 1985), it is important to separate the images held by visitors from those of non-visitors. Non-visitors will include those who would like to visit but have not yet been able to for various reasons, as well as those who have chosen not to visit. Destination image can be enhanced through travel to a destination. Milman & Pizam (1995) demonstrated how familiarity with a domestic USA destination, measured by previous visitation, led to a more positive image and increased likelihood of repeat visits. However, many studies of destination image have excluded those who have chosen not to visit (Ahmed 1991b; Baloglu & McCleary 1999a).

Cognition, Affect and Conation

Fishbein (1967) and Fishbein & Azjen (1975) argued the importance of distinguishing between an individual's beliefs and attitudes. While beliefs represent information held about an object, attitude is a favourable, neutral or unfavourable evaluation. Fishbein was concerned both concepts were frequently subsumed under the term "attitude." Instead, it was proposed attitude comprises cognitive, affective and conative components. Cognition is the sum of what is known or believed about a destination, and may be organic or induced. Such knowledge or beliefs may or may not have been derived from a previous visit. A number of authors (e.g. Milman & Pizam 1995) have cited the World Tourism Organisation's (1979) research finding that images can only exist if there is a small amount of knowledge present. Beliefs are often permanent, but may not always be important (Mayo & Jarvis 1981).

Affect represents an individual's feelings about an object, which may be favourable, unfavourable or neutral (Fishbein 1967). The number of terms used in the English language to describe affect toward a destination is in the hundreds (Russel *et al.* 1981). Following Russel (1980), Russel *et al.* factor analysed 105 common adjectives used to describe environments, and generated the affective response grid shown in Figure 2. Eight adjective dimensions of affect were included in the model, 45 degrees apart. The assumption was that these dimensions were not independent of each other, but represented a circumplex

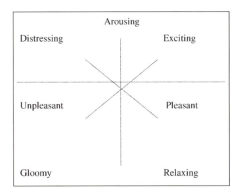

Figure 2: Affective response grid. *Source:* Adapted from Russel *et al.* (1981).

model of affect. The horizontal axis was arbitrarily set to represent pleasantness, while the vertical axis represents level of arousal. In this way "exciting," which is a dimension in its own right, is a combination of arousing and pleasant, while "distressing" is a function of arousing and unpleasant.

Using four semantic differential scales, "pleasant/unpleasant," "relaxing/distressing," "arousing/sleepy" and "exciting/gloomy," Baloglu & Brinberg (1997) demonstrated how the affective response model could be applied to destinations. They used MDS to plot the affective positions of 11 Mediterranean destinations. Baloglu & McCleary (1999a) also reported the use of these four scales, while Baloglu & Mangaloglu (2001) used the four scales in an analysis of images held by travel intermediaries.

Russel *et al.* (1981) suggested two dimensions, "sleepy/arousing" and "unpleasant/pleasant," could be sufficient to measure affect towards environments. Other studies have demonstrated how this can apply to travel destinations. For example, Walmsley & Jenkins' (1993) principal components analysis of Repertory Grid data produced the same two factor labels. While Walmsley & Jenkins' results were based on Australian domestic destinations, a study by Walmsley & Young (1998) concluded the schema was appropriate for international destinations, but not significant for local destinations. However, Hanyu (1993) found pleasantness and arousing levels to be the dimensions of residents' affect towards Tokyo. Also, Pike & Ryan (2004) demonstrated the applicability of using the affective scales in a positioning analysis of domestic short break destinations. Wilkie & Pessemier's (1973) definition of affect bears a striking similarity to Fishbein's (1967) summative multi-attribute model:

> Overall affect is posited to reflect the net resolution of an individual's cognitions (beliefs) as to the degree to which given objects possess certain attributes weighted by the salience (importance) of each attribute to the individual (Wilkie & Pessemier 1973: 428).

It has been suggested that affect usually becomes operational at the evaluation stage of destination selection process (Gartner 1993). However, the evaluative image component has been overlooked in tourism (Walmsley & Young 1998). The majority of destination

Figure 3: Cognition/affect/conation. *Source:* Adapted from Myers (1992).

image studies have focused on cognitive attributes. Pike (2002a) found only 6 of the 142 published destination image papers showed an explicit interest in affective images. Only recently have destination studies studied both cognition and affect towards destinations together (see Baloglu 1998; Baloglu & McCleary 1999a; Dann 1996; MacKay & Fesenmaier 1997; Pike & Ryan 2004).

The conative image is analogous to behaviour since it is the intent or action component. Intent refers to the likelihood of brand purchase (Howard & Sheth 1969). Conation may be considered as the likelihood of visiting a destination within a given time period. Woodside & Sherrell (1977) found intent to visit was higher for destinations in the evoked set, as did Thompson & Cooper (1979) and Pike (2002b). Figure 3 highlights how the cognition/affect/conation relationships apply in decision-making. The process is similar to the AIDA model used by advertisers, where the aim is to guide a consumer through the stages of awareness, interest, desire and action.

Myers (1992) acknowledged the model might not always progress in this manner, since preferences may not need any cognitive antecedents. Therefore the process could begin at any stage of the model. Manstead (1996) suggested cognition, affect and conation toward an object would be correlated. However, this may not always be so, due to intervening or moderating variables (Fishbein 1967). In tourism, Woodside & Lysonski (1989) suggested preferences in the destination decision process are based on a combination of cognitive and affective associations. Baloglu & McCleary (1999a) found cognition, affect and overall image positively influenced intent to visit a destination. Baloglu (1998) found affect influenced intent following experience at a destination.

Motivation

Arguably, motivation begins the holiday travel decision process, when a need arises that cannot be met at home (Gartner 1993). Motives may therefore be viewed as the psychological determinants of demand (Kotler *et al.* 1999). Motivation in tourism is a relatively new field of study, and researchers have consistently reported a lack of understanding (see Baloglu & McCleary 1999a; Dann 1981; Dann *et al.* 1988; Fisher & Price 1991; Mansfield 1992; Pearce 1982b). Tourism motivation theories have mostly been conceptual rather that empirical (Ritchie 1996). However, the lack of theory is not unique to the tourism industry, since the issue of consumer motivation in general is not fully understood (Mansfield 1992; Pearce 1994):

> Since it can be justifiably claimed that these issues are not settled within the field of psychology itself, it is rather demanding to expect that they are satisfied in the context of tourist motivation (Pearce 1994: 119).

One of the first attempts to explain pleasure travel motivation was Gray's (1970) concepts of "wanderlust" and "sunlust," which subsume many of the motivation categories outlined in more recent studies. "Wanderlust" characterised the innate human need to temporarily leave familiar surroundings to experience different cultures and places. It has been suggested that apart from an innate need to explore, all other travel motivations are learnt by individuals (Mayo & Jarvis 1981). For example, no one is born with the need for status. Therefore, an individual's travel preferences and behaviour can change during a lifetime as needs and motives are learned. In this regard, sunlust was described as travel for a specific purpose for benefits not available at home, such as winter sun holidays or visits to a larger city. Related to this was the work of Dann (1977) who used "push" factors, to explain the link between motivation and destination choice. Motivational push factors were proposed to be a logical antecedent to the analysis of "pull" factors such as destination attributes. Within the push category, Dann introduced the concepts of anomie and ego-enhancement from social psychology, to explain the core travel motivations. The anomic traveller seeks escape from the mundane and isolation at home to obtain opportunities for social interaction. Ego-enhancement on the other hand seeks increased self-recognition, such as opportunities to recreate oneself at a place where identity is not known, or trip-dropping at home to reinforce status.

Working on the premise that a state of disequilibria occurs when a need arises, Crompton (1979b) sought to determine the causes of tension that lead to destination choice. Crompton proposed motives were multi-dimensional, and combined in destination decisions. Indeed, most general buying decisions involve more than one motive (Howard & Sheth 1969). Crompton concluded a "break from routine" was the solution to a state of disequilibria. One option for such a break is a holiday, driven by a continuum of socio-psychological and cultural motivations. The socio-psychological motives, "escape from routine," "exploration," "relaxation," "prestige," "regression," "enhancement of family relations," and "social interaction," were found to be unrelated to the attributes of any particular destination. The two cultural motives, "novelty" and "education," were found to be partially associated with destination attributes. For some of Crompton's respondents the actual destination was unimportant.

Related to the study of tourism motivation is the work of Cohen (1972) and Plog (1974) in categorising traveller types. Cohen suggested four types of tourist roles: the organised mass tourist, the individual mass tourist, the explorer and the drifter. While the core motives for most were variety and novelty, each group clearly differed in the level of control and predictability sought from the experience. The key variable in the typology was "strangeness vs. familiarity." Plog introduced psychocentricity and allocentricity to travel. Psychocentrics were posited to be nervous and non-adventurous, who travel to familiar places, preferring to drive rather than fly. Allocentrics on the other hand were more confident and willing to experiment with life. These individuals would prefer new experiences such as non-touristy destinations, and prefer to travel by air. Both Cohen and Plog linked their concepts to the evolution of a destination's lifecycle. For example, Cohen suggested strangeness and novelty were important for travellers. Plog proposed allocentrics would be the first to visit or explore a new destination, while psychocentrics would be attracted at the maturity or even decline stage. However, Cohen suggested mass tourism had created a paradox, where novelty was increasingly difficult to cater to as tourism had become institutionalised.

One of the problems for tourism researchers is the motives for travel may not actually be entirely understood by travellers themselves (Crompton 1979b: 421): "The in-depth interviews caused many respondents to confront for the first time their real motives for going on a pleasure vacation." Therefore the reasons people give for taking holidays are not sufficient to explain motivation (Mill & Morrison 1992). Instead, following Maslow's (1943) theory of motivation as a hierarchy of needs, Mill & Morrison argued the key to understanding travel motivation was through the recognition of travel as a needs and wants satisfier: "Motivation occurs when an individual wants to satisfy a need" (Mill & Morrison 1992: 17). They suggested this view of motivation was the difference between seeing the destination as a collection of attractions and seeing it as a place for satisfying needs and wants. Gilmore (2002) suggested holiday decisions are made on the basis of activity first, destination second, and succinctly summarised the complex field of tourism motivation into three categories: hedonism, self-improvement and spiritual. Recognising the needs of an individual traveller will be physical, psychological or intellectual, Mill & Morrison linked the relationships between needs and motives referenced in the tourism literature, as shown in Table 2. It could be argued the physiological and safety needs are "physical," while the

Table 2: Relationship between needs and tourism motives.

Need	Motive	Tourism Literature
Physiological	Relaxation	Escape, relaxation, relief of tension, sunlust, physical, mental relaxation of tension
Safety	Security	Health, recreation, keep oneself active and healthy
Belonging	Love	Family togetherness, enhancement of kinship relationships, companionship, facilitation of social interaction, maintenance of personal ties, interpersonal relations, roots, ethnic, show one's affection for family members, maintain social contacts
Esteem	Achievement, status	Convince oneself of one's achievements, show one's importance to others, prestige, social recognition, ego-enhancement, professional business, personal development, status, prestige
Self-actualisation	Be true to one's own nature	Exploration and evaluation of self, self discovery, satisfaction of inner desires
To know and understand	Knowledge	Cultural, education, wanderlust, interest in foreign areas
Aesthetics	Appreciation of beauty	Environmental, scenery

Source: Adapted from Mill & Morrison (1992: 20).

belonging, esteem and self-actualisation needs are "psychological." The last two categories are "intellectual" needs.

Destination Decision Sets

When motivated to act, the individual consumer-traveller becomes a decision-maker (Mayo & Jarvis 1981). Decisions must be made about where to go, when to go, how to get there and what to do there. Brand decisions then essentially involve alternative brands and the buyer's own choice criteria (Howard & Sheth 1969). Choice criteria will be associated with motives. Therefore, while a favourable image of a destination is important, it must also be aligned to the traveller's motives, to increase the likelihood of visitation (Henshall *et al.* 1985; Mansfield 1992). Mill & Morrison (1992) suggested one implication of Maslow's hierarchy of needs was that holidays targeting the satisfaction of lower level physical and physiological needs would be treated as a necessity rather than as a luxury. Of particular interest is how travellers select a holiday destination from so many places that could ably provide satisfaction.

Consumer decision set theory offers some explanation of this most complicated aspect of consumer behaviour. Howard (1963) and Howard & Sheth (1969) introduced the evoked decision set concept to propose the number of brands considered in any purchase decision was considerably lower than those available. The evoked set was defined as comprising only those brands the consumer will actually consider in the next purchase decision. Howard proposed the number of brands in an individual's evoked set would remain constant at about three or four. Woodside & Sherrell (1977) were the first to investigate evoked sets of destinations in the holiday decision process. They were motivated by the proposition that the mental processes required to evaluate the features of 15 or more destinations would represent too great a task for most travellers.

Decision sets are formed by a combination of external information sources such as prior experience, general knowledge, advertisements and feedback from friends, as well as internal factors such as needs, motivation and evaluative criteria (Spiggle & Sewall 1987). The reduced set of likely alternatives that form the evoked set is part of the total set. For travellers, this total set would consist of all those destinations that may or may not be available, and which they may or may not be aware of. How many destinations must there now be on the planet? Within this total set of destinations, Woodside & Sherrell (1977) proposed the following possible overlapping sub-sets:

- Unavailable and unaware set
- Awareness set
- Available set
- Evoked set
- Aware and unavailable set
- Available and unaware set
- Inert set
- Inept set
- Chosen destination.

Since consumers will either be aware or unaware of the existence of a product, it is from the awareness set that a purchase choice will ultimately be made (Narayana & Markin 1975). Clearly, a destination must firstly make it into the consumer's awareness set for consideration. However, as simple and logical as this may appear, from a practical perspective this represents a significant challenge for some destinations. Lilly (1984), for example, discussed the difficulties of promoting North Staffordshire, a region with little tourism image outside its own boundaries. It is important to recognise the distinction between this problem and that of a negative image, since the existence of the latter denotes awareness. However, more than simply awareness of a destination is required. For example, Milman & Pizam (1995) found awareness of a popular USA domestic destination was not necessarily a strong indicator of intent to visit. In short, other determinants of choice exist.

Crompton (1992) suggested operationalising the awareness set in tourism would be problematic, since the number of destinations a consumer is aware of will usually be greater than for consumer goods brands. The number of packaged goods brands would probably be limited to the range of 10–30, whereas it would be reasonable to expect that the number of destinations a traveller is aware of would be much greater than this (Oppermann 1999). Due to the number of possible destinations in the awareness set, it is therefore more realistic for the marketer to determine the composition of the early consideration set. These are the destinations the consumer believes could realistically be visited within a given time period. This represents the overlap of the awareness and available sets.

Woodside & Sherrell (1977) found the mean number of destinations available to a small sample of 71 domestic self-drive travellers in South Carolina was only 5.7. Similarly, Thompson & Cooper (1979), who replicated Woodside & Sherrell's survey format, sampling domestic visitors to Tennessee, found respondents considered a mean of 6.2 holiday destinations were available for travel during the next year. Woodside & Sherrell proposed the number of destinations in the early consideration set would be larger for air travellers who would have a greater selection of international destinations. However, Woodside *et al.*'s (1977) study, which used respondents in USA and Finland found this not to be the case.

Miller (1956) cited a number of studies from the consumer psychology literature to suggest the limit to the number of stimuli people would generally be capable of processing would be around seven. Miller even linked this proposition to the use of questionnaire rating scales, where seven points had generally been considered the limit of usefulness. The number seven may have implications for the length of such items as phone numbers, car registration plates and PIN numbers, as well as consumer decision sets. Woodside & Sherrell's (1977) literature review found this limit had generally been consistent in brand recall tests across product categories as diverse as cars and toothpaste.

When a consumer becomes involved in a purchase decision the early consideration set is categorised into three subsets: inert, inept and evoked (Narayana & Markin 1975). The inert set consists of brands for which the consumer has neither a positive nor a negative opinion. The consumer will have some awareness of the destination to stimulate initial interest and inclusion in the early consideration set, but may lack information to make a judgement. Or they may have sufficient information but see no advantage in pursuing it further at that point. The consumer is undecided about visiting these destinations within a certain time period. In Woodside & Sherrell's (1977) study, the mean number of destinations in the inert set was 0.9. Thompson & Cooper (1979) found a mean of 1.8, while Woodside & Lysonski

(1989), who used a convenience sample of 92 New Zealand students found a mean of 1.7 overseas destinations.

The inept set consists of brands the consumer has rejected from the initial purchase consideration within some time period. Destinations in the inept set will have been rejected from the early consideration set due to negative perceptions, perhaps from comments by significant others for example. Woodside & Sherrell (1977) found the mean number of destinations in the inept set was 1.4. Others have found similar means, including 1.8 (Thompson & Cooper 1979) and 1.6 (Woodside & Lysonski 1989). Woodside *et al.*'s (1977) four sample sub-groups generated mean inept sets of between 1.7 and 2.3 destinations.

Once the inert and inept destinations have been eliminated from the early consideration set the remaining destinations form the evoked decision set. The evoked set comprises those destinations the consumer has some likelihood of visiting within a given time period (Woodside & Sherrell 1977). Woodside & Sherrell found perceptions of destinations listed in the evoked set of their respondents were more favourable than for those listed in the inert and inept sets. In their study the evoked set size averaged 3.4 destinations for selection during the following twelve months. Their proposition of four plus or minus two destinations in the evoked set has been supported in other destination studies (see Thompson & Cooper 1979; Woodside & Lysonski 1989). Thompson & Cooper noted that no tourism study had examined the effect of travel context on evoked set size. However, investigations of decision sets in the context of short break holidays in New Zealand (Pike 2002b) and Australia (Pike 2004) found a consistency in the size of the evoked decision sets with 3.9 and 3.2 destinations respectively.

For consumer goods, it has been suggested brands excluded from the evoked decision set may have a purchase probability of less than 1% (Wilson 1981). The concept of the evoked set therefore has important implications for DMOs if it is from this set that final destination selection is made. It must be accepted that a hierarchy of destination brand saliency is formed within the evoked set of destinations, if a final selection is to be made. The higher a brand's position in a consumers mind, the higher the intent to purchase (Wilson 1981). Woodside & Wilson (1985) cited research by Burke & Schoeffler (1980), which supported this proposition. It has been shown that top of mind awareness (ToMA), measured by unaided recall, is related to purchase preference among competing brands (Axelrod 1968; Wilson 1981; Woodside & Wilson 1985). Consequently, for the destination that first comes to mind when a consumer is considering travel, ToMA must surely represent a source of advantage (Pike 2002b). The goal of any promotional campaign is to guide consumers through the hierarchy of awareness to comprehension to favourable attitude to interest and intent (DiMingo 1988). Influencing this decision process of travellers is the focus of DMO activities, since a key challenge in the competitive world of destination marketing is to achieve brand saliency. Importantly the decision set indicates which brands have an affinity with each other in the context of a purchase decision (Wilson 1981).

Travel Context

Attribute importance can vary between situations (Barich & Kotler 1991; Crompton 1992). It has been proposed anticipated usage situations affect brand perceptions. For example,

Belk's (1975) analysis of six product categories found that brand purchase was determined by situational influences. Miller & Ginter's (1979) investigation of situation determinants on brand choice found context becomes important to marketers when the strengths and weaknesses of a brand differ between situations. Travel context therefore should be an important consideration. However, there has been limited attention to the importance of context in consumer research. In an assessment of the tourism marketing research "state of the art," Ritchie (1996: 62) proposed ten key shortcomings: "Unfortunately, as we all know, there are a number of areas which we prefer not to acknowledge, or which we manage to ignore on a fairly regular basis." Among the gaps, which Ritchie labelled the "dark side of the universe," was travel context. Destination image studies have generally been undertaken without explicitly defining the context in which the traveller decision is being made (Hu & Ritchie 1993).

Context in this instance is the specific usage of the product, such as the time of year, type of trip or geographic travel range. For example, destination brand attribute salience will likely differ between the context of a honeymoon and an end of season football team trip. Brand association salience therefore depends on the decision context (Keller 1993). Golf

Table 3: Destination image papers with an explicit travel context.

Author(s)	Year	Travel Context
Mayo	1973	Self drive
Anderssen & Colberg	1973	Overseas winter holiday
Dillon *et al.*	1986	Student Spring break
Perdue	1986	Boating
Woodside & Carr	1988	Foreign travel
Woodside & Lysonski	1989	Foreign travel
Embacher & Buttle	1989	Summer holiday
Chon, Weaver & Kim	1991	Short break
Crompton *et al.*	1992	Winter long stay
Javalgi, Thomas & Rao	1992	Self drive
Hu & Ritchie	1993	Education travel
Amor *et al.*	1994	Sun/beach
King	1994	Sun/beach
Oppermann	1996	Convention
Go & Zhang	1997	Convention
Hudson & Shephard	1998	Snow skiing
McClellan	1998	Short break
Ritchie	1998	Bicycling
Vaughan & Edwards	1999	Overseas winter holiday
Baloglu & McCleary	1999a, b	Summer holiday
Murphy	1999	Backpacking
Chacko & Fenich	2000	Convention

Source: Adapted from Pike (2002a).

excursions, for example, may act as both the catalyst for travel and the destination choice (Woodside 1999). Phelps (1986) found visitors to Menorca had a low awareness of the destination they were travelling to on a package tour, since the package product was more important that the destination. Alford (1998) cited research commissioned by the English Tourist Board, which found consumers were most likely to be influenced by the type of holiday or activity, whereas RTBs were promoting regions or towns. The research suggested consumers found RTB brochures confusing, but that tour operators' brochures were better because they tended to specialise in the type of holiday. Alford found RTBs generally still produced the regional brochure as if trying to be all things to all people.

Hu & Ritchie (1993) claimed the first destination image research to focus on the manner in which the perceived attractiveness of a particular destination varies with travel context. An evaluation of five destinations, using two different contexts, found differences in overall attractiveness, and individual attribute performance. Hu & Ritchie's work supported previous findings in other tourism studies of context in dining choice (see Miller & Ginter 1979) and airline services (see Ritchie *et al.* 1980). Even though it was proposed three decades ago that any list of determinant destination attributes will vary depending on situational context (see Gearing *et al.* 1974), only 23 of the 142 published destination image papers analysed by Pike (2002a) were explicit about a travel context of interest. These are highlighted in Table 3.

Chapter Key Point Summary

Key point 1 — The Importance of Image in Tourism Marketing

Tourism marketing is generally concerned with the selling of dreams, since expectations of an intangible tourism service can only be realised after travel. The images held by consumers therefore play a critical role in their decision-making. Since tourism services can only compete via images, it is imperative marketers understand that "perception is reality." The *brand image* of the destination may or may not be quite different to the *brand identity* intended by the DMO.

Key point 2 — Destination Brand Image

Since the first destination image studies appeared in the 1970s, the topic has become one of the most prevalent in the tourism literature. A destination's image is a repertoire of brand associations held in the mind of the consumer. These associations may be cognitive, affective, conative or a combination of these. They may have been developed through organic sources such as previous visitation or induced sources such as advertising.

Key point 3 — Consumer Decision Sets

An important consideration in market research assessment of destination image is gaining an understanding of consumer decision sets. Consumers are spoilt by choice of available destinations, but will only actively consider a limited number in the decision making process. Also, destination decision set composition will likely vary according to the travel context. The size of the consumer's decision set of destinations will be limited to around four. The implication for DMOs examining the image of their destination is that destinations not included in a consumer's decision set will be less likely to be selected.

Additional Reading

Baloglu, S., & McCleary, K. W. (1999a). A model of destination image. *Annals of Tourism Research*, *26*(4), 868–897.

Echtner, C. M., & Ritchie, J. R. B. (1993). The measurement of destination image: An empirical assessment. *Journal of Travel Research*, *31*(3), 3–13.

Gartner, W. C. (1993). Image information process. *Journal of Travel & Tourism Marketing*, *2*(2/3), 191–215.

Lawton, G. R., & Page, S. J. (1997). Analysing the promotion, product and visitor expectations of urban tourism: Auckland, New Zealand as a case study. *Journal of Travel & Tourism Marketing*, *6*(3/4), 123–142.

Pike, S. (2002a). Destination image analysis: A review of 142 papers from 1973–2000. *Tourism Management*, *23*(5), 541–549.

Chapter 6

Destination Positioning

> A brand position is the part of the brand identity and value proposition that
> is to be actively communicated to the target audience and that demonstrates
> an advantage over competing brands (Aaker 1996: 71).

Chapter Perspective

Positioning can be mutually beneficial for the DMO and the consumer, as it is underpinned by
the philosophy of understanding and meeting unique consumer needs. For the organisation,
the value of positioning lies in the link it provides between the analyses of the internal
corporate and external competitive environments. Positioning can aid the DMO to "cut
through" to the minds of consumers in markets that are crowded with the clutter of
promotional messages of competing destinations and substitute products and services.
However, to do so requires a narrow focus. After all, a brand is "a singular idea or concept
that you own inside the mind of a prospect. It's as simple and as difficult as that." (Ries
& Ries 1998: 172). On the demand side, effective positioning of a brand can enable easier
decision making for the consumer. Consumers don't have time to consider the merits of
all available products in a purchase decision, and will therefore appreciate a memorable
and focused value proposition. Previously, a model of the destination brand construct was
espoused as consisting the concepts of *brand identity*, *brand image* and *brand positioning*.
This is reproduced in Figure 1. Chapter 4 discussed the elements in a brand identity, which
represents the self-image, while Chapter 5 discussed brand image as representing the actual
image held by consumers. The focus of this chapter is on positioning as a means of enhancing
congruence between brand identity and brand image.

Positioning as a Source of Competitive Advantage for Destinations

The conceptualisation of destination attractiveness proposed by Mayo and Jarvis (1981:
203), remains a useful foundation for operationalising destination image. They followed
the work of Goodrich (1978a, b), who used the Fishbein's (1967) multi-attribute model to
conceptualise destination preferences. Mayo and Jarvis suggested destination attractiveness
"has a great deal to do with the specific benefits that are desired by travelers and the
capability of the destination to deliver them." From this perspective it is important to gain
an understanding of what decision criteria will be used by the consumer when differentiating

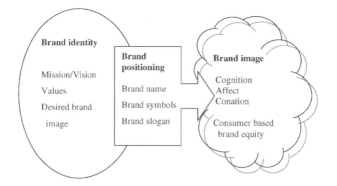

Figure 1: Brand identity, brand positioning and brand image.

destinations under consideration. Effective positioning can be a source of competitive advantage for organisations in any industry consisting of close substitutes (Porter 1980). In most tourism markets, particularly those dominated by charter flights and package deals, competing destinations are indeed close substitutes. After all a beach is a beach. For example, the beach sunset scene in Figure 2 could be almost anywhere in the world.

Therefore, the successful positioning of a destination into a consumer's evoked decision set represents a source of competitive advantage over the majority of competing places

Figure 2: Surfers Paradise beach at sunset.

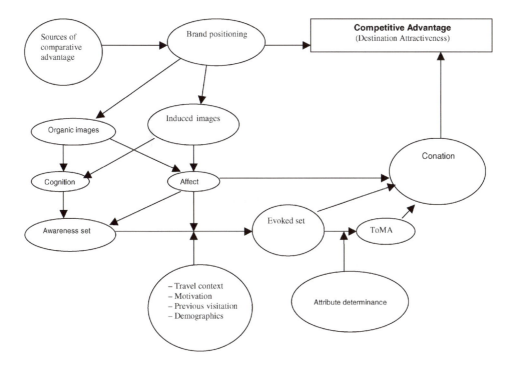

Figure 3: Brand positioning as a source of competitive advantage for destinations.

(Pike 2002b). Building on the work of Pike (2002b), and the literature review of destination image outlined in Chapter 5, Figure 3 presents a proposed model of brand positioning as a potential source of competitive advantage for destinations. The model views positioning as a vehicle for influencing brand image. The following definition is offered to represent destination attractiveness in a way that generates competitive advantage:

> A distinctive ToMA position, which is based on leadership in determinant attributes, in the decision sets of a significant group of travellers who have an intent to visit within a given time period.

The Positioning Concept

> Brand positioning describes how a brand can effectively compete against a specified set of competitors in a particular market (Keller 2003: 150).

Positioning was first introduced to the advertising community as a marketing strategy in 1969 (Trout & Ries 1979), and has been defined as a process of "establishing and maintaining a distinctive place in the market for an organisation and/or its individual product offerings" (Lovelock 1991: 110). At the core of this quest for a distinctive place is recognition that marketing is a battle fought inside the consumer's mind (Ries & Trout 1986: 169):

> Marketing battles are not fought in the customer's office or in the supermarkets or the drugstores of America. Those are only distribution points for the merchandise whose brand selection is decided elsewhere. Marketing battles are fought in a mean and ugly place. A place that's dark and damp with much unexplored territory and deep pitfalls to trap the unwary. Marketing battles are fought inside the mind.

Positioning theory is based on three propositions (Ries & Trout 1986). First, we live in an over-communicated society, bombarded with information on a daily basis, at levels that are unprecedented in our history. Second, the mind has developed a defence system against the clutter. Third, the only way to cut through the clutter to the mind is through simplified and focussed messages. Consequently, not selecting a positioning strategy could lead to head-on competition with stronger brands, an unwanted position with little demand, a fuzzy position where distinctive competence is unclear, or no position, where the product is unheard of (Lovelock 1991). Porter (1980) warned that being "stuck in the middle," with no distinctive position, was the most dangerous place to be.

Effective positioning offers the customer benefits tailored to solve a problem, in a way that is different to competitors (Chacko 1997; DiMingo 1988). The key construct in positioning is product image. However, positioning requires more than an understanding of what a product's image is in the mind of the consumer. While image is clearly important, positioning also requires a frame of reference with the competition. A position is a product's perceived performance, relative to competitors, on specific attributes (Lovelock 1991; Wind & Robinson 1972). Most destination image studies however have analysed only one destination in isolation (Uysal *et al.* 2000). While such studies enable an indication of satisfaction with a destination, a weakness of this approach is the inability to determine relative positioning against competing regions. In this regard, positioning studies have not been prominent in the tourism literature (Grabler 1997b). Although positioning had featured in the economics literature as early as the 1920s (Myers 1992), there had been little mention of the construct in the marketing literature until the 1970s. In particular, studies of destination positioning have been rare (Heath & Wall 1992; Uysal *et al.* 2000; Yau & Chan 1990). Pike (2002a) found 75 out of 142 published destination image papers from the period 1973–2000 had analysed the image of one destination in isolation.

Ries & Trout (1986) emphasised the need for marketers to think in terms of "differentness" rather than "betterness." This has important tourism implications. For example, it has been suggested that few tourism products are unique (Murphy & Pritchard 1997). Differentiation is critical for destinations since they will either become places of status or commodities, with the latter leading to increased substitutability (Gilbert 1990). Plog (2000) lamented the increasing sameness of most destinations around the world, due to the effects of globalisation. "Modernity" has all but destroyed the opportunity for travellers to experience "different" attractions (Dann 2000). This standardisation of facilities enabled mass tourism by providing travellers with necessary familiarity:

As a result, countries become interchangeable in the tourist's mind. Whether
he is looking for good beaches, restful forests, or old cities, it becomes relatively unimportant to him where these happen to be found (Cohen 1972: 172).

Effective differentiated positioning to stand out from the crowd is possible for any product
(DiMingo 1988; Moutinho 1994). The modern tourist is a sophisticated consumer, engaging
in many travel-related decisions, including where to travel to. For any given holiday type,
the traveller will usually have a large range of destinations to choose from. As a decision
maker, the approach used will vary between travellers and may vary between travel situations
(Mayo & Jarvis 1981). Influencing these decisions is arguably the supply-side's key goal.
The fundamental marketing challenge faced by DMOs is to somehow match a large and
diverse product range with the needs of a number of dynamic and heterogeneous markets.
The desired market position, assuming one has been designed and articulated, must be
presented to the market in a way that stands out from other attention-seeking messages of
rival destinations and substitute products. If successful, such a position will establish the
destination as top of mind in the target audience. If top of mind awareness (ToMA) is an
indicator of purchase preference (Axelrod 1968; Wilson 1981; Woodside & Wilson 1985), it
follows that such a position in the mind offers destinations a potential source of competitive
advantage (Pike 2002b).

It is a marketing axiom that corporate strategy should seek to maximise strengths, correct
weaknesses, minimise threats and maximise opportunities. As discussed in Chapter 3,
Porter (1980) suggested a competitive strategy was one that positioned a business to
make the most of strengths that differentiated the firm from competitors. A sustainable
competitive advantage (SCA) is gained when consumers perceive a performance capability
gap that endures over time (Coyne 1986). To gain an advantage the gap must be through a
product attribute that represents an important buying criterion. The most popular approach
for consumer goods has been positioning by product attribute (Aaker & Shansby 1982).
However, not all attributes that differentiate a product from competitors are actually
important to the consumer (Crompton *et al.* 1992; Lovelock 1991).

Attribute Importance, Salience and Determinance

The ideal for any product is to be perceived favourably on product attributes that are
important to the target segment. Different terms have been used in the tourism literature
to describe important attributes. Salience concerns the order in which features are elicited
from consumers, where the most important may be offered first. Important attributes may
be salient but not necessarily determinant. It is essential then to identify those attributes that
determine product choice, to form the basis for any positioning campaign (Lovelock 1991;
Ritchie & Zins 1978). Myers & Alpert (1968: 13) offered the first definition of determinance
in the marketing literature:

> Attitudes toward features which are most closely related to preference or to
> actual purchase decisions are said to be determinant; the remaining features
> or attitudes — no matter how favourable — are not determinant.

Determinant attributes are those where customers see significant differences between competing brands (Lovelock 1991). Prior to the events of September 11th 2001 the example of airline safety was commonly used to illustrate the differences between importance, salience and determinance (e.g. Lovelock 1991; Mayo & Jarvis 1981; Myers & Alpert 1968; Myers & Gutman 1974):

> Air travelers are naturally concerned with an air carrier's safety record, but presumably the safety records of all major carriers are more or less the same. Thus, safety would not be a salient attribute when one is choosing an airline to fly between two major cities. Similarly, when one chooses from among four or five major motels at a particular location, cleanliness would probably not be a salient attribute (Mayo & Jarvis 1981: 192).

It remains to be seen whether the September 2001 terrorist attacks, as an intervening variable, will have a long term effect on the importance, salience and determinance of safety, in terms of differentiating international airlines. Intervening and moderating variables can affect the determinance of destination attributes. Intervening variables are those that may be of a short or long term nature. However, these are situational and so delay rather than deny the choice. Moderating variables on the other hand are those that are longer term or permanent inhibitors. For example, a husband may regard "opportunities for fishing" as a salient attribute but may be limited in holiday choice to destinations preferred by his spouse, and will therefore not be determinant.

From the analysis of over 80 published destination image studies that had used lists of attributes in structured questionnaires, Pike (2003) summarised 18 themes. Of these studies, 37 concluded with proposed determinant attributes or factors. These were summarised into 15 themes. Pike suggested destination market researchers could screen these themes, through focus groups and/or or personal interviews using the Repertory Grid technique, to develop a context-specific list of attributes for use in tailored destination image surveys.

Positioning Destinations

> Few communities have developed a positioning strategy. Instead they yield to the pressure to be all things to all people, and use look-alike promotions and print brochures showing attractions ranging from historic barns to zoos — without any regard to whether these features have any drawing power (Gee & Makens 1985: 29).

Following Aaker & Shansby (1982) and Wind (1980), the destination positioning process involves seven stages. These are shown in Figure 4.

Once the range of determinant attributes is known, a key decision must be made about which should be used as the focus of the brand positioning. While focus may be appropriate for single product marketers, the selection of one determinant attribute by a destination marketer is usually problematic. For destinations, Ries & Trout (1986) used the analogy

1. Identify the target market and travel context.
2. Identify the competitive set of destinations in the target market and travel context.
3. Identify the motivation/benefits sought by previous visitors and non-visitors.
4. Identify perceptions of the strengths and weaknesses of each of the competitive set of destinations.
5. Identify opportunities for differentiated positioning.
6. Select and implement the position.
7. Monitor the performance of the positioning strategy over time.

Figure 4: Destination positioning process.

of postcard images to sum up how a place was positioned in the mind. Another useful example is the ubiquitous roadside billboard. Clearly there is a limit to the amount of information that can be portrayed on a standard size postcard or billboard. To stand out and be noticed and remembered, DMOs must design a positioning strategy focused on one or few attributes, when the region probably contains a wide range of often quite diverse features and products, and where stakeholders who contribute to DMO campaigns may have vested interests in quite different markets. For destinations, as multi-attributed entities, this means making trade-offs. After all, "you can't stand for something if you chase after everything" (Ries 1992: 7). Success is most likely when the range of differentiated features emphasised is small (Crompton *et al.* 1992; Aaker & Shansby 1982). The power of focus is due our mind's dislike of confusion (Trout & Rivkin 1995). In an age when the information flood is increasing exponentially, the message should not try to tell the product's entire story, but rather focus on one powerful attribute, since more brand variations cause confusion. Ries (1992: 5) suggested that owning a word in the target's mind had become the most powerful concept in marketing. Therefore the following question should be asked: "What single idea or concept does my company (or brand) stand for in the mind of the prospect?"

In the brand literature it has been suggested a value proposition is the promise of functional, emotional and self-expressive benefits to influence purchase decisions (Aaker 1996). These are relevant to the concepts of cognitive, affect and conative images. Functional benefits, or product attributes, by themselves do not differentiate and are easy to copy. This relates to the cognitive image or knowledge of a destination's features. Emotional benefits are the stimulation of a positive feeling. This relates to the affective or evaluative image component. For example, how do you feel when you are at destination X? Many destination experiences are hedonic, and so the brand must somehow capture this pleasure dimension (Ritchie & Ritchie 1998). Aaker suggested most functional attributes have an associated feeling. Self-expressive benefits strengthen the link between brand and consumer by representing symbols of our self-concept: "A brand can thus provide a self-expressive benefit by providing a way for a person to communicate his or her self image" (Aaker 1996: 99). These may include for example, "adventurous," "hip," "sophisticated," and "successful" among others. The differences between emotional and self-expressive benefits are that self-expressive emphasises: the self rather than feelings, a public setting rather than private, future aspirations rather than memory, and the act of using the product rather than the consequence of using it. For example, the benefit of the pre and post brag value from visiting an exotic destination may be different to the benefit of feelings attained from being there. Keller (2003) also proposed three positioning deliverability criteria:

(1) Is the position feasible? For a destination this will relate to the ability of the local tourism industry and host community to deliver the promise.
(2) Can the position be communicated? In terms of developing strong, favourable and unique associations, the efficacy of a destination's communications will depend to a large extent on whether the message is reinforcing existing positively held associations of the destination, or whether an attempt is being made to either create awareness or change opinions.
(3) Is the position sustainable? The ability of the destination to strengthen associations over time will depend on how well the position can be defended against imitating rivals.

Undertaking the seven-stage destination positioning process on a segment by segment basis in all markets, for different travel contexts, would present a significant challenge for DMOs. It follows that even with a wide range of attractions, some destinations may not fulfil potential opportunities (Hunt 1975), where, due to poor decision-making, implementation and/or limited budgets, the desired image has not been achieved in the market. Pike & Ryan (2004: 341) proposed the following to enhance destination positioning effectiveness:

• An understanding of the benefits sought by the target audience, and the relative performances of the competitive set of destinations.
• Trade-offs for a focused positioning strategy based on determinant attributes.
• Implementation to "cut-through" and stimulate intent (demand).
• The delivery and monitoring of benefits offered by the position.
• Performance measures to track effectiveness over time.
• Research to stay in touch with target audience needs.

The Positioning Elements

When the focus of the position has been determined, the elements to represent the public face of the brand must be selected. For destinations the most important positioning elements are the place name, a symbol and a positioning slogan.

Destination Names

> In this competitive era, the single most important marketing decision you can make is what to name the product. The name is the hook that hangs the consumer brand on the product ladder in the prospect's mind (Ries & Trout 1982: 28).

At the core of the brand is the product name (Aaker 1991). A well chosen word can trigger meanings in the mind; therefore a good brand name can begin the positioning process by communicating the major benefit of the product (Ries & Trout 1982). However, there has been little empirical research into the contribution of the brand's name in the development of favourable brand associations (Keller 1993), and little if any relating to destination names. Unlike new product developments, where an attempt can be made to select a name that enhances the positioning process through either memorability or development of associations, a destination will already have a place name, for which a history of associations has been developed over time. For all manner of political, economical and practical reasons, it is usually extremely difficult to change a destination's name, even though it might make sense to tourism marketers. For example, in New Zealand during a late 1980s crisis meeting between Rotorua's civic leaders and Japanese tour wholesalers, convened by then Mayor John Keaney to discuss the destination's ailing image in that market, one of the key outcomes was the suggestion that Rotorua change it's name to "Kingstown." This was a deliberate reference to Queenstown, which was the preferred New Zealand resort area for Japanese visitors. In line with Ries and Trout's (1982) view that brand names need aural qualities, Rotorua, which is an indigenous Maori name that translates as "second lake" in English, did not appeal to the Japanese in the same way as destinations with English names such as Queenstown and Christchurch. The "Kingstown" suggestion was however never pursued seriously beyond the meeting for political and cultural reasons.

Admittedly, there are places that owe a lot of their renown to a tricky name, such as Titicaca, Timbuktu, Popocateptl, Ouarzazate and Gstaad (Anholt 2002). Nevertheless there are examples of destination name (re)creation around the world, which in some cases has been for branding reasons. In the Caribbean, Hog Island was changed to Paradise Island to appeal to the tourism market (Ries & Trout 1982). During 2003 the neighbouring Queensland beach towns of Bargara, Moore Park and Woodgate all made moves to add the word "beach" to the destination name. The names Bargara Beach, Moore Park Beach and Woodgate Beach clearly signal an important functional attribute for these small emerging destinations. In effect an association with a desirable tourism product category is being reinforced by adding the word "beach." Similarly, Florida's Lee County, home of USA's best known shell collectors' haven Sanibel Island, changed the destination name to Lee Island Coast. In January 1996 the Republic of Cuervo was created by the well-known tequila brand (see Kotler 1996). The company purchased an island off the coast of Tortola in the Caribbean and declared independence. The company even unsuccessfully petitioned for country status at the United Nations, and for admission of a volleyball team to the Olympics. Today the island is labelled CuervoNation (see www.cuervo.com).

If not able or willing to officially change the name, amendments can be made to the name used to brand the tourism destination. For example, in New Zealand's central North Island the official place name of Taupo has long been promoted by destination marketers as Lake Taupo to take advantage of the district's most noticeable natural feature (e.g. www.laketauponz.com). Likewise, neighbouring district Ruapehu, which features the North Island's major skiing and climbing mountains, is promoted as Mount Ruapehu.

A further opportunity is that of labelling tourism macro-regions with tourism related names, such as Queensland's Gold Coast and Sunshine Coast. Other attempts at establishing emerging macro regions labels within the state include:

- Fraser Coast, in reference to the world heritage listed Fraser Island.
- Coral Coast, in reference to the southern starting point of the Great Barrier Reef.
- Discovery Coast, in reference to Captain Cook's 1770 voyage of discovery, explicit in the name of the popular beach "The Town of 1770."

- Capricorn Coast, in reference to the Tropic of Capricorn.
- Tropical North Queensland.

By comparison, the names of England's macro destination regions indicate a geographic reference point, such as South East England, and miss an opportunity to promote a travel benefit.

Destination Symbols

An interesting example of how the multi-attributed nature of destinations represents a major challenge in the positioning process was experienced by the author, when as General Manager of an RTO, he was presented with a request by a national television network for a graphic image of one local icon for use in the evening news weather segment. Only one image was permitted, which would be used consistently each night alongside images from other major centres. However, this high profile opportunity proved a difficult selection due to the vested business interests in different icons by individual representatives of the RTO's industry advisory board. Indeed, the destination's positioning theme at the time was "Full of Surprises," which was designed to represent the multiplicity and diversity of tourism attractions. Politics aside, symbols can enhance brand recognition and recall (Aaker 1996) by serving as a mnemonic devise for the target (Aaker 1991). A symbol can be a metaphor for the brand's personality, such as Marlboro's cowboy and Esso's tiger (King 1991).

Since destination names have not usually been designed to reinforce or create associations with a product class, logos and slogans can play important roles as identifiers. A logo and/or slogan can be designed to reflect a desirable functional feature such as nature or an affective benefit such as relaxing. Aaker (1996: 205) suggested posing the question: "What mental image would you like customers to have of your brand in the future?" A symbol can help to identify the brand with the product class as well as reflect the brand personality. For example, Virgin's logo, unconventional script and rakish angle support the Virgin personality, which flaunts the rules (Aaker & Joachimsthaler 2000). In particular, symbols that are metaphors for the brand personality are more meaningful. Ries & Ries (1998: 132) were critical of many efforts in this regard:

> The power of a brand name lies in the meaning of the word in the mind. For most brands, a symbol has little or nothing to do with creating this meaning to the mind.

Symbols can emerge from a diverse array of sources, such as a sound (Harley Davidson), architecture (Spanish adobe), the product's founder (KFC's Colonel Sanders), a colour (Hertz' yellow), packaging (Bundaberg Ginger Ale's distinctively shaped bottle), script style (Cadbury chocolate), a programme (Ronald McDonald House), a character (Energizer bunny), a celebrity (Nike's Michael Jordan), or a distinctive logo (Adidas' three stripes). Ownership of such "communication equity" can represent a source of competitive advantage (Gilmore 2002b).

Figure 5: Visit London logo. *Source*: www.londontouristboard.com/.

Figure 6: Brand Australia logo. *Source*: www.atc.net.au.

For destinations, a symbol may represent well established icons: "Such symbols as the Eiffel Tower, the Pyramids of Egypt, and the Great Wall of China are the kinds of unique and enduring symbols that DMOs are prepared to die for" (Ritchie & Ritchie 1998: 113). For other destinations the symbol may be a logo. In Figure 5 it can be seen that the logo for London emphasises the well known underground and taxi icons that play a prominent role in most visits to the English capital. The logo used for Brand Australia, shown in Figure 6,

Figure 7: Visit Florida logo. *Source*: www.flausa.com.

features the nation's favourite icon to provide instant recognition overseas (ATC 2003). The design was developed through extensive research that identified the kangaroo as Australia's most recognisable symbol. Colour variations are used to represent the coastal and interior climates of Australia. Florida launched the new logo FLA USA in 1997, developed at a cost of US$237,000, including US$100,000 in market testing (*Marketing News*, 29/9/97). The report suggested that Sunshine State tourism officials hoped the new logo, shown in Figure 7 would ultimately become as recognizable as the Nike swoosh. The Florida Tourism Industry Marketing Corporation (FTIMC), which changed the organisation name around the same time to Visit Florida, stated the brand was designed for the long term.

Destination Slogans

For most destinations a logo will not be sufficient to communicate a differentiated position. The addition of a slogan offers an opportunity to add more meaning to that which could be achieved by the brand name or symbol (Aaker 1991). A slogan is a short phrase that communicates descriptive or persuasive information about a brand (Keller 2003). Interestingly, it has been suggested the word slogan emanates from the Gaelic term meaning "battle cry" (Boyee & Arens 1992, in Supphellen & Nygaardsvik 2002). Slogans have also been referred to as tag lines and strap lines.

The slogans used during 2003 by NTOs are presented in Appendix 2. The approach used was to record the slogan used on the home page of each NTO's consumer web site. The rationale was the assumption that since one of the basic tenets of integrated marketing communication is a consistency of message across different media, the slogan used on the DMO home page should represent the destination positioning theme. Content analysis of these slogans identified 14 positioning categories, which are listed below in order of popularity:

(1) Leadership
(2) Discovery
(3) Nature
(4) Location
(5) People
(6) Water
(7) Self expressive
(8) Escape
(9) Pleasure
(10) Treasure
(11) Royal
(12) Vibrant
(13) Climate
(14) Culinary.

Too many destination slogans have been less than memorable (see Dann 2000; Morgan *et al.* 2003; Ward & Gold 1994). Best practise in destination promotion has been limited to a few simple slogans, such as the 1970s development of the "I ♥ New York" campaign (Ward & Gold 1994: 4):

> The process of imitation, however, demonstrates a general paucity of creative ideas and effectively ensures that the vast majority of place promotional campaigns rarely manage to cross the threshold of ephemeral indifference.

Some destinations have even resorted to public competitions to unearth a slogan. For example, during 2001 the Tauranga District Council in New Zealand ran a competition inviting the public to design a new slogan for the district. The competition resulted in over 2,500 submitted slogans (Cousins 2001). Slogan competitions have not been limited to small destinations. Holcomb (1999) for example reported a similar initiative by Atlanta in the USA. The obvious danger with competitions is there may be political pressure to use the winning slogan.

Unfortunately, there are few guidelines in the marketing literature for empirically testing brand slogans (Supphellen & Nygaardsvik 2002). One helpful study in the tourism literature concerning differentiation through slogans was reported by (Richardson & Cohen 1993). They developed a hierarchical taxonomy of destination slogans featuring four criteria, based on Reeves' (1961) concept of a unique selling point (USP):

- The foundation of the hierarchy is that the slogan must be prepositional.
- Such propositions should be limited to one or only a few.
- The proposition(s) should sell benefits of interest to the market.
- The benefit(s) must be unique.

Richardson & Cohen categorised the slogans of 46 USA state tourism organisations. Commencing at level zero of the hierarchy, two of the state slogans examined, Yes! Michigan! and Utah!, were deemed not to be propositional. It should be noted however that the development of a proposition is arguably the greatest challenge in branding (Gilmore 2002). Ascending to level one of the hierarchy the slogans of six STOs featured propositions, but which were no more than a plea to "buy our product." Examples at this level included "Discover Idaho" and "Explore Minnesota." At level two, the proposition is equivalent to stating "our product is good." Of the 14 slogans at this level, examples included "Discover the spirit! North Dakota," "The spirit of Massachusetts," and "Vermont makes it special." Level 3a featured nine slogans where the proposition promoted an attribute that represented a potential benefit but that almost every other state could claim. These included "Arkansas — the natural state," "Maine — the way life should be," and "Oregon — things look different here." At level 3b the propositional benefit attribute used in the slogans of six states could be claimed by many states. These included "Ohio the heart of it all!," "Oklahoma — native America" and "Texas, like a whole other country." At level 4a, the proposition features a unique attribute, but one that does not represent a benefit. The three states at this level were "Delaware — the first state," "Pennsylvania — America starts here" and "Rhode Island — America's first resort." At level 4b, the pinnacle of the hierarchy, the slogans of only five states were considered to feature a USP:

- Arizona — the Grand Canyon state
- Florida — coast to coast
- Louisiana — we're really cookin!
- South Dakota — great faces, great places
- Tennessee — we're playing your song.

Chapter Key Point Summary

Key Point 1 — Positioning as the Interface Between Brand Identity and Brand Image

The brand identity development approach outlined in Chapter 5 requires the effective positioning of the brand identity to achieve the desired brand image in the market place. Positioning is therefore the interface between the desired destination image and the actual image held by consumers. Effective positioning is mutually beneficial for DMOs and consumer-travellers.

Key Point 2 — Positioning as a Source of Competitive Advantage

While consumers have an almost limitless number of destinations to choose from, they will only consider the merits of a small number in the actual decision process. A model of positioning as a source of competitive advantage for destinations was proposed. Destination decision set membership and ToMA, which can be achieved through effective positioning, are key indicators of destination attractiveness and competitiveness.

Key Point 3 — Focus

Effective positioning represents a source of advantage for destinations, but requires a succinct, focused and consistent message tailored to meet needs of target segments, to gain "cut through" in crowded, heterogeneous and dynamic markets. Key components of destination positioning are the brand name, and symbols such as logos and slogans.

Additional Reading

Hooley, G., Saunders, J., & Piercy, N. (2004). *Marketing strategy and competitive positioning* (3rd ed). Harlow: Prentice-Hall.

Pike, S., & Ryan, C. (2004). Destination positioning analysis through a comparison of cognitive, affective and conative perceptions. *Journal of Travel Research*, *42*(4), 333–342.

Ries, A., & Trout, J. (1982). *Positioning: The battle for your mind*. New York: McGraw-Hill.

Chapter 7

Destination Marketing

The advertising and promotion program is the most visible activity of a tourism board and is certain to be received with mixed reviews by the community. Criticism is likely, and board members should develop thick skins (Gee & Makens 1985: 29).

Chapter Perspective

There is no end of ways in which a destination can be promoted, and in every destination community there will be a diverse range of opinions on the tactics that should be employed. Local tourism operators' views on promotional priorities will vary for a range of reasons, including: differing levels of professional experience in marketing and tourism, vested business interests in specific types of products and target markets, access to financial resources, and their position within local industry politics. Anyone who has worked within a DMO for any length of time will almost certainly have experienced the frustration of being surrounded by many different types of stakeholders offering conflicting advice. Criticism can emerge at any time and from many quarters, including the media, tourism operators, travel intermediaries, government officials and elected representatives, local residents and even other DMOs. Occasionally the "feedback" is made public, such as in the criticism by local government and tourism operators in Edinburgh aimed at Visit Britain for their "ludicrous" non-promotion of the city's famous arts festivals (see Ferguson 2003). Critics claimed Visit Britain advertising focused on fringe festivals instead of major attractions such as the Edinburgh International Festival and Edinburgh Military Tattoo. However, the NTO argued that given the city is always "booked up" during major events, advertising funds were better directed elsewhere. Clearly, dialogue is required with the business community and host population during marketing planning, and yet the DMO must be careful to avoid the trap of trying to please everyone. The more time and resources directed towards communicating with internal stakeholders the less will be available for communicating with current and future customers.

Outward-Inward Thinking

A market orientation dictates outward-inward market-organisation thinking (Duncan 2002). In tourism this means firstly anticipating travellers' needs, and then developing products and services to meet these. Adopting this approach in destination marketing is problematic. Instead, DMOs generally use inward-outward thinking by attempting to find markets that will be interested in a destination's existing products. A DMO must somehow showcase the destination in a way that offers benefits sought by travellers, represents the interests of tourism suppliers, and does not commodify residents' sense of place. Promoting matches between destination resources and travellers' needs is the focus of DMO marketing activities. With this in mind, the generally accepted steps in destination marketing planning are: a situation analysis, incorporating a resource audit, environmental analysis (Chapter 3) and competitive positioning analysis (Chapter 6); development of goals and strategy (Chapter 3); an action plan, and measures of performance (Chapter 9). A typical table of contents for a DMO marketing plan generally includes the sections as shown in Figure 1.

Often the debate within a destination community about marketing activities is representative of a promotion or selling orientation rather than a market orientation. However, the destination marketing paradigm is quietly undergoing a revolution. Thomas Kuhn's original thesis on paradigms was as science operating within a largely unquestioned framework, governed by fundamental theoretical models (Gregory 1987). When a theory is accepted it becomes a paradigm until it is challenged by way of revolution. This concept applies as much to tourism practices as it does to science. The role and activities of DMOs have evolved slowly over time, and there have been few revolutionary shifts. However, technology in particular is shaping a new paradigm that is currently forcing DMOs to reconsider their marketing activities. The issues highlighted in Chapter 4 to introduce the increasing interest in branding mean that traditional mass media advertising and promotion are quickly becoming less efficient: the recognition of customer-based brand equity, commodification of products, changing distribution channel power, globalisation, sophisticated consumers, and escalating media costs.

Readers will be aware that every marketing text features a section on the marketing mix, otherwise known as the four Ps of "product," "price," "place" and "promotion." The mix has been adapted in the services marketing literature to the seven Ps, with the addition of "participants," "process" and "physical evidence" (e.g. Lovelock *et al.* 1998). Critics of the four Ps argue that the approach is outdated in that it has an internal organisational focus. A customer focused approach views these elements as the four Cs (Schultz *et al.* 1993):

1. Executive summary
2. Mission and vision
3. Situation analysis
   - Macro-environment analysis
   - Resource audit
   - Competitive positioning analysis
4. Goals and objectives
5. Target market selection
6. Marketing mix
7. Action plan timelines
8. Budget
9. Performance measures

Figure 1: Table of contents for a DMO marketing plan.

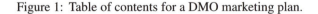

- Customer (product)
- Cost (price)
- Communication (promotion)
- Convenience (distribution).

Nevertheless, some aspects of the mix remain problematic for DMOs. For example, price is clearly an important tourism marketing variable, and is inextricably linked to the destination's approach to branding and positioning. Price is also the most flexible of a tourism product's marketing mix (Heath & Wall 1992). However, with little or no direct control over a destination's products, the influence of a DMO on pricing is usually limited at best.

The emergent shift in thinking towards destinations as brands requires a brand management approach that focuses on developing relationships with customers rather than simply focusing on generating sales. One such approach is integrated marketing communication (IMC), which has emerged relatively recently in the marketing literature but has received little academic research attention to date in the destination marketing field. IMC has been defined as:

> ...a process from managing the customer relationships that drive brand value. More specifically, it is a cross functional process from creating and nourishing profitable relationships with customers and other stakeholders by strategically controlling or influencing all messages sent to these groups and encouraging data-driven, purposeful dialogue with them (Duncan 2002).

Inherent in this description of IMC are five important tenets that provide both opportunities and challenges for DMOs: profitable customer relationships, enhancing stakeholder relationships, cross-functional process, stimulating purposeful dialogue with customers, and generating message synergy. Three decades ago it was suggested DMOs had been slow to adopt an integrated marketing approach:

> To a large number of NTOs, especially in the developing world, the term "integrated marketing" is either unknown or ignored (Wahab *et al.* 1976: 182).

Profitable Customer Relationships

One of the key goals in marketing is enhancing brand loyalty, which as discussed in Chapter 4, is a component of consumer-based destination brand equity. The rationale for stimulating relationships with customers is that these will be more profitable over time than one-off sales transactions, since the cost of reaching a continuous stream of new customers will far outweigh the cost of keeping in touch with existing customers. The topic of destination loyalty has attracted little research attention in the tourism literature (Oppermann 2000). Relationship marketing is an important area of research given the inherent advantages of repeat visitation and the limits to the extent that relationship marketing may be used by

DMOs of destinations that host hundreds of thousands of visitors. Periodic destination marketing newsletter *Eclipse* devoted a special issue to customer relationship marketing (CRM) for destinations. *Eclipse* found only one NTO that employed a specialist CRM senior executive. On the topic of whether CRM was a management fad, *Eclipse* cited the editor of CRM web site www.crmguru.com:

> Third grade — that's about where the CRM industry is today. Lots of software sold, some implemented, but not much to show for it. Do customers think relationships are improving? Are sales and profits increasing? Not very often and not by very much, based on various industry studies on CRM success rates.

Relationship marketing is the attempt to establish a long term bond with the customer. This presents challenges for DMOs. Not the least of which is the difficulty in obtaining quality customer data from service providers over which they have no direct control. Also, effectively collating the information in the mass of consumer coupon responses has also been challenging in the past. For example, three decades ago, South Carolina's promotional program generated almost 100,000 coupon responses in 1972 (Woodside & Reid 1974). Relatively recent advances in technology provide DMOs with a new marketing option to take advantage of such data. In 2002 for example, incoming BTA CEO Tom Wright announced a major customer relationship management strategy that would aim for 6 million active database records by 2006 (*Marketing*, 7/11/02). Following relationship marketing researchers (e.g. Anton & Petouhoff 2001; Egan 2001; Fyall *et al.* 2003; Grönroos 1994), it is suggested DMOs seeking to engage in relationship marketing should consider the following:

- The selection of customers who offer maximum yield. Selection criteria, which may prove problematic for a DMO due to data collection constraints, include frequency and volume of visits, spending patterns and probability of future visitation.
- Ensuring high quality service encounters. This requires the marketing concept to extend to the entire destination. As with service standards the DMO is reliant on the organisational cultures of the destination's many individual businesses. Initiatives include cooperative destination networks, visitor surveys, improving employee satisfaction, and a quality grading system such as Qualmark (see www.qualmark.co.nz). Almost 75% of tourism suppliers at New Zealand's 2004 TRENZ travel exchange were Qualmark accredited (*Inside Tourism*, IT490 18/3/04). Tourism grading schemes are a relatively recent development. For example, in Bermuda the Department of Tourism's emphasis on encouraging the development of a controlled upscale tourism environment led to the introduction of a grading plan in 1988 (Conlin 1995). The plan required properties to meet high standards in a number of areas in order to be able to renew their operating license. The first U.K. accommodation grading scheme was launched by Scotland during the mid 1980s (see Stuart 1986).
- Providing added value to selected customers. The DMO must stimulate cooperative efforts to monitor and provide sources of value. For example, during off season periods, communication could be made with previous domestic visitors offering bundled

packages at an advertising cost saving to the destination and a price saving to the traveller.

• Developing a philosophy of nurturing long term mutually beneficial relationships. Clearly however, the benefits of the relationship for the destination must outweigh the costs.

Direct marketing offers DMOs opportunities for developing dialogue with consumers. Hawes *et al.* (1991) found only 8 of 37 USA STOs used direct marketing, which involves sales communications without the use of other channel members (Clow & Baack 2004). Typical examples include: mail, telemarketing, catalogues, the internet and e-mail. In highlighting the limited degree of destination relationship marketing in practise, Fyall *et al.* (2003) reported two case studies. The first, Project Stockholm, is an example of an introductory attempt to engender more loyalty towards a destination, albeit without loyalty-building tools. The project is a cooperative initiative by the Stockholm RTO, Scandic Hotels and SAS airlines, specifically targeting European weekend tourists. A benefit card was designed for the project, offering added value in the form of free local transport and discounts at shops and restaurants. The second was the Club Program developed to reward repeat visits to Barbados. The programme boasted 1,700 members who had visited the island at least 25 times. Rewards have included luncheons hosted by the Barbados Tourism Authority and unofficial ambassador status. One of the key problems for DMOs highlighted by Fyall, Callod and Edwards (654) was the expense of retaining single visitors in comparison to the predominant transactional marketing activities:

> What thus appears sound in theory and operational in practise, particularly as a weapon to achieve sustainable competitive advantage in the marketplace, is likely to remain in its implementation infancy for destinations for some time.

Identifying Target Markets

The first task in developing profitable customer relationships is the identification of target markets. The DMO marketing approach differs to the generally accepted definition of the "marketing concept," as presented in general marketing theory in at least one significant way. The marketing concept was defined in Chapter 1 as a philosophy that recognises the achievement of organisational goals requires an understanding of the needs and wants of the target market, and then delivering satisfaction more effectively than rivals (Kotler *et al.* 2003). With such an orientation, all marketing decisions are made with the customer in mind. Most DMOs have no control over the tourism services they represent, and devote relatively few resources to new product development tailored to meet identified consumer needs. Therefore the marketing process is not one of designing products to meet market needs, but of attempting to find markets that are likely to be interested in the destination's current products. Admittedly, this approach is not unique to DMOs, with many agricultural product marketers are often forced into this situation in commodity markets. For example, carrot growers around the world have found a new market by packaging "seconds" to take advantage of the consumer trend of juicing. Identifying market segments that may have an interest in the destination's product range is therefore arguably the most important task for DMOs.

While targeting products to the perceived needs of specific segments is a marketing axiom (Assael 1971), most tourism organisations operate in mass markets with millions of consumers. The problem of a broad marketing focus usually occurs for public agencies that have such a broad mandate (Lovelock & Weinberg 1984). Tourism demand does not represent a homogenous group of people with identical motivations (Wahab *et al.* 1976), and as already discussed the market interests of a destination's tourism businesses can be divergent. However, the need to focus resources then leads to the central operational decision for tourism marketers being to prioritise target markets. Market aggregation represents an undifferentiated approach, where all consumers are treated as one, and is often criticised as being a "shotgun approach." At the opposite end of the continuum is total market disaggregation where every consumer is treated individually as a separate segment. There are obvious limits as to how far this can be taken by DMOs, and yet the literature does not provide any ready answers. Admittedly, important trade customers such as inbound tour operators are an example of marketing to the needs of an identifiable individual client. Positioning, which was the focus of Chapter 6, has its roots in segmentation theory (Haahti 1986), and the two concepts have become inseparable in the marketing process (Aaker & Shansby 1982; Hooley & Saunders 1993):

> Positioning usually implies a segmentation commitment. Positioning usually means that an overt decision is being made to concentrate only on certain segments. Such an approach requires commitment and discipline because its not easy to turn your back on potential buyers (Aaker & Shansby 1982: 61).

A destination's image may differ between regional markets (Hunt 1975) and between different segments (Fakeye & Crompton 1991; Phelps 1986). However, DMOs seldom research the differences in the images held by different markets (Ahmed 1996). Pechlaner & Abfalter (2002) criticised many NTOs in Europe for paying insufficient attention to the differences between markets, suggesting they were limited to using undifferentiated, but cost effective, marketing, which targeted common interests and needs of all travellers. However, undertaking needs analyses on a segment-by-segment basis provides marketers with opportunities to understand the needs of target segments better than competitors (Lovelock 1991). As discussed in Chapter 6, positioning is based on communicating one or a few key benefits desired by the target. Destinations operate in mass markets containing individuals with differing needs. Therefore can one positioning theme be adapted for use in all markets, or do the different characteristics of each market dictate a mix of distinct tailored themes as in the "think global, act local" mantra? In theory, this enables separate advertising briefs to be developed that cater to the needs of different segments. However, from a practical perspective, when considering the range of segments that will be of interest to a DMO's stakeholders, both a multi-market assessment and a differentiated promotion approach appear daunting. As discussed by Hooley & Saunders (1993: 154), an organisation taking the multiple segment approach "may face a diseconomy in managing, supplying and promoting in a different way to each of these segments it has chosen." Woodside (1982) also presented a warning in this regard, suggesting it is more effective to offer one set of benefits to one significant segment.

Segmentation can be undertaken either by *a priori* means, where the criterion variable for dividing the market is already known, or by *posteriori* means, where no such prior knowledge exists (Calantone & Mazanec 1991). For practical reasons many smaller DMOs will use an *a priori* approach to segmenting the global market. This is undertaken using criteria relating to easily obtainable information on geographic and demographic characteristics. The target market selection process generally begins by geographic means. For example, destinations in Central America and the Caribbean place a heavy reliance on visitors from cities in North America, while 15% of all USA arrivals are from Latin American countries (TIA 2004, in www.restaurantnewsresource.com, 29/304).

A number of methods for measuring international markets in relative terms have been reported in the literature, such as the Market Potential Index developed by the United States Travel Service (see Lundberg 1990), Western Australia's Market Potential Assessment Formula (see Crockett & Wood 1999), and the Country Potential Generation Index (CPGI) (Hudman 1979 in Formica & Littlefield 2000: 110). For example, the CPGI is expressed as:

$$CPGI = \frac{Nc/Nw}{Pc/Pw}$$

Where: Nc = the number of trips generated by the country, Nw = the number of trips generated in the world, Pc = the population of the country, Pw = population of the world.

A weakness of the CPGI approach is the model utilises simplistic terms and does not consider other important factors such as accessibility and per capita wealth. A more comprehensive method is multifactor portfolio modelling, which has been based on a two dimensional matrix combining measures of market attractiveness and competitive position (see Mazanec 1997). The matrix presents a visual tool similar to the growth-share matrix used by businesses to plot their product portfolio by market share and market growth (e.g. Johnson & Scholes 2002: 284). For destinations, market attractiveness variables considered for inclusion include market size, growth rate, seasonality effects and price levels, while competitive position might include variables related to market share, image, and advertising budgets. Destinations and markets are rated on each variable, which are subjectively assigned a weighting since not all will be of equal importance. For processing such data Mazanec promoted the use of the IAAWIN software, which was freely available from the Vienna University of Economics and Business Administration (see www.wu-wien.ac.at). A variation of this method, using a 3 × 3 matrix, was reported by Henshall & Roberts (1985) in a comparative assessment of New Zealand's major markets.

Another portfolio approach, the Destination-Market Matrix (DMM), which provides more balance between quantitative and qualitative analysis, was promoted by McKercher (1995). The DMM incorporates the destination life-cycle as well as the growth-share matrix, and displays six relationships between the destination and its markets:

- the relative importance of each market
- each market's life cycle stage

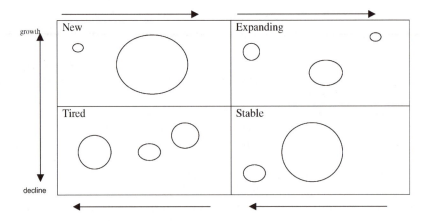

Figure 2: Destination-market matrix.

- the age of each market in each life cycle stage, which forms the basis of the horizontal axis
- a prediction of future performance, which forms the basis of the vertical axis
- the total number of markets attracted to the destination
- the interrelationship existing among all these markets.

The four cells of the DMM, shown in Figure 2, represent the life cycle stages each market would be expected to follow: "new," "expanding," "stable" and "tired." Each circle represents a market of interest, in terms of relative size and future performance. A critical assumption of the model is that markets progress through the matrix in a clockwise direction, starting as a "new" market in the top left hand corner. The horizontal axis represents the age of the market in the cell. McKercher suggested the benefits of the DMM were its flexibility, in that markets could be segmented by whatever means was most suitable to the DMO, and the ability to track the performance over time. Three Australian case studies were provided in the paper to demonstrate its effectiveness as a visual planning tool. The DMM was used by McKercher to graphically highlight unbalanced growth at the Gold Coast, the state of Victoria in decline, and balanced growth for Australia as a whole.

General utilities of market portfolio modelling techniques include aiding DMO decisions relating to promotional budget allocation for each market, and enhancing understanding of the destination's relative reliance on key markets. These can then be graphically presented to stakeholders. Often it is only with hindsight that the full implications of an over-reliance on particular markets is realised. This was particularly evident in Australia and New Zealand during the 1990s Asian economic crisis when an over reliance on markets in the region proved a weakness of many tourism businesses. Similarly, one of the major problems in the downturn in visitors to Majorca during the 1980s was an over reliance on the U.K. and German markets, which accounted for 70% of the island's visitors (Morgan 1991). The portfolio approach can also be used by a DMO on a market-by-market basis to plot current and future attractiveness of the destination's individual products. This is useful for destinations with a diverse range of products that have differing levels of appeal for different markets. A competitive analysis of the attractiveness of other destinations' product portfolios can also be undertaken.

The *posteriori* segmentation approach usually utilises more sophisticated multivariate techniques, such as cluster analysis, to identify groups within a population that exhibit or state similar psychographic characteristics. These will involve more subjectively defined criteria such as attitudes, desired benefits and behavioural intent. Another means is by travel purpose, including special interest groups. An almost limitless list of these include such diverse examples as: business meetings, incentive groups, school reunions, education field trips, bird watchers, calligraphers, collectors, country music fans, bikers and surfers. As examples, this section discusses three significant markets that have emerged in recent years, which provide opportunities for DMOs to generate repeat visitation and destination loyalty, but which have not yet attracted significant academic research attention in many parts of the world: gay and lesbian tourism, short breaks, and family related tourism.

Gay and Lesbian Tourism

In the emerging field of research about gay and lesbian travellers in the tourism literature it is evident there are mixed views about the justification for targeting this market. On one hand there is a stereotypical image of an affluent group with a high propensity for travel. On the other hand there has been criticism from host communities and gay travellers alike, about some negative impacts on society. Hughes' (2002) literature review found a number of reasons for warranting the targeting of gay markets by urban destinations:

* the group represents a new market for existing products
* they are perceived to be interested in urban tourism
* general characteristics of gay men include a propensity for and frequency of travel, high travel spend, high income and education levels, an interest in culture, few family connections, and more free time.

However, Hughes also listed some of the problems of characterising gay men in such a way, including:

* the characteristics are not universally applicable to all gays and lesbians
* segmentation by sexual orientation conceals other characteristics such as age, race, attitudes and interests, which may have a stronger bearing on travel purchase patterns.

Hughes summarised the travel needs of gay men as seeking destinations that meet the usual needs of a holiday, but which also offer "gay space," such as in pubs and clubs, and a lack of homophobia among residents. To this end, in 1999, the BTA produced a brochure entitled "Britain: you don't know the half of it" (later renamed "Britain: Inside and Out") as part of a promotion targeting gay travellers in New York, Chicago and Los Angeles (*Time International* 1999: 28). The brochure, which touted London as the gay capital of Europe, and the seaside resorts of Brighton, Bournemouth and

Torquay as the "queens of the south," provided details of gay pubs, clubs, hotels shops and bath houses. At the time the U.K. was attracting half a million international gay visitors annually. Spokesperson Louise Wood commented on the campaign rationale: "We're actively targeting the pink dollar. American gays are frequent travellers, long stayers and big spenders." One RTB to capitalise on the BTA/Visit Britain campaign has been Marketing Manchester. Manchester features a unique gay space, hosts an annual Gayfest, and is home to the television series "Queer as Folk." Tactics have included advertising in gay media, direct mail, representation at gay pride events and distribution of a dedicated gay Manchester brochure. The campaign focused on emphasising the city's gay space, and provided reassurance about the community's tolerance of alternative lifestyles. In Australia, Tourism Victoria launched an international gay and lesbian tourism campaign in 2003 (www.tourismvictoria.com.au/newsletter/july_2003/story7.htm, 7/7/03). Key elements of the campaign included *The Melbourne Gay and Lesbian Visitors' Guide*, a newly branded gay specific website (see www.visitmelbourne.com/gaytravel), and an image library upgrade.

DMOs targeting the gay market should also be prepared for criticism from the host population. Marketing Manchester's campaign has been criticised by prominent civic leaders as promoting "sex tourism" and therefore alienating other visitors (Hughes 2002). It was as recent as 1994 in New Zealand that the CEO of the RTO for leading resort area Queenstown described the local council's decision to criticise a New Zealand Tourism Board (NZTB) campaign targeting the Australian gay market as "discrimination" (*Inside Tourism*, IT487, 27/2/04: 8). The council passed a motion to not support any tourism promotion based on "ethnic, race, religious or sexual grounds." Earlier, the country's Minister of Tourism, John Banks, stated that he was also against the NZTB's gay campaign, although he did not want to ban homosexual visitors. *Time International* (1999) reported the new sexual openness by the British NTO was only possible following the election of the Labour government in 1997. However, Visit Britain's campaign has been slammed by some in the local gay community for a range of reasons such as welcoming gay money but not extending basic human rights like adequate policing of London's gay quarter, and stimulating "gawping" heterosexual tourists who were creating a fishbowl effect. "You feel like you are in a zoo" suggested one gay travel writer.

Short Breaks

The term "short break" is firmly entrenched in the travel industry vernacular and has regularly been the topic of articles in trade publications such as *Traveltrade*, *Travelweek*, and *Traveltalk Asia-Pacific* (e.g. Burns 1994; Marshman 1995; Speigal 1997), and in the popular press such as *The Australian*, *Age* and *Business Review Weekly* (e.g. McCabe 1998; Sandilands 1997; Tolhurst 1999). Also, in Australia, *The Sunday Mail* features a travel column entitled "Short Breaks." However, in the tourism literature it was as recent as 1990 that Fache (1990: 5) referred to short breaks as a "new form of recreation."

Short breaks have emerged relatively recently as a significant holiday trend in Europe (Euromonitor 1987; Fache 1990; Ryan 1983), Australasia (Pike 2002c; Pike & Ryan 2004) and North America (Kotler *et al.* 1998; Plog 2000). The majority of research into this travel segment has been in the U.K., where the focus has been on commercial hotel packages (e.g. Davies 1990; Edgar 1997; Edgar *et al.* 1994; Middleton & O'Brien 1987; Ryan 1983; Teare *et al.* 1989). Ryan discussed the introduction of domestic weekend-break packages, by U.K. hotels, as one of a range of initiatives to counter static domestic and international visitor growth during the late 1970s. By the 1990s commercial short breaks in the U.K. had evolved from an off-season contribution towards fixed costs, to an all-year growth market (Edgar *et al.* 1994). In Europe it has been claimed short breaks were growing at a faster rate than other holiday types Lohmann (1990, 1991) and generated the highest per day spend (Gratton 1990). Gratton suggested increases in the number of short breaks taken each year had reversed the decline in domestic tourism experienced in many European countries during the 1970s. It has also been suggested increases in leisure time and disposable income had led to one or more shorter holidays being taken each year, which supplemented the annual holiday (Euromonitor 1987). However, there has been little empirical investigation of the extent to which short breaks either replace or supplement the main holiday. Euromonitor also estimated that almost one third of people took more than one such break per year, and that 40% of all holidays taken were short breaks. More recently, research in Australia (Pike 2004) and in New Zealand (Pike 2002) found respondents averaged four short break holidays each year.

The Euromonitor (1987) report suggested short breaks in the U.K. were less seasonal than longer holidays, and that three quarters of domestic short breaks were by private car. In New Zealand it has been estimated that about 80% of domestic travel uses private vehicles (Forsyte Research 2000). Similarly, in Australia it has been estimated 76% of domestic travellers use private vehicles (BTR 2002). BTR also found 70% of domestic travel was within the home state, and that the mean trip duration for these intrastate travellers was three nights.

Short break holidays lack an internationally recognised definition (Edgar 2001). In the U.K. and Europe they have commonly been referred to as short holidays of up to three nights (see Euromonitor 1987; Fache 1994; Ryan 1983; van Middelkoop *et al.* 1999). However, Edgar pointed to emerging thinking that short breaks are more likely to be up to four or five nights. Intuitively, this appears reasonable given four or five nights may or may not be considered a main holiday in many parts of the world. Therefore, it is suggested a short break holiday is a non-business trip of between one and five nights away from the home environment. Fache (1994) summarised the following characteristics of short breaks:

- they do not replace annual holidays
- destinations are usually within the home country
- private cars are the main form of transport
- short breaks are taken throughout the year
- short break takers are relatively high spenders
- short breaks are usually a spontaneous decision.

Despite the clear significance of the short break market, relatively few published market perceptions studies have focused on this travel context. Indeed, only two of the 142 destination image papers reviewed by Pike (2002a) had indicated an interest in short break holidays. Chon *et al.* (1991) investigated the image of Norfolk, Virginia as a "mini-break" destination, while McClellan (1998) analysed perceptions of Cherbourg as a potential short break destination for French and English travellers. Since then, Pike & Ryan (2004) have reported on the short break market positions of a competitive set of destinations in New Zealand.

Family Related Tourism

Travel to visit friends and relatives (VFR) generates repeat visitors to a destination (see Gitelson & Crompton 1984). VFR represents a significant component of the tourism industry. Chon & Singh (1995) cited research by the U.S. Travel Data Centre, which estimated almost half of leisure travel in the USA involved VFR. Clearly this presents opportunities for DMOs. For example, Stephenville in Newfoundland effectively developed a visitor market out of VFR links from marriages between USA military personnel and local women (Butler & Baum 1999). Over 25,000 servicemen served in Newfoundland from the 1940s to 1960s. VFR tourism also offers opportunities for regions that have been characterised by high migration levels. These range from small rural areas that have experienced urban drift to countries such as Ireland, New Zealand and Samoa, which have disproportionately large percentages of expatriates living abroad. The latter in particular enjoys seasonal influxes of visiting expatriates from the USA, Australia and New Zealand, whose regular trips provide valuable cash injections to the fragile economy.

The VFR market also presents a number of challenges for DMOs, not the least of which is that it is not viewed positively by all in the tourism industry, and DMOs must take due care to investigate its feasibility. Critics argue that the market often ties up valuable aircraft capacity, particularly at peak holiday periods, but at the same time makes relatively little use of accommodation and tourist attractions. McKercher (1996, in Bleasdale & Kwarko 2000) described VFR tourism as an invisible activity, given the difficulty in isolating the segment within aggregated statistical sources. Bleasdale and Kwarko investigated the opportunity for Ghana to capitalize on the potential of VFR tourism. Ghana has a poorly developed image as a tourism destination relative to competing destinations in the region such as the Gambia and South Africa. The country also suffers from the existence of health hazards such as malaria, as well as a lack of investment capital and tourism infrastructure. In 1988 it was estimated that half of all international visitors were Ghanaian (Teye 1988, in Bleasedale & Kwarko 2000), and that many others travelling on USA or U.K. passports were of Ghanaian origin. Despite the high proportion of VFR travellers, their survey of Ghanaians residing in London found very few used commercial accommodation or visited tourism attractions. They recommended therefore the Ghana Tourist Board needed to develop pro-active initiatives if the VFR segment was to contribute more to the development of the tourism industry.

Related to VFR is genealogy tourism or kinship tourism. Although there has been little published research to date, many destinations have the opportunity to target markets where settlers either emigrated from or emigrated to. For example, regarding the former, the *Evening News* (4/2/03: 14) reported on an initiative by Edinburgh tourism businesses that involved a sales mission to Canada and the USA to "strengthen bonds of kinship" with Scotland. North America is Scotland's largest overseas market. A report in the *National*

Post (6/1/03) cited a government commissioned study in Canada that found one-third of Canadians are interested in genealogy tourism. Visit Scotland operates a dedicated website (see www.ancesteralscotland.com) under the promotional theme "Follow in the footsteps of your ancestors . . . all the way home." Another notable initiative, "Invite the World," was implemented by Tourism Vancouver in 2002 to urge residents to invite friends and relatives from around the world to visit the destination. The CVB encouraged residents to send an e-postcard from tourismvancouver.com to contacts outside of Vancouver and British Columbia. In doing so, the resident was automatically entered into a weekly prize draw. The campaign ran from March to November at a cost of over C$400,000, three-quarters of which was generated from sponsors. Key results included:

- 14,098 e-postcards sent from tourismvancouver.com compared to 4,122 sent over the same time period 2001; an increase of 242%
- 1,539,573 unique visits to tourismvancouver.com compared to 976,390 over the same time period 2001; an increase of 58%
- 7,966 qualified names collected by permission data capture for future e-marketing efforts.

Product

A "product" has been defined as "anything that can be offered to a market for attention, acquisition, use or consumption that might satisfy a want or a need" (Kotler *et al.* 1998: 344). Globalisation is increasing the homogeneity and commodification of tourism products. For example, the internationalisation of theme parks such as through expansion by Disney and the outsourcing of international consultants is leading to a homogenous approach towards these developments (Swarbrooke 2001). Likewise the westernisation of Asia, standardised format of international hotel chains, the ubiquitous golden arches and the sale of similar types of "souvenirs" has to decreased surprises for experienced travellers and an increasing difficulty in DMOs' ability to differentiate.

A product offering comprises core, actual and augmented elements. The core product is the bundle of benefits sought by the consumer. In the case of destinations these are the ability to cater to travel motivations such as the need for escape and relaxation or adventure and excitement. These will vary between segments, depending on the context or purpose of the travel. Indeed the same individual may seek quite different benefits for travel at different times of the year and also during different stages of their lifetime. Thus the same destination may offer different core products to different markets and at different times of the year. The actual product is that supplied for purchase, such as a travel package. In this regard a destination is viewed by the consumer as both a product in itself, since in general consumers talk about purchasing travel to a destination such as Paris or Germany, as well as an amalgam of individual tourism services. The augmented product represents the added value component. For tourism service providers and intermediaries a satisfaction guarantee to overcome perceived risk is a useful example.

While some DMOs, particularly at the NTO level, have historically been directly involved in developing and managing tourism products, the majority no longer have any direct responsibility, due in the main to the high labour intensity of the activity. For example, Getz *et al.* (1997, 1998) found most Canadian CVBs lacked formal goals for product development, with only one quarter reporting having a policy. They found significant barriers to direct involvement included a lack of resources, an organisational marketing mandate, and concerns from existing members. In some cases the DMO abdicates responsibility to an economic development agency, such as in the case of Rotorua, New Zealand, where the product development has been role has been the domain of the local council's business development unit (see http://rotorua-business.com/index.shtml). Essentially there are three main roles played by DMOs. One DMO product opportunity is the stimulation of new product development. The DMO must determine the extent to which the range of destination products adequately takes advantage of the destination's source(s) of competitive advantage. For example, in New Zealand for many years it has been argued that of all the attributes that country has to offer visitors there is only one that is truly unique on the world stage, and that is the indigenous Maori people and their culture. Everything else, such as fiords and glaciers, geothermal activity, bungee jumping and the like can be found elsewhere. Given that so many travellers are interested in experiencing aspects of other cultures this has been advantageous for New Zealand. However, until very recently there has been a lack of commercial Maori product for visitors to experience, and a lack of access to "authentic" Maori life on the Marae (tribal meeting place).

The marketing concept dictates products are designed to meet the needs of the target. However, a destination's major tourism products are usually rigid in terms of what they can be used for, and therefore difficult to adapt to changing demand. For example, Morgan (1991) reported that the late 1980s price wars by U.K. tour operators, which led to demand for increased accommodation capacity in Majorca, stimulated the development of 70,000 new hotel beds. A later shift in demand from the dominant U.K. and German markets for self catering accommodation then led to a surplus of an estimated 50,000–70,000 hotel beds on the island. Also, since all markets and destinations evolve through a life cycle, DMOs must remain in tune with changing demand and emerging product opportunities. After all marketing is a forward thinking exercise. Arguably most tourism product development occurs without any consultation with a DMO. In an ideal world such consultation during the feasibility stage would enhance identification of potential opportunities and problems that may save business failure.

Another DMO role is stimulating the bundling or packaging of products to meet identified market needs. This type of approach can be undertaken through wholesale and retail package sales. For example, during the 1980s, Bradford, categorised as a "difficult" tourism area, placed a significant emphasis on promoting a series of special interest short break packages. These were based on the following themes, which generated an estimated 85,000 bed nights a year (Buckley & Witt 1985):

- the area's mill shops
- "In the footsteps of the Brontë sisters"
- television and film themes
- industrial heritage
- camera craft with the National Museum of Photography, Film and Television.

The third key area of product involvement by DMOs is special events, which generate significant visitor arrivals. For example, during 2003 the Dublin Chamber of Commerce reported an otherwise flat tourism season was "kept alive" by a series of major events, including the Special Olympics (www.onbusiness.ie, 11/8/04). Recognising this, Tourism New Zealand maintains a team of three staff to leverage the contribution of events to tourism. Governments have long been involved with special events, and in the modern era the first examples were probably the Great Exhibitions of the 19th century that were held in London in 1851, Vienna in 1863 and Paris in 1878 (see Elliott 1997). Today the highest profile events in the world are sports related, and it has been estimated that sports and related recreation make up at least 25% of tourism activity (Research Unit 1994, in Pitts & Ayers 2000). A significant component of sports tourism is special events, such as the Gay Games for example. Held every four years, the event has evolved into one of the biggest on the world sporting calendar. The 1998 Amsterdam games attracted almost 15,000 participants from 78 countries, which was more than the summer Olympics (Pitts & Ayers 2000). The event also attracted over 800,000 spectators at 56 venues, with a total value estimated at US$350 million. As well as the immediate economic impact, events can also provide ongoing tourism opportunities. After hosting part of the 2002 winter games, the city of Ogden in Utah reported a 300% increase in ski groups the following season (*Ski Press Magazine*, 7/2/03). Pitts and Ayers also noted the 2002 Gay games, to be held in Sydney, would for the first time involve the host country's NTO and actively engage in destination marketing. Similarly, in the lead up to the 2006 Commonwealth Games in Melbourne, the Victorian state government announced a commitment to at least A$7 million towards a destination tourism marketing strategy (www.tourismvictoria.com.au/newsletter/july_2003/story3.htm, 7/7/03). Key elements of the strategy include:

- *Global Marketing:* Targeted international tourism operators will be brought to Victoria to highlight Games-related travel opportunities. Cooperative international marketing will be undertaken with the Australian Tourist Commission.
- *National Marketing:* Campaigns will be launched in cooperation with the Victorian tourism industry to bring people to the State from around the country. This will include national advertising and travel packages.
- *Event Cross-Promotion:* The Games will be highlighted during events such as the 2003 Rugby World Cup in Australia and at other international sporting events.
- *International Conferences:* A range of business events and conferences, such as ATE, will be held in Victoria in the lead up to and during the Games.
- *Research:* Various projects will be undertaken to identify opportunities and target markets; for example, backpackers.

Despite the high profile of national and international sports events, as many if not more people attend cultural events. Cultural events are not the sole domain of the major cities. For example, in the USA, *The Age of Rubens* exhibition attracted 234,000 visitors to Toledo, mostly from interstate (Holcolm 1999). Gartrell (1994) reported the Street Art Fairs in Ann Arbor, Michigan, attracted over 500,000 attendees. Another event category could be labelled odd, wacky or off-beat. For example, in August each year the council supported tomato fight the Spanish town of Bunol attracts around

30,000 participants (http://edition.cnn.com/2000/FOOD/news/08/24/spain.tomato.war.ap, 29/03/04). Twenty years ago the downturn in tourism during winter months the town of International Falls, Minnesota, which has been referred to as "the ice box of the USA" introduced a winter festival based on "The Freeze Yer Gizzard Blizzard Fun Run" (Pritchard 1982). In 2004 the four day January festival was still a popular visitor attraction (see www.intlfalls.org/icebox.htm). Examples of off beat events in the U.K. include (Ross 2003):

- The World Bog Snorkelling Championships at Llanwrtyd, Wales
- Shrovetide football, with goalposts 4.8 kilometres apart, at Ashbourne in England
- Up-Helly-Aa Viking festival, which originated in the 19th century, in Lerwick, Scotland
- The Shrove Tuesday Pancake race at Olney, England
- The World Coal Carrying Championships at Onsett, England
- Cheese rolling races, which date back 400 years, at Brockworth, England
- The World Toe Wrestling Championships at Wetton, England
- The World Stinging Nettle Challenge at Marchwood in England
- Gurning competition (pulling grotesque faces) at the Egremont Crab Fair, England
- Stonehaven Fire Balling Festival, England.

Generally, DMO involvement in events can include: ownership and management, promotional support, assistance with event bids, and marketing advice. Getz *et al.* (1997, 1998) found 60% of CVBs had an event policy. Thirty nine percent either owned or produced festivals/events, 48% provided financial support, 65% bid for events and 91% provided advice or other assistance to events.

Cross-Functional Process and Stakeholder Relationships

The responsibilities of destination brand management should not rest solely with the DMO. Arguably the greatest marketing challenge faced by DMOs, certainly in the implementation of IMC, is stimulating a coordinated approach among all those stakeholders who have a vested interest in, and will come into contact with, the target visitors. Ideally, what is required is an understanding by all stakeholders of what the brand identity is, what the brand image is, and what the brand positioning strategy is. The more stakeholders have an understanding of the rational behind the brand strategy, the more effectively they will be able to integrate their own marketing and customer interactions. Clearly, it is too much to expect all stakeholders to do so, and yet in theory the approach represents a powerful opportunity to enhance the destination brand.

There are essentially three main reasons for DMOs coordinating a "cooperate to compete" approach among tourism operators. The first has been driven out of necessity to stretch the promotional budget. DMOs and tourism operators have recognised the value in pooling limited financial resources to create a bigger noise in the market place. The second major driver in developing a cooperative destination marketing approach has been a greater awareness that the traveller experience of a destination can be marred by one bad service encounter. Thus, it makes little long term sense for a small group of large visitor attractions to work on marketing and quality issues independently, if the mass of remaining small businesses become the weak link in the visitor's destination experience by failing to deliver. Thirdly, it has only been relatively recently that the concept of brand synergy has become the third key rationale for a destination's cooperative marketing approach. For example, there has been a lot of work undertaken in Australia between the ATC and STOs, and between STOs, such as Tourism Queensland, and RTOs. However there has been little documented about attempts to synergise the promotional efforts between DMOs and individual tourism businesses.

Purposeful Dialogue and Message Synergy

Anholt (2002: 53) likened marketing to chatting someone up in a crowded bar:

> In effect, you walk up to somebody you have never met, and have a few seconds in which to convince them you are worth getting to know better, and to win the chance of a longer conversation. Often a joke will do the trick, but if the bar is in Finland or Iraq (unlikely), where making strangers laugh is both difficult and unwelcome, a different opening gambit might be preferable. Either way, there are few countries and few people who will fall in love with a stranger who kicks off the conversation with a long list of his natural advantages, impressive family tree and key historical achievement.

Elements of the promotional mix are forms of marketing communication (marcom). All marcom should be about purposeful dialogue with the target market. Marcom is the marketing element over which the DMO is able to exert the most control, and is therefore the focus of DMO operations. The purpose of marcom should be to enhance brand associations and market position, with the communication objective being to inform, persuade or remind consumers about the destination. DMOs use promotion to either "pull" consumers to the destination or "push" them through travel intermediaries. In the competitive markets in which DMOs operate, innovative promotional ideas can very quickly be adopted by rival destinations, and so there tends to be a commonality of DMO activity. Hawes, Taylor & Hampe's (1991: 15) analysis of USA STO marketing plans found few examples of any novel tactics: "In fact, we found that most states do pretty much the same things."

The WTO (1999a) estimated the breakdown of promotional budgets for NTOs was: advertising (47.1%), public relations (11.5%), promotional activities (28.9%), public information (3.7%), research (3.5%) and "other" (5.2%). More recently, a survey of 10 NTOs by Dore & Crouch (2003) also found consumer advertising (35%) represented the largest item in the promotional budget. This was followed by personal selling to the trade (23%), publicity and public relations (17%), trade advertising (12%), direct marketing (7%), sales promotion partnerships (5%) and personal selling to consumers (1%). IMC does not use any different marcom tools. Ideally, the five key promotional tools of advertising, public relations, direct marketing, sales promotions and personal selling should be integrated to provide a consistency of message.

Advertising

Advertising is paid non-personal promotion of ideas or products by an identifiable sponsor (Kotler *et al.* 1998). The role of advertising is to stimulate the desired images of the brand in the mind of the consumer in such a way that it leads to action. There are four generally accepted stages in the design and implementation of any advertising campaign:

- setting the objectives, which include those relating to sales targets and communication purpose
- budget allocation decisions, for which methods include the affordable approach, percent of sales, competitive parity, and objective and task
- message decisions, including both the content of the messages and the type of medium
- campaign evaluation, including the communication impact and resultant sales.

Of these, it is arguably the message decisions that are most problematic for DMOs. Ward & Gold (1994) suggested many destination advertising efforts lack professionalism. In particular they pointed to a tendency towards wordiness in advertisements, which is better suited to direct mail communications, as well as a lack of identification of a USP. These criticisms reflect one of the themes of this text, which is the difficulty in promoting multi-attributed places to a dynamic and multi-dimensional market place. The purpose of all DMO advertising should be to enhance awareness of the destination brand, and to establish favourable, strong and unique associations (see Keller 1993). The segmentation and positioning strategy should therefore guide all message decisions. Advertising should be targeted and have a clear focus and point of differentiation. Politics and substitutability combine to constrain the marketers of destinations. Morgan (2000: 345) cited this comment from an interview with the editor of *Advertising Age*:

> When you look at the ads . . . you can see transcripts of the arguments at the tourist boards . . . the membership of which all wanted their own interests served . . . you can see the destruction of the advertising message as a result of the politics.

The first destination travel guides were printed in France in 1552 (Sigaux 1966). Since the establishment of the first DMOs, brochures have been the most common form of destination advertising. Jeffries (2001: 72) suggested this may have been as much to do with providing tangible evidence to the local tourism industry of "fair" exposure:

> It may be the projection of a political and administrative entity and only coincidentally meaningful from the consumers' point of view, offering too much information in some respects and not enough in others.

For many RTOs the production and distribution of the annual destination brochure is the most important and expensive item in the promotional budget (Pritchard & Morgan 1995). Pritchard & Morgan cited research by the ETB that estimated only 5% of domestic trips in the U.K. used a travel agent. Without the influence of such intermediaries the role of the brochure has traditionally been important. A key decision in the design of a destination brochure is its purpose, of which there are two main categories. The first role is to attract visitors to the destination. The design focus is on developing the image of the destination, and the brochure usually has the style and quality of a magazine, often with no advertising content. Distribution is external to the destination since they are expensive to produce, and will often be the primary sales aids used to service travel exhibitions and direct consumer enquiries. The second role is a "visitors guide" designed as directory of facilities and attractions to aid trip planning. This provides an opportunity for local advertisers to pick up a share of business from travellers at the destination. Distribution may take place both externally, such as in ticket wallets, and locally through the VIC and accommodation outlets. Often for smaller RTOs the purpose will be to achieve both functions with one brochure due to a lack of funds and reliance on advertising revenue.

Visitor guides that are reliant on advertising are often controlled by private sector interests, saving the RTO time and money. However, in other cases ownership by the RTO can raise valuable promotional funds. For example, the author used this approach during the 1990s to raise over $100,000 annually to fund a generic regional television advertising campaign. The visitors guide then became the official destination brochure, used to service campaign responses, which made it easier for local operators to prioritise the multitude of advertising opportunities presented to them. The initiative also enabled the RTO to demonstrate to council funders the direct financial contribution of the private sector towards destination marketing. As was discussed in Chapter 2 generating such financial contributions is otherwise problematic, particularly for generic destination image advertising.

There has been little published research about the role and effectiveness of brochures in traveller decision making. Clearly more research is required; particularly given this traditional form of information dissemination has been threatened by the recent arrival of new technologies such as the WWW. A survey by Wicks & Shuett (1991) of tourism brochure producers in the USA, which included CVBs, found the majority reported the sales aid was produced without any specific target market in mind. Likewise, Alford (1998) cited research commissioned by the English Tourist Board, which found consumers were most likely to be influenced by the type of holiday or activity, whereas RTBs were promoting regions or towns. RTBs generally still produced the regional brochure as if trying to be all things to all people. Pritchard & Morgan's (1995) content analysis of destination image promotion brochures used by local authorities in Wales identified the following key features:

- An eye catching image on the front cover designed to attract attention.
- A single graphic device on the front cover, such as a logo or symbol, intended to reinforce a campaign theme.
- Identifying symbols within the brochure to reinforce the presence of unique destination features.
- Multi-dimensional images to reflect the multi-attributed nature of the destination. The study identified 2000 images in 28 brochures, of which 70% were of scenery.
- An average 54–46% ratio of images vs. information.

Pritchard & Morgan's key criticisms of the Welsh brochures included: a general lack of identifying a distinctively Welsh identity and a lack of images of people. They also found most destinations were using similar images. An interesting example of this recently occurred in Australia. Morely & Stolz (2003: 3) reported the embarrassment of Gold Coast Tourism Bureau officials after the discovery that the destination had been inadvertently using a Sunshine Coast beach scene in 100,000 copies of the Gold Coast's 2003 *Holiday Guide*. In reference to the ensuing national television coverage of the faux pas, the Sunshine Coast's RTO chairman responded: "We appreciate all the publicity we can get."

PR and Publicity

For destinations, publicity represents public exposure, including "word of mouth," which may be favourable or unfavourable. A wit once suggested that any publicity is good publicity unless it is an obituary. In this philosophy the concern is not about what is being said about you but whether you are being talked about at all. Publicity can occur from many sources, with which the DMO may or may not have had any involvement or knowledge of. There has been a lack of research reported in the literature on the use of publicity as a promotional tool by DMOs (Dore & Crouch 2003). Public relations (PR) on the other hand is a concerted effort by the DMO to develop favourable impressions of a destination. This involves both the generation of positive publicity by the DMO as well as the stimulation of positive relations between internal and external stakeholders. The cost effectiveness of PR initiatives is usually not lost on DMOs, particularly given the limited resources of most.

One small Australian LTA with a small limited budget that has been successful in attracting national publicity for the destination is Queensland's Burnett Shire Council. The Burnett Shire is the headquarters for the Coral Coast region (www.coralcoast.org), which is a small coastal community located 350 kilometres north of Brisbane. The region is classified as an "emerging" destination by Tourism Queensland. The council provides a relatively modest financial allocation to destination promotion. However, two council staff, who have other roles but work part-time on tourism initiatives, have been very proactive in terms of attracting high profile media and coordinating industry support for the visits through their work with a Tourism Industry Advisory Committee (TIAC). In October 2003 the shire hosted the weather segment of Australia's leading national breakfast television programme. Presenter Sami Lucas broadcast a series of 12×5 minute segments live from Bargara Beach, Moore Park Beach and Bundaberg over three days. Equivalent advertising value of the airtime was estimated at A$600,000. The total cost of hosting the film crew was approximately A$20,000, of which almost all was provided by tourism industry sponsorship. The previous year the council successfully hosted television programme *Destinations*, which produced a half hour segment on the Coral Coast's attractions. The cost of hosting the programme was A$17,000, which was shared between council and local tourism interests. In a local media release (6/2/03), Mayor Ray Duffy enthused:

> This is an exciting time for Council and the Coral Coast. Through this programme we have the potential to reach over 4 million viewers nationally.

The *Destinations* programme was credited locally as being a major force in the "discovery" of the Coral Coast as a new tourism destination by Australians, and coincided with the council's million dollar redevelopment of the Bargara Beach foreshore. The months following these events represented a new era of tourism development in the area by interstate property developers and investors. The council used the programme to launch a brief television advertising campaign promoting the region. During 2004, the TIAC was in the process of arranging the return of *Destinations*. The programme's producers were keen to highlight the extent of the new developments that had taken place in the two years since the 2002 screening. These examples help to demonstrate how significant national publicity can be generated for a small destination without a large advertising budget. The examples also demonstrate how PR can be cost-effective for a small destination community through council coordination and in-kind contributions spread between industry in the form of accommodation, rental cars and meals.

In a survey of the publicity practice of 10 NTOs from Europe, Africa and Asia/Pacific, Dore & Crouch (2003) found the largest budget item within the PR budget was the visiting journalists programme (VJPs). This is also referred to as a visiting media programme (VMP). While the PR allocation was the third highest in the promotional budget, behind advertising and personal selling, it was rated as the highest in importance by NTO respondents due to cost-effectiveness. Likewise, Hawes *et al.* (1991) found the marketing tactic most common across USA STOs was the use of familiarisations for travel writers and intermediaries, although only 12 of 37 STOs reported using such practises.

News generally has higher credibility that paid advertising, and consumer suspicion about paid advertising is not a new phenomenon, as evidenced by the view of Wahab *et al.* (1976: 73) three decades ago:

> To obtain a buying decision means overcoming the buyer's resistance to yet one more sales message. There are so many, and life has taught him that they promise so much more than they achieve, that the buyer acquires a built-in suspicion and hostility, which we know as sales resistance.

While much publicity about places occurs in the general news and entertainment media without the influence of DMOs or the travel industry, travel writers are a primary target of DMO PR managers. For example, in 2003 the Canadian Tourism Commission (CTC) launched a website specifically for travel media (see www.gomediacanada.com). The site contains travel stories, CTC media releases, links to the tourism industry, information on media tours, market research results, and a photo/video library. Travel articles in newspaper and magazine travel columns are commonly positive about destinations, given the writer has usually been sponsored by the DMO, airline, accommodation and attractions. For this reason, Lundburg (1990) reported that travel writers from the *New York Times, Wall Street Journal* and Washington Post were not permitted to accept "freebies." While other newspapers such as the *Los Angeles Times* and *Dallas News*, also did not allow staff to travel free, stories could be purchased from freelance writers who may have done so.

The Society of American Travel Writers (www.satw.org) was established fifty years ago as a professional association to raise standards in the travel writers profession. Likewise, the

British Guild of Travel Writers (see www.bgtw.metronet.co.uk) was established in 1960. The guild's 220 mostly freelance members contribute to 38 national and provincial daily newspapers, 56 magazines, 86 general interest publications, 37 trade journals, 42 in-flight magazines and travel guidebooks. Travelwriters.com is an example of one of the many resources available to current and aspiring travel writers, and provides advice for PR agents, DMOs and tourism operators, such as: a writer database, travel publications directory, and press release forum. Key problems with VJPs identified by NTOs include: limited funds and staff resources, lack of industry support, short notice arrival of media, quality control of ensuing publicity, and results not meeting expectations (Dore & Crouch 2003).

It is good practise for DMOs to maintain a PR resource library to service the needs of the media and trade. Resources typically include photos, brand images and videos of local attractions. These are useful, for example, for travel writers who are not equipped to replicate professional images that may have been obtained in perfect weather conditions and by special means such as a helicopter. Limited time, resources and inclement weather can inhibit the travel writer's ability to record suitable images during a brief visit. In recent years resource libraries have become digital. In 2002 for example, the Canadian Tourism Commission launched a photo CD, which contained 100 images as well as links to a searchable database on a website with over 800 photos (see www.canadatourism.com). The images are free to use in publicity for Canada, within guidelines on the conditions of use included with the CD. In New Zealand, RTO Tourism Rotorua out sources the image bank to an organisation specialising in the on-line management of brand image integrity:

> The storage, maintenance and effective distribution of brand standards and brand identity artwork is often complex, repetitive, slow and expensive, especially when distributing internationally. Incorrect artwork can be used or corners cut as lead times evaporate. These lapses can jeopardize the success of a brand. The arrival of the Internet as a reliable communications tool has made obsolete the traditional hard copy manual, bromides, couriered disks, etc. (www.e-see.com/marketing/aboutesee2.htm, 29/3/04).

Requests for destination imagery by media and tourism operators, including photos and brand logos, are vetted and distributed by E-see.com.

As well as opportunities in the general and travel media, readers will be aware of numerous examples of notable TV programmes that have generated publicity in various parts of the world for destinations such as *Coronation Street* and *Queer as Folk* (Manchester), *Sea Change* (see Beeton 2001) and *Neighbours* (Australia), *Bergerac* (Jersey, see Tooke & Baker 1996) and *Cheers* (Boston) to name but a few. Movie and television induced tourism is not a new phenomenon. Davidson & Maitland (1997) reported how the West Yorkshire village of Holmfirth became a tourism destination overnight in 1972 following the airing of the BBC TV series *Last of the Summer Wine*. During 2004 the theme was still being promoted by the destination on the home page of the Kirklees District website (see www.kirklees.go.uk/visitors):

> In Holmfirth you can visit various locations including Sid's Café, the Last of the Summer Wine Exhibition and the Wrinkled Stocking Tearoom.

Similarly, Bradford made use of its television and film history to promote short break packages based on *Wuthering Heights, Emmerdale Farm* and *The Last of the Summer Wine*, among others (Buckley & Witt 1985). Voase (2002) cited research indicating the main reason for visiting Austria for three out of every four international visitors was the film *The Sound of Music.* A year after the 1977 movie *Close Encounters of the Third Kind* was released, the level of visitors to the Devil's Tower National Monument increased by 74% (Riley & Van Doren 1992). Other examples of movie induced tourism discussed by Riley & Van Doren included: *Deliverance* (Rayburn County, Georgia), *Dances with Wolves* (Fort Hayes, Kansas), *Thelma and Louise* (Arches National Monument, Georgia), *Field of Dreams* (Iowa), *Steel Magnolias* (Natchitoches, Louisiana) and *Crocodile Dundee* (Australia).

Many DMOs have been proactive in maximising movie and television exposure. Petersburg in Virginia took advantage of the December 2003 release of the movie Cold Mountain to promote tours of the scene of the 1864 civil war Battle of the Crater, which is relived in the opening scenes of the movie (Bergman 2004). The New Zealand government allocated a special fund of $10.4 million in 2001/2002 and NZ$4.4 million in 2002/2003 towards promotion of the *Lord of the Rings* trilogy (Foreman 2003). The state of North Carolina provides a website discussing the importance of the movie industry (see www.ncinformation.com/nc_movie_industry.htm). Since 1980, North Carolina has attracted over 600 feature films. A number of case studies of movie induced tourism have been reported in the tourism literature, including: Nottingham and *Robin Hood — Prince of Thieves* (see Holloway & Robinson 1995), New Zealand and the *Lord of the Rings* trilogy (see Croy 2004), Australia and *Ned Kelly* (see Frost 2003).

While there is evidence that movies do increase visitors to the location (Tooke & Baker 1996), movie induced tourism does have its critics. For example, the director of Natural History New Zealand, a documentary producer owned by Fox Television Studios, described the tourism focus on *Lord of the Rings* as "tacky": "... it's just extraordinary to listen to boring little people trying to quantify it in value (to) tourism. It is sickening" (*Inside Tourism*, IT488, 5/3/04). There has also been criticism in Wales that it was the landscape in that country that inspired Tolkein's Middle Earth, and not New Zealand. In examining the tourism impact of the Australian TV series *Sea Change* on the seaside village of Barwon, Beeton (2001) lamented a change in the visitor mix, which may have long term impacts on the destination's traditional holiday market. DMOs interested in this emerging area of research will find a rich resource of examples of the positive and negative impacts of film locations in the papers of Riley & Van Doren (1992), Tooke & Baker (1996), and Riley *et al.* (1998).

While enhancing travellers' perceptions of a destination is usually the PR priority, initiatives can also be used for political lobbying. For example, Pritchard (1982) reported an interesting PR initiative by Wisconsin's STO. For the constituency of every government representative, the office had its research department prepare a breakdown of the number of tourism businesses, tourism employees, tourism tax revenue and the total value of tourism to the area. The STO then sent this information to each legislator to improve the case for tourism marketing funding. The initiative resulted in 240 press releases being generated by the legislators to their local media around the state. The end results were twofold. The first was an increased public awareness of the value of tourism and the second was an increased awareness of tourism as a re-election vehicle for legislators.

Table 1: Examples of Australian small town icons.

Icon	Town
The Big Apple	Stanthorpe
The Big Avocado	Byron Bay
The Big Banana	Coffs Harbour
The Big Cheese	Bega
The Big Cow	Nambour
The Big Guitar	Tamworth
The Big Lobster	Kingston
The Big Merino	Gouldburn
The Big Oyster	Taree
The Big Peanut	North Tolga
The Big Pineapple	Nambour
The Big Pie	Yatala
The Big Prawn	Ballina

Other DMO initiatives that fall under the labels of PR and publicity include:

- Stimulation of "big things," particularly in small towns, as eye catching roadside icons. Australian examples are shown in Table 1. From the "only in America" category, Schofield (2002) commented on the eight story office building that is built in the shape of a basket, headquarters of the Longaberger Basket Company. Morley (2003) reported on the proposal in Augathella, 660 km west of Queensland's state capital Brisbane, to build a giant monument in honour of the prolific meat ant. The Augathella and District Tourist and Progress Association proposed the idea after the town of 430 residents was bypassed by the Matilda Highway.
- Stimulation of the use of locations in corporate brochures, such as by Canada in Porche's magazine (*Marketing Magazine*, 17/3/03).
- Contra prizes for game shows.
- Sponsorship of media competitions.
- Encouraging department stores to use destination themes.
- Public "film" evenings.
- Use of celebrities as tourism ambassadors, such as the ATC's use of world surfing champion Lane Beachley, model Megan Gale and swimmer Ian Thorpe. Maison France used actor Woody Allen in the trade promotion video "Lets fall in love again." The Queen and royal family participated in the promotion of British Tourism Day 2003 (www.travelmole.com, 10/6/03).

Personal Selling

Arguably the most effective means of stimulating meaningful dialogue with consumers is personal selling. Travel trade events are a common feature of DMO action plans. DMOs with small budgets tend to favour such push strategies as they cost less than consumer advertising (Pearce *et al.* 1998). Surprisingly however, Hawes *et al.* (1991) found only 9 of 37 USA STOs coordinated an official presence at major travel trade shows. Opportunities include consumer travel exhibitions such as Sydney's Holiday and Travel Expo, trade exhibitions such as ITB in Berlin, special interest consumer exhibitions such as the Chelsea Flower Show in London, and special interest travel trade exhibitions such as Business Travel Expo Hong Kong. The WTO maintains a calendar of major travel trade events (see www.world-tourism.org/calendar/menu.html), which is ever expanding. For example, China, the emerging powerhouse of world tourism, opened its first World Travel Fair (WTF) in February 2004 (News@PATA, 25/2/04). Likewise, the first Turkish inbound travel exhibition was announced to take place in June 2004 (www.travelmole.com, 25/3/04). Travel Turkey 2004 was aiming for attendance by 500 tour operators and travel agents from around the world. Included in the four day event are two days "professional days" for information exchanges between delegates and exhibitors.

Tourism exchange meetings are increasingly seen as an effective means of reaching key travel decision by providing tourism suppliers with individual meetings with a limited number of retailers and wholesalers selected by the NTO and major airlines. The trade representatives are generally flown to the destination for the meetings with suppliers and then offered familiarisation tours. Examples include:

- Arab World Travel & Tourism Exchange (see www.awtte.com)
- Australian Tourism Exchange (see www.tradeevents.australia.com)
- Bula Fiji Tourism Exchange (see www.bfte.com)
- International Pow Wow, USA (see www.powwowonline.com)
- South Pacific Tourism Exchange (see www.tcsp.com)
- TRENZ, New Zealand (see www.nztia.co.nz/Tianz-Events/TRENZ.asp).

When the 2002 Australian Tourism Exchange was held in Brisbane, over 2,500 hotel rooms were used by 2,000 tourism suppliers, 80 international and domestic media and 670 travel buyers from 50 countries (Cameron 2002). According to the ATC managing director, it was estimated the A$8 million cost of the event would generate up to A$2 billion in trade for Australia: "This event delivers more export earnings and business than any other in Australia." The importance of the event led to the development of industry briefing seminars by Tourism Queensland and the ATC. Operators were also able to access information from the seminars on-line in the form of PowerPoint slides with voice reproduction (http://www.tq.com.au/ate. 20/4/03). The increasing numbers of international tourism exchanges is forcing competition for the limited numbers of key travel decision makers. Unfortunately in 2004, this competition led to the cancellation of the South Pacific Tourism Exchange, as shown in Figure 3.

Distribution

Distribution is representative of product placement, which in product marketing refers to the physical distribution of goods from the place of manufacture through various

South Pacific Tourism Exchange 2004 — CANCELLED

The SPTO regrets to advise all interested Buyers and Sellers that due to a shortfall in the number of targeted Buyers and Sellers, we have now decided to cancel the event. The cancellation is largely attributable to its similarity and closeness to other tradeshows and tourism exchanges being held in the region at the same time (including ATE, TRENZ and BFTE, where similar Buyers and Sellers are attending. We particularly wish to thank all who expressed their interest and support for SPTE. We apologize for any inconvenience caused to you.

If you have any questions or require further information, please feel free to contact us using our Contact Form.

Figure 3: South Pacific tourism exchange cancellation. *Source:* http://www.tcsp.com/ public/spte2004.shtml, 25/03/04.

channels to the point of sale. This is usually a complex process involving the logistics of supply chain management as well as demand management. In service marketing however, distribution does not involve the physical transportation of a tangible product. The concepts of immovability and inseparability generally mean the destination product is consumed at the place of production and the tourism provider and the consumer must be present for the service to be delivered. The closest function to physical distribution is the means by which a DMO delivers destination tourism information to consumers. A destination visitor guide for example, which is ultimately a form of marcom, must somehow be distributed to the trade and consumers. Also, distribution can be viewed as the "place" of tourism consumption, which includes the destination itself. Key issues are location, accessibility and perceived distance (e.g. McKercher 1998).

In terms of delivering a product to the point of sale, distribution refers to the tourism reservation mechanism. Distribution channel intermediaries for tourism services include tour wholesalers, travel agencies and airlines. Intermediaries often represent the most effective means of reaching travellers, but at the same time can be one of the highest operating costs. Commission to intermediaries represents the distribution cost.

Apart from operating local VICs, most DMOs leave reservation systems to the private sector. However, Tourism Queensland (see www.tq.com.au) operates as a travel wholesaler, through Sunlover Holidays and as a retailer, through Queensland Travel Centres. Sunlover Holidays offers over 3,500 products, which are distributed via Queensland Travel Centres in nine cities, travel agencies, and a consumer call centre and web booking service.

In an effort to improve distribution effectiveness many NTOs have established formal training programmes for selected travel agents in key markets. Initiatives include accreditation of specialist agents. In the USA for example, where there are over 30,000 agents, the NTO can direct consumer advertising responses to the agent nearest the enquirers' post code area. The NTO has the benefit of knowing the specialist agent has the resources to service the enquiry, the agent benefits from the lead generation, and the risk of uncertainty is alleviated for the consumer. Examples of specialist destination agent programmes include:

- Tourism Ireland's Shamrock Club (www.shamrockclub.net)
- Tourism New Zealand's KEA (Kiwi expert agents — www.tourisminfo.co.nz)
- The Australian Tourism Commission's Aussie Specialists (www.atc.net.au).

Tourism distribution has been undergoing a transformation through the development of the internet, albeit still as a work in progress. The world wide web has become a significant opportunity for marketers since its inception in 1996. According to a Travel Industry Association of America's study, there were around 64 million American on-line travel planners using the Internet in 2002 (TIA press release, 12/12/02). This represented a dramatic increase over 1997, when an estimated 12 million Americans were planning and researching travel options online. Forty-two percent of TIA respondents indicated they did all or most of their travel planning online, up from 29% who did so in 2001. In Canada in 2000 it was estimated 80% of air tickets were still being sold by travel agents (CTC 2000, in Hashimoto & Telfer 2001).

While there has been a proliferation of online travel booking sites (e.g. www.lastminute.com), almost all have been developed by the private sector. Sites such as British Airways' "Manage my booking" (see www.BA.com) enable travellers to bypass traditional travel agents by proving functions to manage their own itinerary, including making requests for specific seats and special meals. Such sites facilitate significant savings on distribution for airlines, since commissions have been one of the largest costs of operating an airline. A key advantage of the WWW for DMOs is the ability to develop sites specifically to cater for different segments. This partly overcomes the problem in destination branding of designing and communicating one destination brand for all markets. Niche advertising in traditional media can direct the target to the branded site. Examples include:

- The Finland Tourist Board's family website (see www.finland-family.com/eng/)
- Tourism Victoria's gay and lesbian site (see www.visitmelbourne.com/gaytravel)
- Tourism Queensland launched a website for last minute booking in October 2003 (see www.bestrates.com.au).

In spite of the increasing access to information technologies (IT), such as the WWW, DMOs often struggle to keep up with the rapid advances in IT and their implications for marketing. In summarising a workshop coordinated by the National Laboratory for Tourism and eCommerce for tourism and IT leaders to address this challenge, Gretzel *et al.* (2000) argued future success of DMOs was related to a change in approach rather than technology itself. That is, DMOs must learn to proactively adapt to change to enhance organisational viability:

> Most of the problems organizations face today when designing and implementing online strategies stem from trying to fit everything into existing structures and models. It is suggested that DMOs need to redefine their nature

of business and the underlying models and processes . . . Since the Web is ever evolving and new challenges occur 'at the speed of thought', these changes should be directed toward increasing the organizational flexibility and openness to change (Gretzel *et al.* 2000: 154).

The workshop developed a number of principles for the development of web strategies by DMOs:

- different skills are required due to the characteristics of the WWW
- a combination of online and offline advertising is most effective in utlising the potential of the WWW
- a web site should not be viewed as a stand alone advertising tool
- banners and cross advertising should be used to control web traffic
- the most important points of entry for users searching for tourism information are portals
- a consistent advertising message across different media creates synergy between online and offline strategies
- WWW marketing strategies should be based on personalisation, experience, involvement and permission.

It could be argued that online branding essentially begins with domain names, which have become a digital market akin to real estate. The proliferation of domain name registrations has been such that by 2000 all three letter combinations, as well as 98% of English words, had already been registered (Keller 2003). Intuitively, acquisition of the destination domain name such as NewZealand.com appears a wise move. However, Tourism New Zealand's purchase of the domain for NZ$1 million caused a political stir during 2003. Government opposition tourism spokeswoman Pansy Wong, a former director of the NTO, labelled the purchase rash, embarrassing and made without a prior cost-benefit feasibility study. TNZ CEO George Hickton (2003) responded the purchase was timely given the prediction by www.wordlingo.com that domain names would increase in value tenfold during the next decade. Hickton claimed domain names were the most logical starting point for potential travellers seeking information about a destination, pointing to a claim by www.lee-online.com that 65% of all users type the URL into their browser, either by guesswork or memory. Liscom (2003) entered the debate by suggesting TNZ would be failing in its marketing if it relied on such guesswork by potential travellers, and that domain names were irrelevant to search engines. Minister of Tourism Mark Burton argued the move was a "sound investment" as a portal for tourism and business interests, and suggested the South African government offered $US10 million for SouthAfrica.com while Korea.com sold for US$5 million (*Inside Tourism*, IT448: 1). Wong claimed the government wasted money prior to the purchase, through the incorrect assumption that the name "New Zealand" was a trademark of the government. The USA-based newzealand.com domain name owner was initially taken to court by the government over the trademark violation:

> A domain name is simply a web-based address while a trademark is a name, symbol or device used to identify a product that has been legally registered as such and use of which is therefore restricted to the owner or

Table 2: Non-travel related destination domains.

http://www.usa.com	E-mail and business portal
http://www.canada.com	Canwest Global Communications Corporation
http://www.japan.com	Japan Incorporated Communications
http://www.wales.com	Domain register
http://www.brazil.com	Business portal
http://www.ireland.com	The Irish Times

manufacturer. The idea that the name of a country could be trademarked is ludicrous.

In this regard, one regional city in New Zealand was forced to pay NZ$100,000 to a porn site for the city's domain name. Other examples of destination domain names, belonging to a DMO or a private sector travel company, include: Australia.com, France.com, Italy.com, Fiji.com, Scotland.com and Korea.com. However, as shown in Table 2 a many major destination domains are owned by non-tourism interests.

Chapter Key Point Summary

Key Point 1 — Outward-Inward Thinking

A market orientation is an outward-inward market-organisation approach, dictating marketing decisions are concerned with designing products to meet the unmet needs of target consumers. However, most destination marketing has been limited to an inward-outward approach. DMOs are constrained by having no control over product development and must therefore focus on finding markets for existing products.

Key Point 2 — Implications of Multi-Attributed Destination Communities

The purpose of all marcom is to enhance consumer-based brand equity. However, there has been relatively little research published in the tourism literature dealing with effective design and use of marcom activities such as brochures, relationship marketing and publicity. There has been criticism that the marcom by DMOs has tended to lack focus and differentiation. One the reasons for this has been a theme of the text; that is, the multi-attributed nature of destinations, which manifests in the politics of decision making.

Key Point 3 — Integrated Marketing Communication (IMC)

IMC represents a relatively new approach to marketing. Key tenets of IMC are the development of profitable customer relationships, a cross-functional process, purposeful dialogue with customers, effective relationships with stakeholders, and synergy of messages. IMC represents the way forward for DMOs confronted by significant changes in the destination marketing paradigm.

Additional Reading

Duncan, T. (2002). *IMC: Using advertising and promotion to build brands*. New York: McGraw-Hill.

Heath, E., & Wall, G. (1992). *Marketing tourism destinations*. New York: Wiley.

Nykie, R. A., & Jascolt, E. (1998). *Marketing your city, USA*. New York: Haworth Hospitality Press.

Schultz, D., Tannenbaum, S., & Lauterborn, R. (1993). *Integrated marketing communications*. Lincolnwood, IL: NTC Publishing.

Chapter 8

DMOs, Disasters and Crises

The terrorist attacks in Bali on 12 October 2002 and more recent attacks in Istanbul, Riyadh, Jakarta, and Baghdad underscore the ongoing threat across the world posed by international terrorism . . . Australians are urged to be alert to their personal security practices and to monitor developments that may affect their safety — both through the department's travel advice and the media (Australian Department of Foreign Affairs and Trade, www.Dfat.gov.au/zw-cgi/view/Advice/General, 6/2/04).

Chapter Perspective

All national governments have a responsibility to provide an advisory service for their citizens, identifying where is not safe to travel. Most countries provide regularly updated travel advisories on government web sites, the public profile of which has grown significantly since the events of September 11th 2001. As an example, at the time of writing, the travel advisory web site of the U.K. Foreign and Commonwealth Office (see www.fco.gov.uk/travel) provided citizens with a list of some of the major terrorist attacks that had occurred around the world during the previous 18 months. These are shown in Table 1.

Also at this time the Australian Department of Foreign Affairs and Trade advised against all travel by Australians to the following countries: Afghanistan, Burundi, Haiti, Iraq, Liberia, Pakistan, and Somalia. The department further advised against any non-essential travel to a number of other countries: Algeria, Central African Republic, Colombia, Indonesia (including Bali), Ivory Coast, Saudi Arabia, Sudan, Turkey, and Yemen. The implications for the DMOs of these countries are significant in terms of the damage to the image of their destination and the necessary recovery-marketing efforts. It is important to consider that, unfortunately, the negative images created by publicity surrounding a disaster can last far longer than any physical destruction to infrastructure or tourism facilities. Of the above destinations, Bali was Australia's most popular overseas destination until the October 2002 terrorism bombing of a tourist precinct left the destination in a state of crisis, from which it had not recovered, in terms of visitation levels, by 2004.

The ILO (2003) estimated the total loss of jobs in world tourism at over 11 million since the terrorist attacks of September 11th 2001, representing a loss of one in every seven jobs in tourism and travel. Government travel advisories have been regarded as extremely controversial in many quarters for their significant role in exacerbating these negative economic impacts, particularly on poorer nations. Rarely is a travel advisory posted about

Table 1: Global terrorist attacks during 2002–2003.

- A suicide car bomb against a synagogue in Djerba, Tunisia in April 2002, that killed 18 European tourists and local Tunisians
- A suicide attack against a bus in Karachi carrying French engineers in May 2002
- A series of ETA bombings during the summer of 2002 in resorts on the Costa Blanca and the Costa del Sol and other cities in Spain
- The bombs in Bali in October 2002 that killed over 200 tourists and local Indonesians
- The attacks in Mombassa in November 2002 that killed 17 Kenyans and Israelis
- The shooting of three American medical charity workers in Yemen in December 2002
- An attack on a hotel nightclub in Colombia on 17 February 2003
- A British national was shot and killed in Saudi Arabia on 20 February 2003
- A campaign of terrorist bombings in March and April 2003 in the Philippines and Indonesia, including attacks on an airport and a ferry terminal in the southern Philippines and at Jakarta airport
- Al Qa'ida were almost certainly responsible for the suicide bombings in Riyadh on 12 May that targeted the homes of westerners, including British Citizens, living in the Kingdom
- Over 40 people were killed in a series of suicide attacks in Casablanca on 16 May, including at a hotel and restaurant used by westerners
- There were suicide bomb attacks in Istanbul on 15 November and further attacks on 20 November, which were on British related targets, the British Consulate General and the HQ of HSBC

---

western industrial countries. For example, few countries issued advisories against visiting the U.S.A. post-September 11, or the U.K. during the 2002 foot and mouth outbreak. Unfortunately most advisories are issued against less developed countries that can ill afford the resultant tourism downturn. Philippine tourism secretary and PATA associate chairman Richard Gordon suggested travel advisories reward the terrorists (Alcantara 2003):

> It is really a cover-your-behind memo issued by a foreign bureaucrat. Jobs have been lost and it's time issuing countries take responsibility for their actions.

Opanga (2003) strongly suggested travel advisories from U.K. and U.S.A. governments were responsible for the collapse of tourism in Kenya:

> The irony is, it is Kenyans, not Americans or Israelis, who have borne the brunt of terrorist attacks on Americans and Israelis.

Beirman (2003b) reported on a recovery seminar in Kenya during 2003, which was convened by the Kenyan Association of Tour Operators to "establish what was required to alter the negative travel advisories which had crippled Kenyan tourism during the first half of 2003." Beirman questioned the motives for the continuation of travel advisories by the U.S.A. and Australian governments that warned of an "imminent terrorism attack," even though this had not materialised after six months. Kenya's minister of tourism visited the U.K. in mid-2003 in a failed attempt to urge the government to change the travel advisory (www.travelmole.com, 6/6/03).

Jordan Tourism's worldwide director reacted strongly to a 2003 travel advisory of the U.K. Foreign and Commonwealth Office (FCO) recommending against travel to the country, claiming misperceptions of what was a safe country:

> Whenever there is trouble in the Middle East we expect the FCO to issue a statement that inevitably includes Jordan . . . but for us it is business as usual. Jordan is a safe country.

In response to member states' concerns about the nature of government travel advisories, PATA established a website in 2003 to disseminate "impartial" advice for travellers (see www.travelwithpata.com). PATA recommended to travellers that the best advice regarding travel advisories was to use a wide range of sources. However, travel advisories are also announced by organisations other than governments. For example, the World Health Organization issued SARS travel advisories for a number of destinations in 2003, including parts of China, Toronto, Hong Kong and Taiwan. Universities also provide travel advisories for students and staff. For example, Australia's Griffith University maintains a travel advisory website (see www.gu.edu.au/travel/). Public pressure groups can also exert pressure on private tour companies. Australian environmental groups have been urging tourists to boycott travel to Tasmania, in a protest against the felling of native forests there (www.travelmole.com, 23/3/04). Leading U.K. tour operator Abercrombie and Kent reportedly bowed to pressure from pressure groups and agreed to stop promoting tours to Burma (www.travelmole.com, 29/7/03). The report cited a spokesperson of pressure group Burma Campaign U.K.:

> Abercrombie and Kent were one of the last significant tour operators in Burma. It further isolates Orient Express, Carnival Cruises and Noble Caledonia — we will be stepping up pressure for them to withdraw as well.

Travel warnings may also come from terrorist groups. For example, a report in *The Independent* newspaper cited the Basque separatist terror group ETA as warning foreign travellers not to visit Spain in 2003 (www.travelmole.com, 4/8/03):

> In 2003 ETA will once again strike hard against the Spanish tourist industry and it cannot guarantee that anyone who enters the war zone will not be injured.

Although a destination in crisis is not a modern phenomenon, the field of study has only emerged recently in the tourism literature. As David Beirman stated in the opening line of his text *Restoring Destinations in Crisis*, the first to focus on the topic: "No tourism destination is immune from crisis" (2003: xiii). It could be expected that preparing contingency plans for crises would be an important element of any DMO planning. However, from the author's experience, at a RTO level at least, it is rare for such a topic to dominate much meeting time. Observations of publicly available strategic plans for NTOs and STOs also indicate contingency planning for many has not been a priority. In the quest for increased visitors and spending, which is how a DMO is ultimately judged, crisis planning may be viewed as a luxury of time if a disaster hasn't actually occurred nearby to stimulate discussion. The author is aware of one RTO that had regularly ignored pleas from the local civil defence co-ordinator to consider contingency plans in what is a recognised earthquake zone. The co-ordinator's concern was the fact that all entrances to the destination were via bridges, which risk collapse in a significant quake. This would severely impact the ability to evacuate visitors. The rationale for contingency planning was that a major earthquake was likely to strike the destination at some unknown time in the future — maybe not for 10,000 years, but maybe next week. The approaches literally fell on deaf ears at the RTO. To be fair to the tourism industry however, until recently there has also been an absence of any case studies in the literature to guide DMO crisis planning.

Some crises may be caused by relatively short term or one-off events, such as the 1996 Port Arthur massacre in Tasmania and 1992 Hurricane Andrew in Florida. Others might be long term, such as the political ban on U.S.A. citizens visiting Cuba. The ban was imposed by President JF Kennedy in 1963, was later lapsed by President Carter and then reimposed by President Reagan in 1982 (www.travelmole.com, 27/10/03). The Middle East is a region that has suffered from ongoing acts of war and terrorism, with the key agenda item at the 2003 Arab World Travel and Tourism Exchange in Beirut being tourism crises affecting the region (www.travelwirenews.com, 21/7/03). Mansfield (1999) outlined six major cycles of tourism decline and recovery in Israel due to different security situations since 1967. The cycles were caused by:

- the six day war in 1967
- the 1973 Yom Kippur war between Israel, Egypt and Syria
- the 1981 intensity of Palestine Liberation Organization attacks
- the late 1980s double cycle of international and domestic terror
- the 1990–1991 Gulf War
- the terrorized peace cycle of the 1990s.

As a result, Israel has suffered a prevailing image of a high risk destination. Unfortunately however, from the analysis of these events, Mansfield concluded that once each crisis had ended and recovery in visitor arrivals was evident, neither the government nor tourism industry planned for a future crisis event. Like Israel, Northern Ireland tourism has suffered a negative image from terrorism over three decades. However, Leslie (1999) found the even though the violence associated negative publicity of the 1970s had decreased considerably, Northern Ireland had become increasingly substitutable as a destination for U.K. travellers. O'Neill & McKenna (1994) found by comparison that in the 1990s visitor numbers to Northern Ireland had merely re-established the 1960s "pre-trouble" levels, whereas volumes in Great Britain and the Republic of Ireland had increased by over 50%.

Some crises have been the result of an "Act of God," such as earthquakes, tsunamis, hurricanes, bushfires, eruptions, tornados and avalanches. Other crises have been man-made, including such diverse events as pollution, crime, war, terrorism, economic recession, and labour strikes. Whether short term or long term, natural or man made, the common characteristics of disasters with the potential to impact on the tourism industry are threefold:

(1) No destination is immune in the long term
(2) Rarely has a disaster been predictable
(3) Causes of disasters have been beyond the control of the tourism industry.

Tourism destinations have always been, and will continue to be, at risk to exogenous events. Arguably the greatest impact of these on the tourism industry is uncertainty:

- Uncertainty of travellers to risk personal safety on what is after all a discretionary activity. During periods of insecurity, consumers can choose either to travel somewhere perceived to safe or delay travel plans. For example, Hopper (2002) reported that within hours of the September 11 strikes in the U.S.A., hotels in London were receiving cancellations from all over the world. Over 140 business events were cancelled in one week, at an estimated immediate loss to London of over £2 million.
- Uncertainty of investors and small business owners to invest or reinvest in repairs, maintenance, upgrades or new developments.
- Uncertainty of tourism staff on the future of their career. This even extends to tourism degree and diploma courses, which can suffer from reservations held by prospective students and parents.

At the time of writing, the WTTC forecast a "robust" recovery for global tourism in 2004, with a 5.9% increase over 2003 (www.travelmole.com, 15/3/04). However, this would not reach pre-September 11th levels. The WTTC report, which was revealed at the London Stock Exchange, attributed the growth to factors such as: the end of the slump in the stock market, supportive macro-economic policy, the end of uncertainty of the war in Iraq, and growth in Chinese tourism. On a global basis the tourism industry has historically proven resilient, with remarkably quick recoveries following major crises. For example, IATA CEO Giovanni Bisignani suggested that following the 1991 Gulf War, a year when tourism arrivals only increased by 1%, growth in 1992 was 8% (www.travelmole.com, 26/3/03). Even with the events of September 11 2001, international arrivals exceeded 700 million for the first time, representing an increase of 3% over 2001 and 19 million more than "Millennium year" (WTO media release, 27/1/03). Following the 1998 Australia Day flood that devastated the tourism industry in Katherine, Northern Territory, visitor arrivals in 1998 to the area increased by 15% over the previous year (Faulkner & Vikulov 2001).

It is important to note there is a distinction between the terms disaster and crisis. Faulkner (1999: 7) suggested a crisis was representative of a self-inflicted situation caused by such problems as inept management practises or inability to adapt to a changing environment. A disaster on the other hand is a sudden catastrophic change over which the organisation has little control:

> Good management can avoid crises to some degree, but must equally incorporate strategies for coping with the unexpected event over which the organisation has little control.

From this perspective a crisis could be considered as occurring during the period between when a natural or man-made disaster strikes a destination and recovery is achieved. The degree of "internal" crisis caused by the "external" disaster will vary between organisations, depending on the nature of the event as well as management's preparedness, availability of resources and ability to react.

War and Terrorism

The CEO of the International Air Transport Association (IATA), Giovanni Bisignani, predicted the 2003 war in Iraq would cost the global airline industry U.S.$10 billion in losses, on top of the U.S.$30 billion in losses following September 11 2001 (www.travelmole.com, 26/3/03). Bisignani suggested the crisis was the worst in the history of the travel industry. At the time, a survey by the Tourism Association of America estimated over 70% of Americans were not interested in travelling overseas (www.travelmole.com, 15/4/03). Six months after the 2002 Bali bombings, visitor arrivals were still below 40% of normal levels, according to a report in *The Independent* (www.travelmole.com, 12/5/03). One year after the Bali bombings, a United Nations report estimated unemployment rate to be up by almost one third and that street vendors' sales down by 50% (www.eturbonews.com, 14/10/03). The decrease in tourism employment had led to increasing numbers of prostitutes one year after the Bali bombings (Munro & Taylor 2003). In France, visitors from the U.S.A. declined by an estimated 90% in the month immediately following September 11 2001. The effects of September 11, and the ensuing fall of the U.S. dollar against the Euro continued to effect travel to Europe by Americans during 2003, with visits down by about one third (Litchfield 2003).

Recent events have increased the global profile of the link between terrorism and tourism. Terrorists have recognised the symbolism of tourism and the vulnerability of tourists. Unfortunately the issue is one that is likely to confront the tourism industry for generations. It therefore behoves DMOs to consider contingencies for the effects of such events in their own region and in other parts of the world. The emerging literature on destinations in crisis contains a number of case studies that will be of value. For example, in 1999 the *Journal of Travel Research* published a special issue on tourism crises caused by war, terrorism and crime (Vol. 38/1). The guest editors advised the 11 published articles represented a cross section of those presented at the 1997 *War, Terrorism: Times of Crisis and Recovery* conference held in Dubrovnik, Croatia. The conference was the second, following a meeting in Sweden in 1995, to focus on the relationship between tourism, security and safety. *The Journal of Travel Research* papers covered a wide range of issues:

- Classification of crime and violence at destinations (Pizam 1999)
- Managing the effects of terrorism (Sönmez *et al.* 1999)
- New Orleans tourism and crime (Dimanche & Lepetic 1999)
- Tourism potential of the peace dividend (Butler & Baum 1999)
- Management and recovery of tourism in Israel (Mansfield 1999)
- The Northern Ireland situation (Leslie 1999)

- Lessons of rebuilding tourism in the Philippines, Sri Lanka and Pakistan (Richter 1999)
- Dark tourism (Lennon & Foley 1999)
- Political instability, war, and tourism in Cyprus (Ionnides & Apostolopoulos 1999)
- The role of tourism in the aftermath of violence (Anson 1999)
- U.S.A. policy on traveller safety and security (Smith 1999).

More recently, Beirman (2003a) examined the crises and responses of 11 case studies, most of which are related to war, crime or terrorism:

- U.S.A. and 9/11
- Egypt's terrorist attacks against tourists 1990–1998
- Israel and the Palestinian uprising 2000–2002
- Sri Lanka's civil war 1995–2001
- Fiji's political coups of 1987 and 2000
- Turkey's Izmit earthquake 1999
- Britain's foot and mouth disease 2001
- South Africa's crime wave 1994–2000
- Australia's Port Arthur massacre 1996
- Croatia and the Yugoslavia war 1991–1995
- Philippines' multiple crises 1990–2001.

Natural Disasters

At the time of writing, the most recent significant natural disaster had been the 2003 SARS outbreak. During the first half of 2003, Severe Acute Respiratory Syndrome (SARS) caused panic in the travel industry worldwide. SARS was estimated to have affected over 8,000 people and was responsible for over 800 deaths (Manning 2003). China was the worst affected, with the emerging destination giant experiencing its first decline in international visitor arrivals in 2003 (www.eturbonews.com, 7/8/03). Other than the loss of life, the most significant aspect of the SARS outbreak to impact on the tourism industry was the mass media coverage. A March 2003 press release by PATA called for "accurate, restrained and sensible travel advice and media reporting" of SARS (patanews@pata.th.com, 17/3/03). PATA urged all reporting to be geographically specific and avoid alarmist statements. The following day in an e-mail to the TRINET online tourism research community, Associate Professor Bob McKercher of The Hong Kong Polytechnic University, lamented how the global media frenzy was feeding perceptions of a "disaster":

> While the health scare is no doubt of concern, we must keep a proper perspective on it. The local and global media is in something of a feeding frenzy. As a resident of HK, it is worrying, but remember that, out of a population of 7 million, only 100 people have fallen ill, so far.

McKercher (2003) later introduced the term SIP (SARS induced panic) to the tourism lexicon, arguing strongly that SIP was a greater threat to tourism than SARS. A KPMG report estimated Toronto's tourism industry lost $190 million in the first two months of SARS (McClelland 2003). During May, at the height of the SARS publicity, holiday visitor arrivals to New Zealand decreased by 24% (TNZ 2003).

The Federal Emergency Management Agency (FEMA) listed over 50 declared natural disasters that occurred in the U.S.A. during 2003. The FEMA website (see www.fema.org) provides a valuable resource on disaster management, including education and training information. The range of other natural disasters to impact on destinations have included:

- In 2003 Bermuda's worst hurricane for 80 years struck the destination, forcing the tourism industry to virtually shut down due electricity failures and road closures (www.travelmole.com, 8/9/03).
- During 2003, overseas visitors were injured by a 15 minute tornado in Costa Blanca (www.travelmole.com, 8/9/03).
- The 2002 outbreak of foot and mouth disease in the U.K. highlighted how other destinations can suffer from a disaster in another country. For example, one politician from the Republic of Ireland labelled Britain as the "leper of Europe" for the negative image being tagged to the wider region (Frisby 2002). Ironically, it was London, an urban destination with minimal farming activity and no incidence of foot and mouth, which experienced the greatest negative economic impact of the foot and mouth disease (Hopper 2002).
- The 1999 Izmit eruption in Turkey (see Beirman 2003a).
- The 1995 Kobe earthquake.
- The 1993 Sydney bushfires (see Christine 1995).
- Hurricane Andrew on Florida in 1992 forced the closure of Miami Beach for a week (Portorff & Neal 1994).
- The Philippine's 1991 Mt. Pinatubo eruption.
- The 1982 Mt. Usu eruption in Japan (see Hirose 1992, in Faulkner 1999).
- In the winter of 1981/82, Florida's STO was forced to spend US$600,000 on an emergency three week advertising campaign to counter negative media publicity about a brief and unseasonal cold spell (Pritchard 1982).

Management Failures

In addition to acts of God, destinations are at the mercy of man made disasters, which are in effect representative of management failures. Other than war and terrorism, the most recent significant man-made disaster to impact negatively on the tourism industry was the 1997/1998 Asian Economic Crisis. Heavy, and some would argue reckless, short term borrowing by banks and businesses in the region for investments in real estate and the share market were poorly managed (Henderson 2002). Consequently, the withdrawal of capital and loss of confidence in the region's financial sector created a domino effect through national economies, which at one point created fears of a collapse of the world economy. Prior to the economic crisis, the Asia-Pacific region was experiencing the world's fastest growth in international visitor arrivals. For example, Asia Pacific had been the world's fastest growing tourism region, increasing its share of international arrivals from 1% in 1960 to 13% in 1992 (PATA 1996). PATA had forecast the region to grow at 7.5% per annum until 2000 and then 6.5% until 2010. International tourist arrivals were expected to increase to 101 million in 2000 and 190 million in 2010. The immediate effect of the crisis on tourism was a reduced growth of 1% in arrivals in 1997 and a loss of 1% in 1998 (WTO 1998, 1999, in Henderson 2002). As a result of the boom in intra-regional travel within the Asia-Pacific region many businesses became over exposed to markets within the region, and paid the price when the crisis emerged.

In 1996 at Port Arthur in Tasmania a lone gunman killed 35 people, including domestic and overseas tourists. During October 2003 there was violent rioting in the streets in leading Jamaican destination, Montego Bay (www.eturbonews.com, 28/10/03). A month earlier, the tranquil Maldives was hit by rioting that led to late-night curfews (www.travelmole.com, 23/9/03). Arguably, violent crimes such as these are representative of a management failure by government to manage security. Excessive crime and unruly behaviour can affect the image of a destination, and crime against visitors has led to negative reputations for many urban destinations around the world. For example, violent crimes in Miami and Orlando reached such a level in 1993 that they caused a decrease in visitor arrivals to the entire state (Pizam 1999). Dimanche & Lepetic (1999) provided a case study of the impact of crime levels on tourism in New Orleans, where the murder rate was eight times the national average and five times that of New York. In 1997 the New Orleans CVB hired an outside consultant to develop a marketing plan to address the negative crime image of the city. However, Dimanche and Lepetic found that while the tourism industry in the city was under siege from a high crime rate, there was a lack of concern among the tourism community, due to no noticeable drop in revenues. They strongly urged operators to heed the warning signals before the situation became a crisis.

Ironically, the source of a crime problem at a destination can often be visitors to the area. For example, business in the Greek Island of Faliraki was estimated to be down by almost one third in 2003 as a result of anti-social behaviour by visitors (www.travelmole.com, 21/7/03). TravelMole.com was citing a report in the *Daily Telegraph*, which suggested British tourists in particular were responsible for the high levels of bad behaviour that included sexual assaults, drunkenness and lewdness. Initiatives introduced by authorities to counter the resultant "image problem" included extra police on the beat and a requirement for tour operators to provide police with details of planned pub crawls.

Other examples of management failures to have impacted negatively on the tourism industry, either directly or indirectly, have included:

- The 2002 collapse of Australia's major domestic air carrier Ansett Airlines
- Nuclear testing in the South Pacific in 1995 (see Elliott 1997)
- Labour strikes such as those by Australian airline pilots in 1989/90 (see Lavery 1992) and U.S.A. air traffic controllers in 1981.
- The 1989 Exxon Valdez oil spill at Prince William Sound, Alaska
- The 1989 conflict in Tiananmen Square (see Roehl 1990; Gartner & Shen 1992)
- The 1970s global oil crisis. The impact in New Zealand was so significant that the government ordered the closure of petrol stations on Sundays. Another initiative that

impacted on tourism was the introduction car-less day stickers, where every car was forced to carry a sticker indicating one day of the week when it could not be used.

Poor planning can also eventually lead to a crisis phase for a destination, such as in the case of Rotorua, New Zealand, during the 1980s and 1990s. Rotorua is one of New Zealand's two most popular resort areas, attracting 1.3 million visitors each year. The district has traditionally been known for its geothermal resources and Maori culture. Tourism is a key element of the local economy, employing one in every five workers. In 1978, two hundred delegates at a New Zealand Travel and Holidays Association branch meeting reached consensus that Rotorua was losing its "oomph" in tourism against other centres (Stafford 1988). However, denial from local government was strong in the mid-1980s, perhaps best encapsulated in a quote by then Mayor John Keaney: "It is in the interests of other centres to carry out a vendetta against Rotorua to put tourists off coming here" (Rotorua Daily Post, 13/8/86). Keaney's comments came in the wake of a report in Wellington's *Dominion* newspaper under the heading "Death of a Tourist town," and an associated national television news item. The frustration of local tourism operators was so bad by 1988 that the industry co-operative that was contracted to the council to undertake destination promotion resigned en masse and withdrew from the council contract. Rotorua's image problems were compounded by a number of significant issues, including:

• The third highest unemployment in New Zealand, at 13% (Stafford 1988).
• National media coverage of protests by geothermal bore owners, over the closure of geothermal bores within a 1.5 kilometre radius of the famous Pohutu Geyser at Whakarewarewa. Hindley (1989) reported scientists had come to regard geysers as an endangered species, since of 11 Whakarewarewa geysers that were active before 1950 only three were erupting frequently.
• Staff strikes at the Rotorua's most popular visitor attraction, the New Zealand Maori Arts and Crafts Institute (Stafford 1988).
• A national recession that brought Rotorua commercial property development to a standstill (Stafford 1988).
• High rent from out of town landlords forcing retail closures, which led to an abundance of empty shops in the central business district.
• A tired cityscape due to local government expenditure being directed towards much needed sewerage infrastructure.

Problems came to a head during the 1980s, which proved a challenging decade for the New Zealand tourism industry in general, due to changing travel patterns. For example, domestic person nights decreased from 61.4 to 53.1 million between 1983 and 1988 (NZTP 1989/2), while international visitor arrivals doubled during the 1980s (Pearce 1990). Changes in international arrivals led to a greater diversification of the market. Prior to this, tourism in New Zealand had mostly focused on "passive sightseeing of a range of natural scenic resources" (Cushman 1990: 13). Rotorua tourism operators had relied on the district's status as the country's most popular holiday area and prominence in NTO promotions overseas. At this time, Pearce (p. 40) claimed that at the time overseas marketing by the New Zealand regions had been limited to "modest campaigns on the East Coast of

Australia." Also, the Government Tourist Bureaux (GTB), including the Rotorua branch, were sold in 1990. The GTB had been the main tourist information office in Rotorua since 1903, almost the last remaining icon of the Rotorua tourism industry's strong reliance on central government. This reliance on government left Rotorua tourism interests unprepared for the new era of competition and market changes. The negative image of Rotorua in the market was so serious it had become a concern to national tourism interests, and in 1992 the New Zealand Tourism Board conducted an analysis of the local tourism industry:

> The study is being carried out in the context of industry concern that Rotorua as one of New Zealand's major tourism hubs could be in decline and unless rejuvenated could lose its focus as a major tourism destination, either as part of the traditional touring circuit or as a regional tourism hub. Taupo has been suggested as a potential challenger to Rotorua's position as the central North Island main tourism hub (NZTB 1992: 2).

The withdrawal of direct involvement by central government forced the local government to be more proactive. Recognising the labour intensiveness of the tourism industry in relation to the district's other major industries, forestry and farming, the Rotorua District Council embarked on a major investment in destination marketing and central business district (CBD) beautification during the late 1980s and 1990s. A NZ$30 million CBD redevelopment included a complete remodelling of the streetscape, a refurbished entertainment and convention centre, a state-of-the-art visitor information centre, and feasibility studies leading to the construction of new hotels. The council owned and operated RTO, Tourism Rotorua, was acknowledged three times as "best RTO" at the New Zealand tourism awards during the 1990s, and now boasts an annual marketing budget in excess of NZ$1 million. Through coordination by the council funded Tourism Rotorua, the district has achieved unprecedented levels of cooperation within and between industry, strong community support, and a vastly enhanced image in the domestic and international market place. The case of Rotorua (see also Ateljevic 1998; Ateljevic & Doorne 2000; Horn *et al.* 2000) is a useful example of how the fortunes of a holiday resort area have peaked and troughed in line with levels of government intervention.

Other examples of destinations in decline that have been discussed in the literature have included Hamm in Germany during the 1970s and 1980s (Buckley & Witt 1985), Majorca during the 1980s (Morgan 1991), Canada during the 1990s (Go 1987), Bermuda in the 1990s (Conlin 1995), and Amsterdam in the 1990s (Dahles 1998).

DMO Responses to Disasters

> The intensity of the moment during a crisis is clearly not the time to commence such planning (Litvin & Alderson 2003: 189).

Any destination thrown into a crisis situation will be forced to implement recovery strategies. Since no destination is immune to disasters, it surely behoves the DMO to develop a crisis recovery strategy in conjunction with civic authorities. However, as has been suggested, there have been few resources available to advise DMOs on crisis management. While some guidelines have been developed for recovery from natural disasters there has been little published on crisis management strategies following acts of terrorism (Sönmez *et al.* 1999). Clearly the purpose of a crisis management plan is to be prepared. A plan should guide the DMO at a time when distress and panic are likely. Sönmez *et al.* suggested a guidebook can include: roles and responsibilities, action checklists, a directory of contacts, and media guidelines such as sample press kits and what to do/not do at media conferences. Following a recommendation of the PATA Bali Tourism Recovery Taskforce, PATA created a crisis manual for member governments (see PATA 2003). The manual provides a checklist of critical tasks to be undertaken during a crisis, as well as a directory of crisis specialists.

While ensuring the safety of visitors and rebuilding infrastructure and tourism facilities will be paramount, these activities are beyond the scope of the vast majority of DMOs. This section is therefore limited to discussing the marketing aspects of recovery from disasters. One RTO that did have a crisis plan on September 11 2001, was Charleston in South Carolina (Litvin & Alderson 2003). The first meeting of the Charleston Area Convention & Visitors Bureau (CACVB) crisis team took place on the afternoon of September 11. However, the CACVB plan immediately proved to be of limited value as all scenarios were based on local events such as hurricanes and floods. There was no scenario for an incident 500 miles away.

Faulkner & Vikulov (2001) examined the role of a tourism disaster management plan in the case of the 1998 Australia Day flood at Katherine. Located in the Northern Territory, in Australia's tropical north, Katherine receives heavy rainfall that is a routine of the wet season. However, the 1998 flood was the worst in the town's history, inundating half of the homes, all of the CBD, and most tourism businesses. This natural disaster challenged the survival of the local tourism industry, and occurred so quickly that the Katherine Regional Tourism Association (KRTA) was involved in a surprise crisis with a very limited decision time (343):

> The urgency of the disaster situation means that operators and the RTA did not have the luxury of reflecting on the most appropriate action to take. Nor was there time to engage in the consultations necessary to produce a fully coordinated response.

Faulkner and Vikulov found that despite the possibility of a "100 year flood" no tourism operators had disaster management plans, other than regulatory evacuation plans. Following the recovery period, the KRTA proceeded to develop a destination disaster management plan in conjunction with emergency service organisations. Concurrently, the RTO also decided to be more proactive in enhancing disaster awareness among local operators. The downside however was, as a result of directing resources to these efforts, the KRTA's ability to continue strategic marketing planning was restricted.

Clearly a DMO's ability to respond effectively will depend on the level of resources available. Depending on the scale of the crisis, this will likely require strong lobbying by DMOs for government intervention. For example, following the events of 9/11 the Southern Governors' Association adopted a resolution that endorsed the following six points (Kubiak 2002: 19):

- federal funds to supplement state government expenditures on tourism advertising
- a $500 individual tax credit for personal travel expenses
- development of a national tourism policy
- a substantial federal investment in an international advertising and marketing program, including funding of the "In-Flight Survey" and national travel and tourism satellite
- an account to collect important statistics on international travellers and other tourism data
- ensuring travelers' efficient expedition, comfort and convenience while screening security.

In 2002, the British government announced a £40 million marketing package to reverse the estimated £2 billion drop in tourism revenue from the foot and mouth outbreak (Kleinman & Bashford 2002). In response to the 1989/1990 pilot's strike in Australia, which resulted in a decrease of over 100,000 international visitor arrivals, the Australian federal government provided an additional "Recovery Plan" fund of A$18.5 million to the ATC (Lavery 1992). In 2003, Hong Kong Tourism Board executive director Clara Chong announced funding of HK$400 million for a series of special events to repair the post-SARS image of Hong Kong (www.eturbonews.com 19/8/03). The Indonesian government allocated $44.6 million for a global campaign to lure visitors back to Bali following the October 2002 bombings (Osborne 2003). The Canadian federal government pledged an additional C$15.5 million to promote Toronto and Canada as safe destinations (www.eturbonews.com, 17/6/03). The Florida state government provided US$20 million for tourism advertising post-September 11 (Word 2003). The *Financial Times* reported the Thailand government took the unusual step of promising US$100,000 to any tourist catching SARS while visiting the country (www.travelmole.com, 21/5/03). Authorities made the offer due to concern over the April arrival Figures which were down by almost half, even though Thailand had been declared a SARS-free zone. The initiative followed a U.S.$100,000 SARS-free guarantee by Thai Airways.

Not all DMOs are fortunate to receive extra funding during a crisis. For example, during the Asian economic crisis, the Indonesian Tourist Promotion Board was forced to close important overseas offices in Frankfurt, London, Los Angeles, Singapore, Taipei and Tokyo, as a result of a lack of funding and huge debts (Henderson 2002). The CEO of the British Incoming Tour Operators Association criticised the British government for failing to adequately support the tourism industry during the foot and mouth crisis (www.travelmole.com, 13/3/03). The criticism was fuelled by reports that the tourism industry received £20 million in additional funds while facing a loss of £5 billion, and yet the agricultural sector received compensation payments of £1 billion.

From the literature published to date on destinations in crisis, the following tactics have been implemented by DMOs in crisis situations.

Disaster Management Taskforce

The purpose of a crisis management taskforce is to minimise the level of guesswork during a crisis. The DMO is in an ideal situation to coordinate immediate and ongoing marketing responses, working closely with any damage response entity to ensure consistency of messages. However, PATA (1991, in Litvin & Alderson 2003) noted the majority of its members, including NTOs, did not include crisis management in strategic planning. This, despite an average estimation they stood a 40% chance of facing a crisis. In most cases a taskforce is instigated during the crisis. For example, the PATA Bali Recovery Taskforce was established immediately following the October 2002 bombings to assist Indonesia. Within a week of the 2001 outbreak of foot and mouth disease in the U.K., the BTA had set up its Immediate Action Group (Frisby 2002). Two weeks after the September 11 terrorist strikes, the London Tourist Board (LTB) established the London Tourism recovery Group (London Tourist Board 2001, in Hopper 2002). The main purpose of the group was to implement tracking research on the impacts to tourism. As a result of the findings, the London Tourism Action group was established by the Mayor to develop a recovery plan.

The first role of any marketing taskforce is to assess the situation for impact on visitor arrivals. Primary impact concerns will be the level of visitation decrease (visitor numbers, nights, spend) and for what period of time. The second role is to respond as quickly as possible, initially focusing on information dispersal in a manner that fosters a sense of trust in the DMO by the media and travelling public. This may be necessary to clearly demarcate where the problem is, particularly if a number of areas have been unaffected. For example, Florida has a coastline of over 1,000 miles, and Hurricane Andrew in 1992 only affected 10 miles of beaches (Portorff & Neal 1994). They cited a U.K. newspaper headline that read "Hurricane Bearing Down on Disney Beaches," and yet the distance between Orlando and the affected beaches was over 200 miles.

DMOs at all levels may form a taskforce that fits within the existing governance structure. Meetings need not have the same frequency as other panels, but should draw on expertise from relevant fields, such as civil defence, public health and infrastructure. Sönmez *et al.* (1999) suggested organising teams within the taskforce with different responsibilities, such as: public relations, promotion, information coordination, and fundraising. Other initiatives worth considering, particularly in high risk areas, include:

- working cooperatively with neighbouring destinations
- communicating the current contingency plan to industry
- providing annual workshops for DMO staff and industry on crisis management and scenario building.

Risk Analysis

Disasters, whether natural or man-made, are not predictable (Faulkner 1999). If destinations are to prepare contingency plans for possible disasters, it is important to look forward as well as backwards. DMOs can benefit from the lessons learnt during previous disasters, and yet history is no predictor of the future. While it would be futile to attempt to predict the future (Drucker 1995), what can be valuable is the use of scenarios. Scenario building attempts to construct views of possible futures, in an effort to better plan for uncertainty (see Johnson & Scholes 2002; Schwartz 1992). Strategic choices can be made based on how the different scenarios might unfold. In theory, this then offers the relative security of being prepared for, to varying degrees, whatever scenario happens. Scenarios should be seen as carefully constructed plots, rather than predictions. When attempting to envision the future, assumptions must be made for each scenario. Since the assumptions are the key elements in determining the basis for each plot, the number should be kept to a minimum, to reduce complexity. For each scenario, a number of questions can be developed, including for example:

- What might lead to success or a speedy recovery where others may fail?
- What might happen to current customers?
- What might happen to future suppliers?
- What type of businesses will fare best/worst?
- What are the most important activities that need to be addressed first?
- Where should marketing resources be directed?

Public Relations

Effective media relations is the most important aspect of a destination recovery response, since negative reporting in the mass media can affect the viability of a destination. The media has a propensity for relaying "bad news" rather than positive coverage of the destination's recovery. Beirman (2003a: 25–26) advised DMO media managers should be prepared for the following questions:

- What is being done to assist victims?
- What is the extent of the damage/casualties?
- What is being dome to reduce, minimise or eliminate future risks?
- What can the government/destination authorities do to guarantee safety?
- Why did this event occur in the first place?
- Who is to blame?
- How long will the crisis last?

During a serious crisis all international marketing should cease, given these will be worthless if consumers are bombarded with negative news images on their televisions (Mansfield 1999). The focus of communications at this stage should be on providing accurate information dissemination. Strengthening of relations with the mass media will be necessary to generate greater positive publicity, since misinformation is one of the greatest challenges to tourism. Quarantelli (1996, in Faulkner 1999) observed four key characteristics in the role of the media in U.S.A. disasters. Interestingly, the first has been a lack of disaster preparedness planning by the mass media. Second, tensions have emerged between local media and national media over disaster ownership. Third, the media have tended to selectively report activities of organisations with which they have an established relationship. Fourth, television has been prone to perpetuate disaster myths. Hopper (2002) reported that misinformation in the U.S.A. about the 2001 outbreak of foot and mouth disease in the U.K., led to perceptions the disease being a human condition and that all of England was "closed." One of the greatest communication challenges was maintaining a positive outlook in destination promotion, while simultaneously promoting the negative impacts to government (83):

> At the height of FMD, the LTB was conducting around six broadcast interviews a week with media, which were focused heavily on the negative.

Frisby (2002) provided a detailed first hand account of the PR activities undertaken by the BTA during the 2001 U.K. outbreak of foot and mouth disease. Initiatives undertaken during the crisis included: media releases, fortnightly newsletters, sponsored overseas media visits, video news releases and background tapes, and development of a media extranet. At the peak of the outbreak the BTA's call centre in New York received an average of 700 calls each day about the crisis (Frisby 2002). Frisby (90) claimed media misinformation was such that enquiries included, for example, "Should we bring our own food?" and "Can we travel around safely?"

Outsourcing

Few DMOs are likely to have the resources to employ a permanent disaster management specialist, and few DMO staff are likely to have been trained in crisis management. Depending on the level of crisis, such a specialist will need to be outsourced to work with the disaster management taskforce. Likewise, outsourcing of PR specialists may be needed to temporarily coordinate public information dissemination. For example, at the RTO level, the Katherine Regional Tourism Association employed a journalist to work with the media following the 1998 Australia Day flood (Faulkner & Vikulov 2001). In 2003 the London Tourist Board took the step of offering a three month contract for a marketer to focus on encouraging Londoners to spend more in their own city during the war in Iraq (*Marketing*, 6/3/03). The temporary position reported to a committee formed by the LTB, the Greater London Authority and the London Development Agency. At the NTO level, during the 2001 U.K. outbreak of foot and mouth disease the BTA contracted a global PR agency to minimise the negative perceptions of Britain overseas (Frisby 2002). However, BTA PR director Frisby candidly acknowledged a post-crisis recommendation to not outsource to a global agency in the future (99):

> Although the appointed agency performed well in the initial rebuttal phase, after six weeks it became clear that a lack of product knowledge meant that enormous inputs of time and expertise were required in order to continue to produce results.

Coordinating Cooperative Campaigns

Key advantages of a coordinated marketing response include (Mansfield 1999):

• economies of scale
• consistency of image-related messages

- more effective assessment of performance
- reduced infighting between different tourism sector groups
- positive signals for the travel industry and target markets.

Regarding the last point, during the 2001 U.K. foot and mouth disease outbreak a feature of the BTA's response was working closely with national and regional tourist boards and key government departments, in an effort to minimise negative media coverage and to provide reassurance to the public (Frisby 2002). Interestingly, September 11th enabled the CACVB to successfully implement cooperative packages, which it had previously been unable to stimulate in more settled times (Litvin & Alderson 2003). Similarly, Hopper (2002) reported one of the key lessons learned by the London Tourism Board in the wake of September 11 was the need for effective dialogue with tourism operators. Hopper suggested a legacy of the improved public-private sector relationship established during the crisis has become a model for future marketing of the destination.

Trade familiarisation visits are also an important function coordinated by DMOs. Following the 2003 terrorism attacks in Turkey, the Balkan Federation of Travel and Tourist Agencies Associations planned initiatives to develop solidarity between tourism interests in the region. On the assumption that negative images of Turkey would affect tourism to nearby member countries, the federation planned familiarisation visits to Istanbul for leading world tourism authorities during 2004 (www.eturbonews.com, 25/11/03). Hosting large groups of travel industry personnel on familiarisations by the Turkish Ministry of Tourism was a major reason for that country's rapid recovery following the 1999 Izmit earthquake (Beirman 2003a).

Supporting Local Tourism Businesses

Mansfield (1999) suggested governments in high risk areas should provide financial incentives for tourism investors, given the probability of future losses. A number of cases in the literature have reported initiatives to support local tourism operators during a crisis:

- In China, post-SARS initiatives included visa exemptions for some nationalities (www.eturbonews.com, 7/8/03).
- One of the first activities of the Katherine Regional Tourism Association, following the devastating 1998 Australia Day flood was an audit of the destination's tourism businesses (Faulkner & Vikulov 2001). The purpose was to assess damage and prospects of recovery.
- VAT was reduced from 13% to 3% on hotels in Jordan during the 2003 war in Iraq (www.travelmole.com, 9/6/03).
- The Israel Ministry of Tourism has provided subsidies for tourism operators marketing the destination (Beirman 2002).
- Post September 11, the CACVB enlisted an online booking company to conduct workshops for local tourism businesses (Litvin & Alderson 2003).

- During the 2001 U.K. outbreak of foot and mouth disease, the BTA used the organisation's website to update industry with information and advice (Frisby 2002).

Stimulating Discounts and Adding Value

The introduction of special deals has been a regular component of Israel's post-crisis recovery programmes (Beirman 2002). Beirman (2003a) provided the examples of Delta Airlines, which provided 10,000 free seats to New York, and Insight Vacations, which provided a one week package in Egypt for U.S.$1 as a value add-on to its European tour product following the 1997 Luxor massacre. During the 2001 U.K. outbreak of foot and mouth disease, the BTA used the organisation's trade website to ask operators to provide details of special deals, details of which were used in media releases and publicised on the organisation's consumer web site (Frisby 2002). Following the events of September 11, one of the recovery initiatives of the London Mayor was a £500,000 contribution towards free and discounted tickets to the city's theatres.

Market Concentration

One of the most important crisis decisions is the tradeoffs about which markets to focus recovery efforts on. During the Asian Economic crisis the STB concentrated on markets unaffected by the economic downturn (Henderson 2002). During the U.K. foot and mouth disease outbreak in 2001 the BTA focused attention on 11 key markets (Frisby 2002). On the correct assumption that Americans would be reluctant to fly in the short term following September 11, the CACVB focused attention on cities within a 10 hour drive (Litvin & Alderson 2003). All scheduled advertising was pulled immediately and replaced with a new campaign featuring the tagline "A short drive down the road, a million miles away."

Beirman (2003a) proposed DMOs facing a continuing crisis could segment the market into three distinctive categories — stalwarts, waverers/fair weather friends, and disaffected/discretionary. *Stalwarts* represent those likely to have solidarity with the destination. Examples include the stimulation of a "travel local" campaign in the U.S.A. domestic market following September 11, and the promotion by Israel to Diaspora Jews and Christian Zionists. *Waverers* are those who form the mainstay of the visitor market during periods of normality, and will be the first to return when a crisis is resolved. Examples include business travellers and those with an affinity for the destination. The *discretionary market* will select substitute destinations at the sign of any trouble that might add stress to a visit. Such holidaymakers are the major segment of tourism and will be the group most influenced by mass media reporting.

During the foot and mouth disease outbreak in the U.K., the London Tourism Board (LTB) directed attention towards the domestic market (Hopper 2002). The LTB particularly focused on promoting domestic short breaks to the capital. By February 2002, the Pacific Asia Travel Association (PATA) had stated concern at the trend towards stronger domestic promotion in many PATA countries (PATA 2002). The concern was due to the potential for discouraging outbound travel, resulting in lower inbound arrivals within the region, which would further impact on airline profitability.

Dark Tourism

There is a dark side to image marketing, where some travellers are attracted to the negative images of places that have suffered disasters (Ahmed 1991c). This phenomenon has been labelled "dark tourism" (Lennon & Foley 2000), and "thano tourism" (Seaton 1996), where tourists visit scenes of death and disaster for reasons of remembrance, education or entertainment. Lennon and Foley's text provided examples of such sites in Europe and U.S.A., including: the death camps of Poland, World War Two occupation sites in the Channel Islands, the death site of U.S. President John F. Kennedy, war sites and the U.S. Holocaust Memorial Museum. That so many travellers are attracted to scenes of disaster is perhaps representative of our innate sense of curiosity, which in part manifests in our desire for travel to explore, rather than a purely morbid inclination. Alternatively, the visit might represent a pilgrimage or merely a photo opportunity. There has been little research however into the significance of such visits by travellers (Lennon & Foley 2000). In some cases curiosity might be immediate to view the devastation. For example, immediately following the 2003 War in Iraq, U.K. travellers were signing up for tours of the country. A report in the *Daily Express* cited bookings by travellers to a tour organised by Hinterland Travel to "see what has happened to the country" (www.travelmole.com, 6/8/03). Although armed guards were employed to accompany the travellers, a spokesperson of the U.K. Foreign and Commonwealth Office warned against such a trip: "Anyone organising a trip or planning to go should not do so." In other cases a sustained curiosity is developed. In New Zealand, disaster struck in June 1886 when Mount Tarawera erupted, destroying three Maori villages with the loss of 150 lives, and obliterating the fledgling destination's most notable tourism attraction at the time, the Pink and White terraces. This was a devastating blow for tourism (Stafford 1986), only 40 years after the first tourist arrivals. However, by 1888 Rotorua's annual visitor arrivals were higher than pre-eruption levels (Reggett 1972). Part of the continued interest in Rotorua was the eruption aftermath and new volcanic craters, which remain attractions today.

The diversity of other examples of sites of death or disaster attracting visitors include:

- The Alma tunnel in Paris where Princess Diana was killed in 1997
- Robin Island, near Cape Town in South Africa where Nelson Mandela was jailed
- Lenin's tomb in Moscow
- The house in Winchester, England, where Jane Austin died
- Hawaii's USS Arizona memorial
- New York's Ground Zero
- Elvis Presley's gravesite in Memphis
- World War Two prisoner of war camps, such as Colditz Castle, Germany
- The site of the 1985 air crash in which 256 members of the U.S. 101st Airborne Division were killed remains one of the most popular visitor attractions in Gander, Canada (see Butler & Baum 1999).
- U.S.A.'s civil war Petersburg National Battlefield

- Auschwitz-Birkenau Memorial and Museum, Poland
- Turkey's World War One battle field at ANZAC Cove, Gallipoli
- Peace Memorial Park, Hiroshima.

Visits to sites of death is not a modern phenomenon (Seaton 1996). Lennon & Foley (2000: 8) arbitrarily selected the 1912 sinking of the Titanic and the First World War of 1914–1918 as the start of the modern dark tourism era. These events coincided with the introduction of cinemas:

> The First World War graphically demonstrated the consequences of modernity to populations using the technology of modernity to achieve its effect.

The popularity of sites of death and disaster has demonstrated there can also be a positive effect of such events. Admittedly with some moral dilemmas DMOs should (sensitively and chronologically) be alert to new marketing opportunities. Lennon & Foley (2000) suggested there is a pattern that western mass tourism has followed regarding the appropriateness of visiting such "celebrated" sites. Immediately following events visitation to show respect for the dead is acceptable, such as following the massacre of Scottish schoolchildren at Dunblame. Often, floral tributes are laid at the site. This is followed by a period in which a memorial may be erected and consequently visited. It then takes much longer for any form of interpretation for visitors to be accepted, for fear of it being seen as a tourist experience.

Chapter Key Point Summary

Key Point 1 — The Likelihood of a Disaster

No destination is immune to disaster. Every DMO should consider the possibility of a disaster at some stage in the future. Disasters can be man-made or acts of God. They can be short term or long term. Almost all will be unpredictable and beyond the control of the DMO. The level of preparedness for a disaster at a destination will determine the extent to which a crisis manifests.

Key Point 2 — DMO Responses

Since a state of crisis can affect the viability of the destination, DMOs have a responsibility to prepare marketing contingency plans. The level of such planning has until recently been very low. However, the recent increase in acts of war and terrorism has forced more destinations to act. The topic of destination crisis management is an emerging research field within the tourism literature. A number of case studies have been reported in recent years, and provide a valuable resource for DMOs considering contingency planning. Key activities that DMOs should consider include: the formation of a permanent disaster taskforce, scenario building and risk analysis, coordinated marketing responses, market concentration, outsourcing of media relations, and initiatives to support local businesses.

Additional Reading

Beirman, D. (2003). *Restoring destinations in crisis*. Crows Nest, NSW: Allen & Unwin.

Faulkner, B. (2001). Towards a framework for tourism disaster management. *Tourism Management*, *22*, 135–147.

Lennon, J., & Foley, M. (2000). *Dark tourism*. London: Continuum.

PATA (2003). *Crisis: It won't happen to us! Expect the unexpected. Be prepared.* Bangkok: Pacific Asia Travel Association.

Chapter 9

Performance Measures

Good management starts with good measurement (Aaker 1996: 316).

Chapter Perspective

It is fitting to conclude by considering how effective DMOs are. Do they generate an appropriate return for the millions spent on promotion? What is an appropriate return on investment? Is it actually possible to quantify the contribution of DMO efforts? If so, are such quantifiable short run measures actually appropriate for DMOs? With no direct control over tourism businesses there is no direct profit return from marketing spend, with which to reinvest in future marketing. DMOs are instead relying predominantly on grants provided by government and are not therefore accountable to shareholders in the same way as a commercial enterprise would be. Destination marketers find themselves accountable to a board of directors, tourism sector groups, local taxpayers and government. Is, as suggested by Ward & Gold (1994) destination marketing more akin to social marketing? After all, there must be a more lasting legacy of other less tangible effects of DMO efforts over time, such as enhancement of destination image and the support and education of fledgling tourism businesses. Effectiveness of DMOs therefore needs to be evaluated based on a combination of specific sales, communication and social objectives.

Currently there is no model to quantify the relationship between the work of DMOs and overall visitor levels, length of stay and spending at a destination. Reflect for a moment on the visitors who are in London, for example, at the time you are reading this. To what extent are they there as a result of induced initiatives by the former ETC and BTA, the current NTO Visit Britain, the RTB Visit London, airlines, tour wholesalers, or individual tourism businesses? To what extent are they there as a result of their own organic attitude development through word of mouth referrals, movies, media news or school geography lessons? If visitor arrivals are up or down this year, to what extent can this be attributed to the DMO, relative to exogenous factors such as interest rates, hallmark events or disasters? Consider also the destination you are likely to travel to next. Are you able to recall what initially stimulated your interest, and what role the DMO has played in shaping your image of the destination and intent to visit? The most challenging and least reported aspect of destination marketing is that of measuring performance. Even so, the extent to which DMOs are able to monitor the effectiveness of their activities is a key destination marketing management function, not only for improving future promotional efforts but also for accountability, funding purposes, and in some cases their very survival as an entity. Woodside & Sakai's (2001: 370)

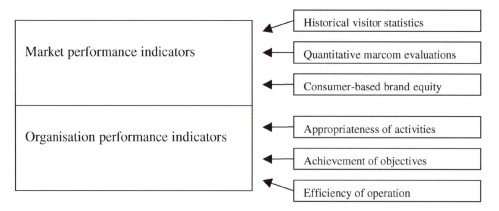

Figure 1: Indicators of DMO effectiveness.

meta-evaluation of government tourism marketing performance audits suggested evaluations that included the following were most likely to achieve the goals of all stakeholders:

*   inclusion of both (post)positivistic and relativistic research methods and both objective and subjective views of realities
*   valuing both the programme activities and results
*   use of a working party of three to five organizations.

The two main categories of indicators to address in the evaluation of DMO effectiveness as shown in Figure 1 are evaluations of: (i) market performance; and (ii) organisation effectiveness.

Market Performance

The theme of the 2004 Travel and Tourism Research Association conference was billed as *Measuring the tourism experience: When experience rules, what is the metric of success?* (see www.ttra.com). Performance metrics is a topical issue, and in the tourism literature has appeared relatively recently, particularly for DMOs. For example, Sheehan & Ritchie's (1997) literature review found very little interest in DMO market performance measures, while Faulkner (1997) suggested most evaluations reported had been ad hoc. From a survey of local government tourism offices in Australia's state of Victoria, Carson *et al.* (2003) suggested up to one third of shire councils lacked a system of performance monitoring for tourism objectives. In the USA, Pizam (1990) cited research indicating only a minority of STOs actually bothered to evaluate the effectiveness of their promotions. Likewise, Hawes *et al.* (1991) found only 7 of 37 STOs used measurable objectives and performance measures. In an examination of the Italian NTO's promotional plans, Formica and Littlefield (2000: 113) discovered the entire section on evaluation of the plan was missing: "Instead, spurious correlations often led to subjective evaluations of promotional performances." This section discusses three categories of market performance. The first two, visitor monitors and marcom evaluations, are quantitative indicators. The third, consumer-based brand equity, represents a longer term and more subjective approach to DMO effectiveness.

Visitor Monitors

Counting the number of visitor arrivals has long been an obvious measure of the health of a destination's tourism industry. In the early years this was probably not an onerous task with small numbers of visitors, and today most NTOs today have access to international visitor arrivals data through collection by immigration officials at arrival gateways. However, the collection of visitor data is more difficult for STOs and RTOs. It was as recent as 2000, in a keynote address at the TTRA conference in Hollywood, that the director of the Los Angeles CVB asked delegates for assistance in developing a valid method for tracking visitor flows to the area. At that time the CVB did not have an accurate measure of visitation, which impeded marketing performance evaluation.

The emergence of visitor monitors, as a means for achieving this, has occurred only recently for most DMOs. Indeed, there are still many RTOs that do not operate a visitor monitor and rely on data captured in NTO or STO surveys. In other cases, RTOs have established a visitor survey through the help of academics, such as in the case of Mt. Alexander in Victoria, Australia. Dr. Warwick Frost of Monash University coordinates an ongoing visitor survey for the Mt. Alexander Shire Council. The survey, which was initiated in 2001 to enhance local understanding of the value of tourism to the shire, collects data from visitors to the VICs in two towns. This is an example of an intercept survey, which can capture often detailed information from a sample of visitors to the destination. In this case survey items include the origin of visitors, length of stay, accommodation, activities, and information needs. The programme has proven mutually beneficial to the Shire and to Dr. Frost, with the results having been used in the following ways:

- provided to consultants to develop a marketing strategy for the Shire
- regularly circulated to the local tourism industry
- used by key decision makers in state government departments, particularly those involved in an application for World Heritage Listing
- industry seminars and academic conferences
- academic publications.

The independent development of the Mt. Alexander survey does however highlight the lack of a lack of national standard of regional visitor surveys in Australia. To guide Australian RTOs on regional data collection methods, the Centre for Regional Tourism Research has established a web site (see www.regionaltourism.com.au/localdata/). One of the aims of the project is to progress the development of a national standard in data collection and reporting. A range of resources is available to RTOs, including case studies, as indicated in Figure 2. Similarly, to foster the development of global standards in tourism data collection the WTO (1995) produced a manual for the collection of tourism statistics by NTOs. The

centre for
REGIONAL TOURISM
research

Southern Cross
University

Managing Regional Tourism Data

The availability of local level data about tourism markets and business performance has consistently been identified as a critical issue for the development of Australia's regional tourism industries. The Centre for Regional Tourism Research has commenced a program to identify the need for local level tourism data, and develop standards and protocols which will help tourism managers collect, analyse, and use locally collected data. This web site has been developed as a companion to a national series of workshops on collecting and managing regional tourism data. It attempts to summarise the principles behind good data collection, and provide some insights into the sorts of regional collections currently available, and the lessons in resource management learnt in those collections. Any comments on the nature of this web site, and its usefulness to managers considering or undertaking local data collection would be most welcome. It is also possible to arrange for a data workshop in your region.

This site provides information about what regional tourism data can be about, and how it might be used in managing destinations. It examines existing sources of regional tourism data and the quality of those sources. It provides a framework (BAD) for helping you decide whether to use existing data sources or collect your own. It illustrates management principles through a number of case studies of regional data collections. It highlights the resource management issues involved in collecting and maintaining locally collected data, and identifies some strategies for dealing with these issues. It also points to a small number of resources which might assist you further.

As part of the research project, the Centre is seeking case studies of local level data collections from across regional Australia. If you have a case study from your region, please send an email with your contact details and a brief description of the data collection to dcarson@scu.edu.au.

Figure 2: Centre of regional tourism research.

manual provides a comprehensive guide to a range of data issues, including: visitor surveys, measuring outbound tourism, measuring domestic tourism, describing tourism supply, and measuring economic costs and benefits of tourism.

One country that has developed a national standard in regional tourism statistics is New Zealand, which has been operating a commercial accommodation monitor (CAM) since the late 1990s. Coordinated by central government (see www.statisticsnz.govt.nz), the CAM requires all commercial accommodation providers to participate. Statistics New Zealand publishes monthly data on capacity, occupancy rates, visitor nights, length of stay and employee numbers. Among the benefits of a national standard visitor monitor is the ability for regions to undertake market share analysis. RTOs have access to month on month CAM data for all regions. This enables benchmarking of performance by each RTO in comparison to previous points in time and relative to competing regions. Also, accommodation operators are able to compare their visitor mix, length of stay and occupancy rate, with the local and national averages. Arguably easier to implement in a small country, the New Zealand CAM evolved out of a desire to establish a national standard, at a time when RTOs were developing their own measurement instruments. The first regional visitor monitor was developed by the Queenstown Promotion Board in 1990. The author established the country's second monitor six months later in Rotorua, which also featured a monthly survey of local households to provide a measure of visitors staying privately with friends or relatives. Many aspects of the national CAM are based on the Queenstown and Rotorua models.

Critics of visitor monitors argue they are flawed, due to a reliance on individual accommodation operators completing the monthly forms accurately and honestly. A key issue in the development of visitor monitors is gaining the confidence of accommodation operators; convincing them their individual data will be pooled and not accessible by a third party. In the Rotorua case it took months of sometimes heated debate with accommodation representatives to gain acceptance of the need for, and benefits of, a visitor monitor. The end result was a tracking system that became a key element of the RTO's six-weekly reporting to the Rotorua District Council, which funded destination marketing. Clearly however, visitor monitor results should only be promoted as an indicator of destination competitiveness, and not, for the reasons indicated in the chapter introduction, used as a singular measure of DMO effectiveness.

Marcom Evaluations

> In boom times, tourist bodies typically take the credit for increased visitation and infrastructure development, while, in downturns, the same bodies blame the lack of government funding and seek increases to budgets (Craik 1991: 24).

Advertising

Slater (2002: 155) cited the Louisiana cabinet secretary to the Department of Culture, Recreation and Tourism: "The more money we spend, the more visitors we get." However, the relationship between advertising and sales has yet to be established in the marketing literature. A number of studies have concluded the link between destination advertising and tourist receipts was tenuous (e.g. Faulkner 1997: 27). Nevertheless, there have been many claims over the years about the success of DMO advertising campaigns. For example, it has been suggested the "I ♥ New York" promotion was so successful that it generated an increase of almost 12% in tourism receipts over the previous year (Holcolm 1999). Between 1977 and 1981 the US$32 million campaign was estimated to have generated at least eight times that amount in additional tax revenues, and US$2 billion in extra tourism revenue for the state (Pritchard 1982). It was estimated that an initial six-week campaign in the U.K., which launched Western Australia's new destination brand, resulted in 5,886 visitors who spent AUD$7.3 million within the state (Crockett & Wood 1999). The April 28th (2003) internet newsletter of the Colorado Tourism Office reported results of a 2002 advertising effectiveness study, designed to measure the return on investment for tourism advertising (www.colorado.com). The report claimed 1.86 million visitors, who spent US$522 million, visited Colorado as a "direct result" of the STO's US$2.5 million advertising campaign. On this basis it was claimed every advertising dollar generated US$205 in visitor spending and US$12.74 in tax revenue. Celebrating success is important for public agencies such as DMOs, to enhance their credibility in the minds of stakeholders. However, readers should also be aware of the complexities in measurement when interpreting any such claims.

In terms of measuring the specific results of campaigns, Hopper (2002) reported the results of the London Tourist Board's £720,000 foot and mouth outbreak recovery strategy included 202,000 views of the campaign web page and 7,290 bed nights. The problem is of course the DMO never knows the long term effect of campaigns on future visitor arrivals, and of course those travellers who purchased travel independent of the campaign sponsors. Johnson & Messmer (1991) found television advertising had an effect on visitation that was independent of inquiries. McWilliams & Crompton's (1997) study of the impact of advertising on low involvement travel decisions estimated only 24% of leisure travellers over a two year period requested travel literature. Hughes (2002: 158) discussed the difficulties in measuring the effectiveness of Manchester's gay tourism campaign:

> The campaign is ongoing and its success since 1999 has been difficult to assess given that, for obvious reasons, no record is kept of the number of gay and lesbian tourists, and even if there was it would be difficult to attribute any increase to any one cause.

In addressing the question of whether destination advertising increases sales, Woodside (1990) found no published research in the tourism literature other than conversion studies. A conversion study estimates how many enquiries from advertising are converted to visitors, and what the characteristics are of the converted visitors. To do so involves surveying a sample of consumers who have responded to a DMO promotion during the year. A number of authors have been critical of tourism conversion studies. For example, Faulkner's (1997) literature review identified a number of common methodological deficiencies in their application, of which two of the most significant were:

- improper sampling techniques, and a failure to not take sampling error into account when interpreting results
- not considering non response bias, since those who visit a destination are more likely to respond to a survey.

Other difficulties identified in McWilliams & Crompton's (1997) literature review included:

- respondent problems in recalling expenditure at the destination
- problems of measuring without considering the stage of the decision process
- failure to take into account advertising by competitors
- a lack of focus on programme objectives.

The cost effectiveness of print media advertisements can be compared by circulation figures, such as cost per thousand readers, and by level of response, such as cost per inquiry.

In destination advertising these measures were first reported in the tourism literature by Woodside & Reid (1974), in a comparison of the effectiveness of upscale and downscale magazines. In surveying responders they were also able to estimate and compare the return on investment (ROI) across different publications. Responding to criticism of the method by Ellerbrock (1981), improvements to this conversion study technique were outlined by Woodside (1981) and Woodside & Ronkainen (1994). While acknowledging advertising conversion studies will capture some respondents who had already made a decision to visit the destination prior to requesting the information package, Perdue & Pitegoff (1990) proposed four major benefits for DMOs:

- the ability to monitor changes that result from advertising campaigns over time
- the ability to assess how well the advertising is reaching the target segment
- the opportunity to assess the quality of the information package and its contribution to visitor satisfaction
- the opportunity to undertake pre and post campaign surveys.

Woodside (1990) proposed the most effective means of examining the relationship between advertising and sales was through field experiments. Separate groups can be exposed to different advertising in what are termed split-run techniques. An example of a split-market variation was reported by Schoenbachler *et al.* (1995) in an analysis of the effectiveness of an advertising campaign run by a USA STO. Three geographic markets were selected, of which two were exposed to the same radio and television advertising. The third market was treated as the control group. At the conclusion of the campaign a questionnaire was sent to 3,000 residents in each of the three markets to assess: unaided recall, image, awareness and behavioural intent. The results indicated the level of awareness of destination attributes featured in the advertising, as well as stated intent to visit, were significantly higher in the two test markets than in the control group.

Publicity

Equivalent advertising value (EAV) has been a popular means for DMOs to monitor the results of their VMP. EAV is a simplistic measure of the amount of advertising dollars required to purchase the equivalent amount of air time or column centimetre generated by the by the PR initiative. As an example, for 1996–1997 the ATC reported EAV in excess of A$675 million (ATC 1998, in Dore & Crouch 2003). Measuring EAV has been an important aspect of marketing for the Colorado Tourism Office, which has suffered from a lack of state government funding. For the year ending June 2003, the STO claimed EAV of US$22 million through the placement of 1,172 media clips. While EAV can be a useful public relations tool in a DMO's efforts to enhance credibility among stakeholders, there are a number of problems that should be factored into reporting:

- EAV figures do not provide any indication of who actually read the article or viewed the screening, and more importantly how many were part of the DMO's target segment(s).

- the old adage "any publicity is good publicity" should be considered in terms of how the publicity reinforced brand associations.
- not all media articles included in EAV figures can be directly attributed to DMO initiatives.
- there can be a significant time lag between organising and hosting a media visit and subsequent publication, which can skew reporting of year on year activities and results.

Qualitative analyses are also required. Corporate press officer for the BTA, Frisby (2002: 98) indicated the results of the NTO's PR campaign during the foot and mouth outbreak included: 600 articles and broadcast features, 151,000 square centimetres of print and 2,700 seconds of broadcast coverage of Britain as a tourism destination. While Frisby calculated the overall result represented "216 million positive opportunities to see" worth £1.9 million, he also advised the results were measured using both qualitative and quantitative assessment of media coverage:

> The media evaluation system measures individual items of overseas print and broadcast coverage, incorporating the type of publication, content, story angle, audience and readership and impact — scoring each. Other information is also recorded to develop data and aid customer relationship management with individual journalists.

Travel Trade Events

Travel trade events can be difficult to evaluate. The success of familiarisation tours of a destination by intermediaries could be assessed in terms of image improvement and bookings. However, it has been suggested formal evaluations of these initiatives have not generally been conducted by DMOs (Perdue & Pitegoff 1990). Likewise, monitoring the effectiveness of travel exhibitions has proven difficult and time consuming, and as a result often neglected by DMOs. At one level the influence of travel show interaction on actual travel is difficult to measure. At another level, it is even difficult at consumer shows to screen genuine enquirers from brochure collectors, and identify those with a propensity to visit the destination. However, most consumer exhibitions now charge admission fees, which does provide an element of screening compared to setting up a display in a shopping mall. DMOs often distribute coupons, for which the redemption rate can be measured or attempt to collect database listings through competitions. Pizam (1990) reported USA STOs had generally used "rough" measures of travel show effectiveness. The most common methods included: numbers of enquiries, numbers of contacts, amount of literature distributed, staff evaluations, conversion studies, number of group bookings, and surveys.

Consumer-Based Brand Equity

> The power of a brand lies in the minds of consumers (Keller 2003: 59).

Generally, there has been a tendency in tourism marketing to focus on short run measures of marcom effectiveness. This is a reflection of the short term focus that pervades many boardrooms. Relatively few current DMO decision makers are likely to still be in office in ten years time, since the high profile and political nature of DMOs management inhibits long periods in governance and senior management. While short run indicators are important they should also be supplemented with indicators addressing a longer term view of sustainable destination competitiveness. A worthwhile supplement to the more quantitative indicators discussed above is the development of measures for monitoring market perceptions, based on the model of consumer-based brand equity. Therefore it is important to develop means for understanding how marketing initiatives are impacting on consumer learning and recall of brand information (Keller 1993). However, given the time consuming, costly and more subjective nature of market research, it is perhaps not surprising that this has been a relatively new activity for DMOs at state and regional levels. For example, in evaluating the initial effects of the Brand Oregon campaign, Curtis (2001: 76) lamented the lack of perceptions research:

> In terms of evaluation of the initial campaign, the Tourism Commission essentially took account of two factors; first the number of visitor enquiries received, and second, the number of awards won from the advertising industry for the campaign. Unfortunately, no consumer evaluation of the image campaign, nor a critical analysis of the campaign's effectiveness was ever conducted.

Hawes *et al.* (1991) found only 10 of 37 USA STOs commissioned market research on a regular basis. In examining the priority of research for CVBs in the USA, Masberg (1999) found the activity was regarded as essential for improving productivity, and yet the bureaus were devoting little time or funding. For example, the person responsible for research was more likely to hold a management position rather than hold the title of "research manager," and almost 80% of respondents indicated spending less than 10% of their time on research. Masberg (38) summarised the research findings as "grim and bleak." Similarly, in an investigation of the perceived importance of research in Austria by the NTO and RTOs, Dolnicar & Schoesser (2003) found:

- an underestimation of the importance of market research
- minimal research budgets relative to promotional spend
- a lack of formal criteria for evaluating market research needs
- a lack of coordination between research and marketing staff.

Sheehan & Ritchie's (1997: 113) survey of CVBs identified the following as the most significant barriers to measuring non-financial performance:

- subjectivity of measures, and the difficulty in proving their importance to sceptics
- the lack of ability to measure tourism activity
- lack of research funds
- consistency in the collection or reporting of data
- lack of cooperation from partners.

In Chapter 4, Aaker's (1991) model of consumer-based brand equity was introduced as comprising brand awareness, brand associations, brand loyalty and perceived value.

Destination Awareness

The first goal of marcom is to enhance awareness of the brand. However, as discussed in Chapter 5, measuring the number of destinations in a consumer's awareness set is likely to be prohibitive and indeed pointless, given the sheer number of destinations consumers are likely to be aware of. Awareness in itself is not therefore an indicator of attitude. What is important is understanding where the destination lies within the hierarchy of awareness levels, which range from non-awareness to an intent to visit. Of particular interest are the issues of top of mind awareness (ToMA), decision set composition and behavioural intent. One approach to this was reported by Pike (2002b), in a study of the positioning of a destination in the domestic short break market. ToMA was operationalised using an unaided question. Fishbein & Ajzen (1975) proposed any question exploring of the relationship between attitude and behaviour must include the following:

- The *behaviour*, which for the study was a holiday.
- The *target object* at which the behaviour is directed, which were domestic destinations.
- The *situation* in which the behaviour is to be performed, which was self-drive short breaks.
- The *time* at which the behaviour is to be performed, which was within the next 12 months.

The question designed to incorporate all four points was: *Of all the short break holiday destinations that are available for you to visit in the next 12 months, if you were driving, which destination first comes to mind?* The destination named is representative of ToMA at that point in time. Following this, the decision set composition was addressed by asking respondents to list the names of any other destinations they would also *probably* consider. Some researchers (e.g. Woodside & Carr 1988) have prompted respondents to mention at least three destinations. Such a prompt can however limit respondents' thinking. Identification of the decision set composition is important in understanding the competitive set of destinations, which is critical in positioning analysis. Intent to visit was measured using a seven point scale. However, without a longitudinal research component any stated intent to visit cannot be regarded as an accurate indicator of future behaviour. Tourism New Zealand reported research indicating the success of its 100% PureNZ global campaign (*Inside Tourism*, IT454, 10/6/03: 1–2). The research in the USA, U.K. and Japan focused on interactive travellers, described as "TNZ's target market of high spending, environmentally and socially aware travellers." The report cited CEO George Hickton as describing key success indicators as being the extent to which respondents in the target market expressed a desire to visit New Zealand. In each market the number of respondents indicating such intent had increased since a previous survey in 2000. It must be acknowledged that little has been published in the tourism literature concerning the relationship between stated intent and actual travel. Nevertheless, Pike's (2002b) results for ToMA, decision set composition and stated intent did provide benchmarks for five destinations, which can subsequently be tracked at future points in time as further indicators of marcom effectiveness.

Destination Loyalty

Repeat visitation is the ultimate measure of a consumer's loyalty towards a destination. Milman & Pizam (1995) demonstrated how familiarity with a domestic USA destination, measured by previous visitation, led to a more positive image and increased likelihood of repeat visits. While repeat purchase behaviour was introduced in the marketing literature during the 1940s (Howard & Sheth 1969), little research has been undertaken in the area of destination loyalty (Oppermann 1999). Accurately measuring this is likely to be beyond the capacity of most regional visitor monitors. Instead, approaches to collecting information range from intercept surveys of visitors at the destination (e.g. Gitelson & Crompton 1984; Gyte & Phelps 1989; Oppermann 1996b; Pyo *et al.* 1998) to mail surveys that captured previous visitors and non-visitors (see Crompton *et al.* 1992; Fakeye & Crompton 1991; Pike 2002b). Such studies can be useful in identifying demographic characteristics, influences, motivations, as well as behavioural patterns such as expenditure and length of stay, of those most likely to have the propensity for repeat visits. This can in turn inform more targeted promotional efforts, which are likely to be more cost-efficient than attempts to attract first time visitors (e.g. Reid & Reid 1993).

Destination Brand Associations

An important area of market research for DMOs is investigating the congruency between brand identity and brand image. This is a measure of how successfully the positioning strategy has enhanced the desired destination brand associations over a given period of time. As previously discussed what is most critical is that brand associations are strong, favourable and unique, in that order (Keller 2003). A range of qualitative and quantitative techniques are available to measure these. Pike's (2002a) review of 142 destination image studies provided a categorisation of approaches used in measuring the strength and favourability of associations.

Perceived Value

One of the most important destination brand associations is perceived value. Not surprisingly, a number of destination image studies have found attributes such as "price" and "good value for money" to be rated amongst the most important features of destinations. However there have been few investigations of the relationship between destination price and tourist demand (Crouch 2000). In particular, Crouch highlighted the need for more research into: (i) seasonality and demand management; and (ii) price bundling or collusion and anti-competitive laws. It is important for DMOs to regularly assess perceived value from non-visitors as well as visitors to the destination. Perceptions of a destination's value for money can be affected by any number of service encounters, even including the purchase of a cup of coffee. For example, TravelMole.com (24/7/03) cited a report by *The Guardian* that claimed Athens was the most expensive in Europe for a coffee and bottled water. The research, carried out by Mercer Human Resource Consulting Group, found a cup of coffee within a view of the Acropolis was double that of cafes near Paris' Eiffel Tower. The report cited the head of Greece's independent consumers' association as stating "Greeks and foreigners, a lot of foreigners, have been calling to complain about inflated prices. They are really distressed."

Organisational Performance

The organisation performance evaluation is concerned with the degree to which an entity has achieved its objectives, the appropriateness of those objectives, and the efficiency of implementation. Akehurst *et al.* (1993: 59) found the main performance indicators for European NTOs to be:

- the amount of activity of the NTO, such as the number of trade fairs attended
- promotion cost per tourist or per additional tourist, or per dollar of expenditure
- grants per job created.

An independent marketing audit is recommended as a systematic process for evaluating marketing practise. An audit would be expected to examine the following (Hooley *et al.* 2004):

- marketing environment audit — to assess changes in the macro and operating environments
- strategy audit — to assess the appropriateness and clarity of corporate and marketing objectives and the appropriateness of the resource allocation
- analysis of the structure, efficiency and interface efficiency of the marketing department
- analysis of marketing systems such as information system, planning system, and control system
- cost-effectiveness analysis
- analysis of marketing mix.

Heath & Wall (1992: 185) offered the following questions:

- Is the mission of the DMO for the region clearly stated in market-oriented terms? Is the mission feasible in terms of the region's opportunities and resources? Is the mission cognizant of tourist, environmental, business, and community interests in a balanced way?
- Are the various goals for the region clearly stated, communicated to, and understood by the major tourism businesses in the region?
- Are the goals appropriate, given the region's competitive position, resources and opportunities?

- Is information available for the review of progress toward objectives, and are the reviews conducted on a regular basis?

Elliott (1997: 12–14) proposed the following questions to address organisational efficiency:

- Have objectives been achieved for the lowest cost?
- Have resources been used efficiently?
- Has the return on public investment been reasonable?

Hunt (1990) found little correlation existed between the size of USA STO budgets and the rank or size of tourism receipts in the state. Sheehan & Ritchie (1997) suggested Hyde's (1989) measures for associations may have relevance for DMOs. These included: ratio of staff to members, ratio of staff to operating budget, and personnel costs as a percentage of operating budget.

From an analysis of the budget trends of seven NTOs from the world's top 20 destinations, Lavery (1992) proposed a set of meaningful performance indicators. One of the most critical was expenditure (cost) per visitor attracted. Of the seven destinations analysed, all but one achieved an increase in market share between 1981 and 1990. This should not be confused with increases in visitor arrivals. For example, during the same period, Canada, the destination with a decrease in market share, achieved a 20% increase in visitor arrivals. Singapore spent S$5.1 per visitor attracted in 1981, which rose to S$10.4 in 1990. In contrast, Canada's cost ratio decreased, which represented a decrease in relative spend and appears related to the decline in market share.

Destination Marketing Awards

At the 53rd annual PATA conference in 2004, Tourism New Zealand was awarded the Grand Award for Marketing, for reversing a declining share in major tourism markets during the 1990s. Under the heading "TNZ 100% Pure Champion," PATA (http://patanet.org/archives/news@pata/17mar04.htm#3) summarised the "100% Pure New Zealand" campaign success factors as:

- Pre-planning research showed that of those international travellers who recognised New Zealand as a potential destination, 87% never intended to visit — the problem was branding and proposition
- TNZ defined its target market as "interactive travellers," constituting about 4% of the international holiday travel market
- "100% Pure New Zealand" branded New Zealand's natural beauty and indigenous culture by portraying warm welcomes, interactive experiences, freedom of movement and "being at one with the way the world should be"
- The campaign's promotional media and materials were consistent, creative and of high quality, the two highlights being the PATA Gold Award-winning Web site www.newzealand.com and poster

- TNZ has successfully captured its target market, contributed to a significant increase in visitor arrivals and helped New Zealand tourism recover from recent global crises much faster than its competitors.

Other recent examples of award winning best practise in destination marketing include:

- The 2003 National Council of Destination Organizations (USA) marketing program award — Albuquerque Convention and Visitors Bureau (www.abqcvb.org).
- The IACVB 2003 Idea Fair award for Cooperative Marketing and Promotion — Tourism Vancouver (www.tourismvancouver.com)
- The 2003 National Council of State Tourism Directors (USA) award for best overall state tourism marketing program — Minnesota Office of Tourism (www. exploreminnesota.com).
- The Travel and Tourism Web Awards promoted by TravelMole.Com selected Australia.com as the "Best Tourist Board Site" for 2003. The awards are the only one in the U.K. to recognise excellence in travel trade use of the internet, and success criteria focus on clarity of purpose and ease of use.
- Best Australian destination promotion (2004) — Murraylands Tourism Marketing, South Australia (see www.murraylands.info).
- The best Victorian product marketing (2003) — Bendigo Tourism (www.bendigotourism. com).

Chapter Key Point Summary

Key point 1 — Quantification of the DMO Contribution

Isolating and quantifying a DMO's contribution to destination competitiveness is currently an impossible task. Ultimately the success of a destination will be as a result of a combination of factors, many of which will be exogenous to the DMO. Examples include the global economy, hallmark events, government visa policies, the weather, disasters, and the marketing activities of others. DMOs at all levels should be wary of staking claims to overall credit for the success of a tourism season, in exactly the same way they should not accept sole responsibility for a poor industry performance.

Key point 2 — Measures of Destination Marketing Effectiveness

There are three dimensions in modelling measures of DMO effectiveness. The first two are internal organisation measures: the appropriateness of activities, and the efficiency of the plan in relation to stakeholder expectations. The third, and more challenging task, is that of measuring the effectiveness of marcom. With the exception of advertising conversion studies there has been relatively little published about measuring the success of DMO marcom.

Key point 3 — Measuring Consumer-Based Destination Brand Equity

The reliance on short run return on investment measures of effectiveness misses the DMO's full contribution to destination competitiveness. Efforts should also be made to model and measure consumer-based destination brand equity. This requires market research to estimate levels of destination awareness, brand associations, perceived value and destination loyalty.

Additional Reading

Advertising Conversion Studies

Woodside, A. G., & Ronkainen, I. A. (1994). Improving advertising conversion studies. In: J. R. B. Ritchie, & C. R. Goeldner (Eds), *Travel, tourism, and hospitality research: A handbook for managers and researchers*. New York: Wiley.

DMO Programme Evaluations

Faulkner, B. (1997). A model for the evaluation of national tourism destination marketing programs. *Journal of Travel Research* (Winter), 23–32.
Woodside, A. G., & Sakai, M. Y. (2001). Meta-evaluations of performance audits of government tourism-marketing programs. *Journal of Travel Research, 39*, 369–379.

Determining Appropriate Advertising Budgets for Different Markets

Mazanec, J. A. (1986). Allocating an advertising budget to international travel markets. *Annals of Tourism Research, 13*, 609–634.

Destination Decision Support Systems

The concept of destination manage information systems (MIS), which represents yet another emerging area of research in the tourism literature, is beyond the scope of the chapter. Readers are referred to the following publications:

Buhalis, D., & Spada, A. (2000). Destination management systems: Criteria for success — An exploratory research. *Information Technology and Tourism, 3*, 41–58.
Chang, D. Y. (2003). Six fundamentals of strategic implementation of information systems for destination management organizations. *E-Review of Tourism Research (eRTR), 1*(4), http://ertr.tamu.edu.
Frew, A. J., Hitz, M., & O'Connor, P. (Eds) (2003). *Information and communication technologies in tourism*. New York: Springer Wein.
Ritchie, J. B. R., & Ritchie, J. R. B. (2002). A framework for an industry supported destination marketing information system. *Tourism Management, 23*, 439–454.

Sheldon, P. J. (1993). Destination information systems. *Annals of Tourism Research, 20,* 633–649.

Wöber, K. W. (2003). Information supply in tourism management by marketing decision support systems. *Tourism Management, 24,* 241–255.

You, X., O'Leary, J., & Fesenmaier, D. (2000). Knowledge management through the web: A new marketing paradigm for tourism organizations. In: B. Faulkner, G. Moscardo, & E. Laws (Eds), *Tourism in the 21st century — Lessons from experience* (pp. 181–197). London: Continuum.

Measuring Consumer-Based Brand Equity

Keller, K. L. (2003). *Strategic brand management: Building, measuring, and managing brand equity* (2nd ed.). Upper Saddle River, NJ: Pearson Education.

Visitor Surveys

WTO. (1995). *Collection and compilation of tourism statistics.* Madrid: World Tourism Organization.

Acknowledgments

Destination Marketing Organisations is a result of a combination of my experiences as a destination marketer and as an academic. In both of these worlds I have benefited from wise counsel. In the academic arena I must firstly acknowledge my appreciation to Professor Stephen Page, series editor for *Advances in Tourism Research* and external monitor for Waiariki Institute of Technology's Bachelor of Tourism degree programme, where I was previously a member of the teaching team. As an emerging academic I learned much from Stephen's candid and practical approach to tourism theory and pedagogy. During the same period I benefited immensely from the mentoring of Professor Chris Ryan at the University of Waikato. I am also indebted to many of my colleagues and students in New Zealand at Waiariki Institute of Technology, Bay of Plenty Polytechnic, and the University of Waikato, and in Australia at Central Queensland University and Queensland University of Technology. In the tourism industry I am grateful in particular to two mentors: the late Greg Fraser at Rotorua District Council, and Owen Eagles, formerly of the New Zealand Tourism Department and currently Managing Director of a leading travel wholesaler in Australia.

Most of the period of the preparation of this manuscript took place while at Central Queensland University (CQU), and I can think of no better place to write a book than Bargara Beach. I was fortunate to have much support at CQU. In particular, I acknowledge Head of School of Marketing and Tourism Associate Professor Les Killion, Associate Dean of Research in the Faculty of Business and Law Associate Professor Gayle Jennings, and the staff of the CQU library. Thanks also to those members of the on-line TRINET community who responded to calls for information.

On a more personal level, the text would simply not have been possible without the support and patience of my wife Louise, son Jesse and daughter Alex.

Glossary

ATB	Area tourist board
BHAG	Big hairy audacious goal
CAM	Commercial accommodation monitor
CVB	Convention and visitors bureau
DMO	Destination marketing organisation
EAV	Equivalent advertising value
IMC	Integrated marketing communication
LTA	Local tourism administration or Local tourism association
Marcom	Marketing communication
NTA	National tourism administration
NTO	National tourism office
PPP	Public-private partnership
ROI	Return on investment
RTB	Regional tourist board
RTO	Regional tourism organisation
ToMA	Top of mind awareness
TTRA	Travel and Tourism Research Association
VIC	Visitor information centre
VFR	Visiting friends and/or relatives
VMP	Visiting media programme

References

Aaker, D. A. (1991). *Managing brand equity*. New York: Free Press.

Aaker, D. A. (1996). *Building strong brands*. New York: Free Press.

Aaker, D. A., & Joachimsthaler, E. (2000). *Brand leadership*. New York: Free Press.

Aaker, D. A., & Shansby, J. G. (1982). Positioning your product. *Business Horizons* (May/June), 56–62.

Ahmed, Z. U. (1991a). Marketing your community: Correcting a negative image. *The Cornell HRA Quarterly* (February), 24–27.

Ahmed, Z. U. (1991b). The influence of the components of a state's tourist image on product positioning strategy. *Tourism Management* (December), 331–340.

Ahmed, Z. U. (1991c). The dark side of image marketing. *The Tourist Review*, 4, 36–37.

Ahmed, Z. U. (1996). The need for the identification of the constituents of a destination's tourist image: A promotion segmentation perspective. *Journal of Professional Services Marketing*, *14*(1), 37–60.

Ahmed, Z. U., & Krohn, F. B. (1990). Reversing the United States' declining competitiveness in the marketing of international tourism: A perspective on future policy. *Journal of Travel Research*, *29*(2), 23–29.

Akehurst, G., Bland, N., & Nevin, M. (1993). Tourism policies in the European Community member states. *International Journal of Hospitality Management*, *12*(1), 33–66.

Alcantara, N. (2003). Travel advisories reward terrorists, says Gordon. www.eturbonews.com, 24/10/03.

Alford, P. (1998). Positioning the destination product: Can Regional Tourist Boards learn from private sector practice? *Journal of Travel & Tourism Marketing*, *7*(2), 53–68.

Alison, R. I., & Uhl, K. P. (1964). Influence of beer brand identification on taste perception. *Journal of Marketing Research* (August), 36–39.

Amor, F., Calabug, C., Abellan, J., & Montfort. (1994). Barriers found in repositioning a Mediterranean 'sun and beach' product: The Valencian case. In: A. V. Seaton *et al.* (Eds), *Tourism the state of the art* (pp. 428–435). Chichester, England: Wiley.

Anderson, J. (1983). *The architecture of cognition*. Cambridge, MA: Harvard University Press.

Anderssen, P., & Colberg, R. T. (1973). Multivariate analysis in travel research: A tool for travel package design and market segmentation. *Proceedings of the 4th Annual Conference, Travel Research Association*.

Anholt, S. (2002). Nation brands: The value of 'provenance' in branding. In: N. Morgan, A. Pritchard, & R. Pride (Eds), *Destination branding* (pp. 42–56). Oxford: Butterworth-Heinemann.

Anson, C. (1999). Planning for peace: The role of tourism in the aftermath of violence. *Journal of Travel Research*, *38*, 57–61.

Anton, J., & Petouhoff, N. L. (2001). *Customer relationship management*. Sydney: Pearson Education Australia.

Ashworth, G., & Goodall, B. (1990a). *Marketing tourism places*. New York: Routledge.

Ashworth, G., & Goodall, B. (1990b). Tourist images: Marketing considerations. In: B. Goodall, & G. Ashworth (Eds), *Marketing in the tourism industry: The promotion of destination regions* (pp. 213–238). London: Routledge.

Ashworth, G. J., & Voogd, H. (1990a). *Selling the city: Marketing approaches in public sector urban planning*. London: Belhaven Press.

Ashworth, G. J., & Voogd, H. (1990b). Can places be sold for tourism? In: G. Ashworth, & B. Goodall (Eds), *Marketing tourism places* (pp. 1–16). New York: Routledge.

Assael, H. (1971). Perceptual mapping to reposition brands. *Journal of Advertising Research, 11*, 39–42.

ATC (2003). http://www.atc.net.au/brand.asp, Accessed 20 December.

ATC (2004). *Corporate Plan: 2004–2009*. Australian Tourist Commission. Accessed on-line at: http://www.atc.net.au/cms/pdf/atc_corporateplan_0409.pdf, 04/04/04.

Ateljevic, I. (1998). *Circuits of tourism: (Re)Producing the place of Rotorua, New Zealand*. Unpublished Ph.D. thesis, University of Auckland.

Ateljevic, I., & Doorne, S. (2000). Local government and tourism development: Issues and constraints of public sector entrepreneurship. *New Zealand Geographer, 56*(2), 25–31.

Australian Department of Industry, Tourism and Resources (2001). *Destination competitiveness: Development of a model with application to Australia and the Republic of Korea*. Canberra: Industry Tourism Resources Division.

Axelrod, J. N. (1968). Attitude measures that predict purchase. *Journal of Advertising Research, 8*(1), 3–17.

Baker, K. G., Hozier, Jr., G. C., & Rogers, R. D. (1994). Marketing research theory and methodology and the tourism industry: A nontechnical discussion. *Journal of Travel Research* (Winter), 3–7.

Baloglu, S. (1998). An empirical investigation of attitude theory for tourist destinations: A comparison of visitors and nonvisitors. *Journal of Hospitality & Tourism Research, 22*(3), 211–224.

Baloglu, S., & Brinberg, D. (1997). Affective images of tourism destinations. *Journal of Travel Research* (Spring), 11–15.

Baloglu, S., & Mangaloglu, M. (2001). Tourism destination images of Turkey, Egypt, Greece, and Italy as perceived by U.S. based tour operators and travel agents. *Tourism Management, 22*, 1–9.

Baloglu, S., & McCleary, K. W. (1999a). A model of destination image. *Annals of Tourism Research, 26*(4), 868–897.

Baloglu, S., & McCleary, K. W. (1999b). U.S. international pleasure travelers' images of four Mediterranean destinations: A comparison of visitors and nonvisitors. *Journal of Travel Research, 38*(November), 144–152.

Barich, H., & Kotler, P. (1991). A framework for marketing image management. *Sloan Management Review, 32*(2), 94–104.

Barney, J. (1991). Firm resources and sustained competitive advantage. *Journal of Management, 17*(1), 99–120.

Barney, J. (1996). *Gaining and sustaining competitive advantage*. Reading, MA: Addison-Wesley.

Baum, T. (1994). The development and implementation of national tourism policies. *Tourism Management, 15*(3), 185–192.

Beeton, S. (2001). Smiling for the camera: The influence of film audiences on a budget tourism destination. *Tourism, Culture & Communication, 3*, 15–25.

Beirman, D. (2002). Marketing of tourism destinations during a prolonged crisis: Israel and the Middle East. *Journal of Vacation Marketing, 8*(2), 167–176.

Beirman, D. (2003a). *Restoring destinations in crisis*. Crows Nest, NSW: Allen & Unwin.

Beirman, D. (2003b). Kenyan tourism's recovery. www.eturbonews, 1 October.

Belch, E. G., & Belch, M. A. (2004). *Advertising and promotion* (6th ed.). New York: McGraw-Hill.

Belk, R. W. (1975). Situational variables and consumer behavior. *Journal of Consumer Research*, 2(December), 157–164.

Bergman, J. (2004). A peek into hell's pit. *The Sunday Mail* (February 22), 6, Brisbane.

Blalock, C. (2000). Slow, steady approach might win funds for tourism promotion. *Hotel & Motel Management*, 215(11), 10.

Bleasedale, S., & Kwarko, P. (2000). Is there a role for visiting friends and relatives in Ghana's tourism development strategy? In: M. Robinson, N. Evans, P. Long, R. Sharpley, & J. Swarbrooke (Eds), *Management, marketing and the political economy of tourism* (pp. 13–22). Sunderland: Centre for Travel & Tourism.

Bonham, C., & Mak, J. (1996). Private versus public financing of state destination promotion. *Journal of Travel Research* (Fall), 3–10.

Bowes, S. (1990). The role of the tourist board. In: B. Goodall, & G. Ashworth (Eds), *Marketing in the tourist industry: The promotion of destination regions*. London: Routledge.

Bramwell, B., & Rawding, L. (1996). Tourism marketing images of industrial cities. *Annals of Tourism Research*, 23(1), 201–221.

Braynart Group (1980). *100 Years of Rotorua*. Rotorua.

Brewton, C., & Withiam, G. (1998). United States tourism policy: Alive, but not well. *Cornell Hotel and Restaurant Administration Quarterly* (July), 50–59.

Brown (2003). Albania bids to boost tourism. www.eTurboNews.com, 21 July.

BTR (2002). *Travel by Australians 2001: Annual results of the national visitor survey 2001*. Canberra: Bureau of Tourism Research.

Buck, R. C. (1978). Towards a synthesis in tourism theory. *Annals of Tourism Research*, 5(1), 110–111.

Buckley, P. J., & Witt, S. F. (1985). Tourism in difficult areas: Case studies of Bradford, Bristol, Glasgow and Hamm. *Tourism Management* (September), 205–213.

Buhalis, D. (2000). Marketing the competitive destination of the future. *Tourism Management*, 21(1), 97–116.

Buhalis, D., & Cooper, C. (1998). Conference report: The future of traditional tourist destinations. *Progress in Tourism and Hospitality Research*, 4, 85–88.

Buhalis, D., & Spada, A. (2000). Destination management systems: Criteria for success – An exploratory approach. *Information Technology & Tourism*, 3, 41–58.

Bull, A. (1995). *The economics of travel & tourism*. Melbourne: Longman.

Burke, W. L., & Schoeffler, S. (1980). *Brand awareness as a tool for profitability*. Strategic Planning institute, Boston: Cahners.

Burns, J. (1994). The 1990s spawn a new boom market. *Travelweek*, 16(February), 23–24.

Butler, R. W., & Baum, T. (1999). The tourism potential of the peace dividend. *Journal of Travel Research*, 38, 24–29.

Cahn, L. I. (1994). All New York cheers tax cut. August, 19.

Cai, L. A. (2002). Cooperative branding for rural destinations. *Annals of Tourism Research*, 29(3), 720–742.

Calantone, R. J., & Mazanec, J. A. (1991). Marketing management and tourism. *Annals of Tourism Research*, 18, 101–119.

Cameron, M. (2002). Free-for-all at tourism event. *The Courier Mail* (24 May), 9.

Carroll, P. (1991). Policy issues and tourism. In: P. Carroll, K. Donohue, M. McGovern, & J. McMillen (Eds), *Tourism in Australia* (pp. 20–43). Sydney: Harcourt Brace Jovanovich.

Carson, D., Beattie, S., & Gove, B. (2003). Tourism management capacity of local government – An analysis of Victorian local government. In: R. W. Braithwaite, & R. L. Braithwaite (Eds), *Riding the wave of tourism and hospitality research – Proceedings of the Council of Australian*

University Tourism and Hospitality Education Conference. Coffs Harbour: Southern Cross University, Lismore. CD-ROM.

Chacko, H. E. (1997). Positioning a tourism destination to gain a competitive edge. *Asia Pacific Journal of Tourism Research*, *1*(2), 69–75.

Chacko, H. E., & Fenich, G. G. (2000). Determining the importance of U.S. convention destination attributes. *Journal of Vacation Marketing*, *6*(3), 211–220.

Chamberlain, J. (1992). On the tourism trail: A nice little earner, but what about the cost? *North & South* (September), 88–97.

Chon, K. (1990). The role of destination image in tourism: A review and discussion. *The Tourist Review*, *45*(2), 2–9.

Chon, K. (1991). Tourism destination image: Marketing implications. *Tourism Management* (March), 68–72.

Chon, K., Weaver, P. A., & Kim, C. Y. (1991). Marketing your community: Image analysis in Norfolk. *The Cornell HRA Quarterly* (February), 31–36.

Chon, K. S., & Singh, A. (1995). Marketing resorts to 2000: Review of trends in the USA. *Tourism Management*, *16*(6), 463–469.

Choy, D. J. L. (1991). Tourism planning – The case for 'market failure'. *Tourism Management*, *12*(4), 313–330.

Choy, D. J. L. (1993). Alternative roles of national tourism organizations. *Tourism Management*, *14*(5), 357–365.

Christine, B. (1995). Disaster management: Lessons learned. *Risk Management* (October), 19–34.

Clow, K. E., & Baack, D. (2004). *Integrated advertising, promotion, and marketing communications* (2nd ed.). Upper Saddle River, NJ: Prentice-Hall.

Cohen, E. (1972). Toward a sociology of international tourism. *Social Research*, *39*, 164–182.

Collier, A. (1997). *Principles of tourism – A New Zealand perspective* (4th ed.). Auckland: Addison Wesley/Longman.

Collins, J. C., & Porras, J. I. (1997). *Built to last*. New York: Harper-Collins.

Conlin, M. V. (1995). Rejuvenation planning for island tourism: The Bermuda example. In: M. V. Conlin, & T. Baum (Eds), *Island tourism: Management principles and practice*. Chichester: Wiley.

Cossens, J. (1994a). *Destination image: Another fat marketing word? Tourism Down Under Research Conference Proceedings*. Palmerston North: Massey University.

Cossens, J. J. (1994b). *The application of branding and positioning to destination Marketing: A study of the relationship between destination image and destination position using multidimensional scaling*. Unpublished Ph.D. thesis. Dunedin: University of Otago.

Cousins, J. (2001). 2500 slogans vie for prize. *Bay of Plenty Times*, *1*, Tauranga.

Coventry, N. (1998). *Inside Tourism* (April 24), 205.

Coventry, N. (2001). *Inside Tourism* (May 03), 352.

Coyne, K. P. (1986). Sustainable competitive advantage – What it is, what it isn't. *Business Horizons* (January–February), 54–61.

Craik, J. (1991). *Government promotion of tourism: The role of the Queensland tourist and travel corporation*. Brisbane: The Centre for Australian Public Sector Management, Griffith University.

Crockett, S. R., & Wood, L. J. (1999). Brand Western Australia: A totally integrated approach to destination branding. *Journal of Vacation Marketing*, *5*(3), 276–289.

Crompton, J. (1992). Structure of vacation destination choice sets. *Annals of Tourism Research*, *19*, 420–434.

Crompton, J. L. (1979a). An assessment of the image of Mexico as a vacation destination and the influence of geographical location upon that image. *Journal of Travel Research* (Spring), 18–23.

Crompton, J. L. (1979b). Motivations for pleasure vacation. *Annals of Tourism Research* (October/December), 408–424.

Crompton, J. L., Fakeye, P. C., & Lue, C. (1992). Positioning: The example of the Lower Rio Grande Valley in the winter long stay destination market. *Journal of Travel Research* (Fall), 20–26.

Crouch, G. I. (2000). Services research in destination marketing: A retrospective appraisal. *International Journal of Hospitality & Tourism Administration, 1*(2), 65–85.

Croy, G. (2004). The Lord of the Rings, Middle Earth, New Zealand and tourism. Presentation. 14th International Research Conference of the Council for Australian University Tourism and Hospitality Education. Brisbane: University of Queensland.

Curtis, J. (2001). Branding a state: The evolution of Brand Oregon. *Journal of Vacation Marketing, 7*(1), 75–81.

Cushman, G. (1990). Tourism in New Zealand – 1990. *World Leisure and Recreation, 32*(1), 12–16.

Dahles, H. (1998). Redefining Amsterdam as a tourist destination. *Annals of Tourism Research, 25*(1), 55–69.

Dann, G. M. S. (1977). Anomie, ego-enhancement and tourism. *Annals of Tourism Research* (March/April), 184–194.

Dann, G. M. S. (1981). Tourist motivation: An appraisal. *Annals of Tourism Research, 8*(2), 187–219.

Dann, G. M. S. (1996). Tourists' images of a destination – An alternative analysis. *Journal of Travel & Tourism Marketing, 5*(1/2), 41–55.

Dann, G. M. S. (2000). Differentiating destination in the language of tourism: Harmless hype or promotional irresponsibility. *Tourism Recreation Research, 25*(2), 63–72.

Dann, G., Nash, D., & Pearce, P. (1988). Methodology in tourism research. *Annals of Tourism Research, 15*, 1–28.

Dascalu, R. (1997). Romania plans reparations for nationalised hotels. *Reuters* (August 11).

Davidson, R., & Maitland, R. (1997). *Tourism destinations*. London: Hodder & Stoughton.

Davies, B. (1990). The economics of short breaks. *International Journal of Hospitality Management, 9*(2), 103–109.

de Chernatony, L. (1993). Categorizing brands: Evolutionary processes underpinned by two key dimensions. *Journal of Marketing Management, 9*, 173–188.

de Haan, T., Ashworth, G., & Stabler, M. (1990). The tourist destination as product: The case of Languedoc. In: G. Ashworth, & B. Goodall (Eds), *Marketing tourism places* (pp. 156–169). New York: Routledge.

d'Hauteserre, A.-M. (2000). Lessons in managed destination competitiveness: The case of Foxwoods Casino Resort. *Tourism Management, 21*(1), 23–32.

Dichter, E. (1985). What's in an image. *The Journal of Consumer Marketing, 2*(1), 75–81.

Dillon, W. R., Domzal, T., & Madden, T. J. (1986). Evaluating alternative product positioning strategies. *Journal of Advertising Research* (August/September), 29–35.

Dimanche, F., & Lepetic, A. (1999). New Orleans tourism and crime: A case study. *Journal of Travel Research, 38*, 19–23.

DiMingo, E. (1988). The fine art of positioning. *The Journal of Business Strategy* (March/April), 34–38.

Dobni, D., & Zinkhan, G. M. (1990). In search of brand image: A foundation analysis. *Advances in Consumer Research, 17*, 110–119.

Doering, T. R. (1979). Geographical aspects of State travel marketing in the USA. *Annals of Tourism Research* (July/September), 307–317.

Dolnicar, S., & Mazanec, J. A. (1998). Destination marketing: Reinventing the wheel or conceptual progress. In: P. Keller (Ed.), *Destination marketing – Reports of the 48th AIEST Congress* (pp. 55–87). Marakech.

Dolnicar, S., & Schoesser, C. M. (2003). Market research in Australian NTO and RTOs: Is the research homework done before spending millions? In: R. W. Braithwaite, & R. L. Braithwaite (Eds), *Riding the wave of tourism and hospitality research – Proceedings of the Council of Australian University Tourism and Hospitality Education Conference*. Coffs Harbour: Southern Cross University. CD-ROM.

Donnelly, M. P., & Vaske, J. J. (1997). Factors affecting membership in a tourism promotion authority. *Journal of Travel Research* (Spring), 50–55.

Dore, L., & Crouch, G. I. (2003). Promoting destinations: An exploratory study of publicity programmes used by national tourism organizations. *Journal of Vacation Marketing*, *9*(2), 137–151.

Dredge, D. (2001). Local government tourism planning and policy-making in New South Wales: Institutional development and historical legacies. *Current Issues in Tourism*, *4*(2/4), 355–380.

Driscoll, A., Lawson, R., & Niven, B. (1994). Measuring tourists' destination perceptions. *Annals of Tourism Research*, *21*(3), 499–511.

Drucker, P. (1995). *Managing in a time of great change*. Oxford: Butterworth-Heinemann.

Duncan, T. (2002). *IMC: Using advertising and promotion to build brands*. McGraw-Hill.

Dwyer, L., Forsyth, P., & Rao, P. (1999). Tourism price competitiveness and journey purpose. *Tourism*, *47*(4), 283–299.

Dwyer, L., Forsyth, P., & Rao, P. (2000). The price competitiveness of travel and tourism: A comparison of 19 destinations. *Tourism Management*, *21*(1), 9–22.

Echtner, C. M. (1991). *The measurement of tourism destination image*. MBA Thesis. University of Calgary Faculty of Management.

Echtner, C. M., & Ritchie, J. R. B. (1991). The meaning and measurement of destination image. *The Journal of Tourism Studies*, *2*(2), 2–12.

Echtner, C. M., & Ritchie, J. R. B. (1993). The measurement of destination image: An empirical assessment. *Journal of Travel Research*, *31*(3), 3–13.

Edgar, D. A. (1997). Capacity management in the short break market. *International Journal of Contemporary Hospitality Management*, *9*(2), 55–59.

Edgar, D. A., Litteljohn, D. L., Allardyce, M. L., & Wanhill, S. (1994). Commercial short break holiday breaks – The relationship between market structure, competitive advantage and performance. In: A. V. Seaton (Ed.), *Tourism the state of the art* (pp. 383–401). Chichester: Wiley.

Edgell, D. (1984). U.S. government policy on international tourism. *Tourism Management*, *5*(1), 67–70.

Edlin (1999). Too much tax to tourism? *Management* (May), 60.

Egan, J. (2001). *Relationship marketing*. Sydney: Pearson Education Australia.

Ehemann, J. (1977). What kind of place is Ireland: An image perceived through the American media. *Journal of Travel Research*, *16*, 28–30.

Ellerbrock, M. J. (1981). Improving coupon conversion studies: A comment. *Journal of Travel Research*, *4*, 37–38.

Elliott, J. (1997). *Tourism   Politics and public sector management*. London: Routledge.

Embacher, J., & Buttle, F. (1989). A repertory grid analysis of Austria's image as a summer vacation destination. *Journal of Travel Research* (Winter), 3–7.

English (2000). Government intervention in tourism: Case study of an English seaside resort. In: M. Robinson, N. Evans, P. Long, R. Sharpley, & J. Swarbrooke (Eds), *Management, marketing and the political economy of travel and tourism* (pp. 86–101). Sunderland: Centre for Travel and Tourism.

Euromonitor (1987). *Weekend breaks and day trips: The U.K. market for short break holidays and day trips*. London: Euromonitor.

Fache, W. (Ed.) (1990). *Shortbreak holidays*. Rotterdam: Center Parcs.

Fache, W. (1994). Short break holidays. In: S. Witt, & L. Moutinho (Eds), *Tourism marketing and management handbook* (2nd ed., pp. 459–467). Hertfordshire: Prentice-Hall.

Fakeye, P. C., & Crompton, J. L. (1991). Image differences between prospective, first time, and repeat visitors to the Lower Rio Grande Valley. *Journal of Travel Research, 30*, 10–16.

Faulkner, B. (1997). A model for evaluation of national tourism destination marketing programs. *Journal of Travel Research* (Winter), 23–32.

Faulkner, B. (1999). *Tourism disasters: Towards a generic model.* Gold Coast: CRC Sustainable Tourism.

Faulkner, F. (2001). Towards a framework for tourism disaster management. *Tourism Management, 22*, 135–147.

Faulkner, B., Oppermann, M., & Fredline, E. (1999). Destination competitiveness: An exploratory examination of South Australia's core attractions. *Journal of Vacation Marketing, 5*(2), 125–139.

Faulkner, B., & Vikulov, S. (2001). Katherine, washed out one day, back on track the next: A post-mortem of a tourism disaster. *Tourism Management, 22*(4), 331–344.

Fayos-Solá, E. (2002). Globalization, tourism policy and tourism education. *Acta Turistica, 14*(1), 5–12.

Ferguson, B. (2003). Tourism chiefs under fire for festivals snub. *Evening News* (15 August), Edinburgh.

Ferrario, F. F. (1979a). The evaluation of tourism resources: An applied methodology. Part 1. *Journal of Travel Research* (Winter), 18–22.

Ferrario, F. F. (1979b). The evaluation of tourism resources: An applied methodology. Part 2. *Journal of Travel Research* (Spring), 24–30.

Fishbein, M. (1967). *Readings in attitude theory and measurement.* New York: Wiley.

Fishbein, M., & Ajzen, I. (1975). *Belief, attitude, intention and behavior: An introduction to theory and research.* Philippines: Addison-Wesley.

Fisher, R. J., & Price, L. L. (1991). International pleasure travel motivations and post-vacation cultural attitude change. *Journal of Leisure Research, 23*(3), 193–208.

Flagstaff, A., & Hope, C. A. (2001). Scandinavian winter Antecedents, concepts and empirical observations underlying a destination umbrella branding model. *Tourism Review, 56*(1/2), 5–12.

Foreman, M. (2003). Tourism chomping through old grants. *The Independent*, 17 July.

Formica, S., & Littlefield, J. (2000). National tourism organizations: A promotional plans framework. *Journal of Hospitality & Leisure Marketing, 7*(1), 103–119.

Forsyte Research (2000). Topline results of the 1999 domestic tourism study. New Zealand Tourism Conference. Wellington.

Frew, A. J., Hitz, M., & O'Connor, P. (2003). *Information and communication technologies in tourism 2003.* New York: Springer Wien.

Frisby, E. (2002). Communicating in a crisis: The British Tourist Authority's responses to the foot-and-mouth outbreak and 11th September 2001. *Journal of Vacation Marketing, 9*(1), 89–100.

Frost, W. (2003). Braveheart-ed Ned Kelly – Destination image and historic films. Taking Tourism to the Limits – An International Interdisciplinary Conference in the Waikato. University of Waikato.

Fyall, A., Callod, C., & Edwards, B. (2003). Relationship marketing: The challenge for destinations. *Annals of Tourism Research, 30*(3), 644–659.

Galbraith, J. R., & Lawler, E. E. (1993). *Organizing for the future.* San Fransisco: Jossey-Bass.

Gardner, B. B., & Levy, S. J. (1955). The product and the brand. *Harvard Business Review* (March–April), 33–39.

Gartner, W. C. (1986). Temporal influences on image change. *Annals of Tourism Research, 13*, 635–644.

Gartner, W. C. (1993). Image information process. *Journal of Travel & Tourism Marketing, 2(2/3)*, 191–215.

Gartner, W. C. (1996). *Tourism development – Principles, processes, and policies*. New York: Wiley.

Gartner, W. C., & Hunt, J. D. (1987). An analysis of state image change over a twelve-year period (1971–1983). *Journal of Travel Research* (Fall), 15–19.

Gartner, W. C., & Shen, J. (1992). The impact of Tiananmen Square on China's tourism image. *Journal of Travel Research* (Spring), 47–52.

Gartrell, R. B. (1992). Convention and visitor bureau: Current issues in management and marketing. *Journal of Travel & Tourism Marketing, 1(2)*, 71–78.

Gartrell, R. B. (1994). *Destination marketing for convention and visitor bureaus*. Dubuque, IA: Kendall/Hunt Publishing Company.

Gatty, B., & Blalock, C. (1997). New organization brings new energy to marketing the U.S. *Hotel & Motel Management, 17*(17 February).

Gearing, C. E., Swart, W. W., & Var, T. (1974). Establishing a measure of touristic attractiveness. *Journal of Travel Research, 12(4)*, 1–8.

Gee, C. Y., & Makens, J. C. (1985). The tourism board: Doing it right. *The Cornell Quarterly, 26(3)*, 25–33.

Getz, D., Anderson, D., & Sheehan, L. (1997). Destination planning and product development among Canadian convention and visitor bureaus. In: M. Joppe (Ed.), *From the ground up – Tourism infrastructure – Proceedings of the TTRA Conference*. Calgary.

Getz, D., Anderson, D., & Sheehan, L. (1998). Roles, issues, and strategies for convention and visitors' bureaus in destination planning and product development: A survey of Canadian bureaux. *Tourism Management, 19(4)*, 331–340.

Gilbert, D. (1990). Strategic marketing planning for national tourism. *The Tourist Review, 1*, 18–27.

Gilmore, F. (2002). Branding for success. In: N. Morgan, A. Pritchard, & R. Pride (Eds), *Destination branding* (pp. 57–65). Oxford: Butterworth-Heinemann.

Gilmore, F. (2002b). A country – Can it be repositioned? Spain – The success story of country branding. *Journal of Brand Management, 9(4/5)*, 281–293.

Gitelson, R. J., & Crompton, J. L. (1984). Insights into the repeat vacation phenomenon. *Annals of Tourism Research, 11*, 199–217.

Gnoth, G. (1998). Branding tourism destinations. Conference report. *Annals of Tourism Research, 25(3)*, 758–760.

Gnoth, G. (2002). Leveraging export brands through a tourism destination brand. *Brand Management, 9(4/5)*, 262–280.

Go, F. (1987). Selling Canada. *Travel & Tourism Analyst* (December), 17–29.

Go, F., & Zhang, W. (1997). Applying importance-performance analysis to Beijing as an international meeting destination. *Journal of Travel Research* (Spring), 42–49.

Go, F. M., & Govers, R. (2000). Integrated quality management for tourist destinations: A European perspective on achieving competitiveness. *Tourism Management, 21(1)*, 79–88.

Godfrey, K., & Clarke, J. (2000). *The tourism development handbook*. London: Continuum.

Goeldner, C. R., Brent Ritchie, J. R., & McIntosh, R. W. (2000). *Tourism – Principles, practices, philosophies*. New York: Wiley.

Gold, J. R., & Ward, S. V. (1994). *Place promotion*. Chichester: Wiley.

Goodall, B., & Ashworth, G. (1990). *Marketing in the tourism industry: The promotion of destination regions*. London: Routledge.

Goodall, B., Radburn, M., & Stabler, M. (1988). *Market opportunity sets for tourism*. Reading: University of Reading.

Goodrich, J. N. (1978a). The relationship between preferences for and perceptions of vacation destinations: Application of a choice model. *Journal of Travel Research* (Fall), 8–13.

Goodrich, J. N. (1978b). A new approach to image analysis through multidimensional scaling. *Journal of Travel Research, 16*(3), 3–7.

Grabler, K. (1997a). The city travellers' view. In: J. A. Mazanec (Ed.), *International city tourism* (pp. 167–184). London: Pinter.

Grabler, K. (1997b). Perceptual mapping and positioning of tourist cities. In: J. A. Mazanec (Ed.), *International city tourism* (pp. 101–113). London: Pinter.

Gratton, C. (1990). The economics of shortbreak holidays. In: W. Fache (Ed.), *Shortbreak holidays*. Rotterdam: Center Parcs.

Gray, H. P. (1970). *International travel – International trade*. Lexington, MA: Heath Lexington Books.

Greenwood, J. (1993). Business interest groups in tourism governance. *Tourism Management, 14*(5), 335–348.

Gregory, R. (1987). *The Oxford companion to the mind*. Oxford University Press.

Gretzel, U., Yuan, Y., & Fesenmaier, D. R. (2000). Preparing for the new economy: Advertising strategies and change in destination marketing organizations. *Journal of Travel Research, 39*(2), 146–156.

Gronhaug, K., & Heide, M. (1992). Stereotyping in country advertising: An experimental study. *European Journal of Marketing, 26*(5), 56–67.

Grönroos, C. (1994). From marketing mix to relationship marketing: Towards a paradigm shift in marketing. *Management Decision, 32*(2), 4–20.

Gunn, C. (1988). *Vacationscape: Designing tourist regions* (2nd ed.). Austin: Bureau of Business Research, University of Texas.

Gunn, C. (1994). *Tourism planning: Basics, concepts, cases* (3rd ed.). London: Taylor & Francis.

Gyte, D. M., & Phelps, A. (1989). Patterns of destination repeat business: British tourists in Mallorca, Spain. *Journal of Travel Research* (Summer), 24–28.

Haahti, A. J. (1986). Finland's competitive position as a destination. *Annals of Tourism Research, 13*, 11–35.

Hall, C. M. (1994). *Tourism and politics – Policy power and place*. Chichester: Wiley.

Hall, C. M. (1998). *Introduction to tourism: Development, dimensions and issues* (3rd ed.). Sydney: Pearson Education Australia.

Hall, C. M. (1999). Rethinking collaboration and partnership: A public policy perspective. *Journal of Sustainable Tourism, 7*(3/4), 274–289.

Hall, D. (1999). Destination branding, niche marketing and national image projection in Central and Eastern Europe. *Journal of Vacation Marketing, 5*(3), 227–237.

Hall, D. (2002). Brand development, tourism and national identity: The re-imaging of former Yugoslavia. *Journal of Brand Management, 9*(4/5), 323–334.

Hanyu, K. (1993). The affective meaning of Tokyo: Verbal and non-verbal approaches. *Journal of Environmental Psychology, 13*, 161–172.

Harvey, C. (2003). Farce looms as France opts for reserves. *The Australian*, 21.

Hashimoto, A., & Telfer, D. J. (2001). Tourism distribution channels in Canada. In: D. Buhalis, & E. Laws (Eds), *Communication issues in NTO distribution strategies* (pp. 243–258). London: Continuum.

Hawes, D. K., Taylor, D. T., & Hampe, G. D. (1991). Destination marketing by States. *Journal of Travel Research* (Summer), 11–17.

Hazbun, W. (2000). Enclave orientalism: The state, tourism, and the politics of post-national development in the Arab world. In: M. Robinson, N. Evans, P. Long, R. Sharpley, & J. Swarbrooke (Eds), *Management, marketing and the political economy of travel and tourism* (pp. 191–205). Sunderland: Centre for Travel & Tourism.

Heath, E., & Wall, G. (1992). *Marketing tourism destinations: A strategic planning approach.* New York: Wiley.

Hefner, F., Crotts, J. C., & Flowers, J. (2001). The cost-benefit model as applied to tourism development in the state of South Carolina, USA. *Tourism Economics, 7*(2), 163–175.

Henderson, J. C. (2000). Selling places: The new Asia-Singapore brand. In: M. Robinson, N. Evans, P. Long, R. Sharpley, & J. Swarbrooke (Eds), *Management, marketing and the political economy of travel and tourism* (pp. 207–218). Sunderland: Centre for Travel & Tourism.

Henderson, J. (2002). Managing a tourism crisis in Southeast Asia: The role of national tourism organizations. *International Journal of Hospitality & Tourism Administration, 3*(1), 85–105.

Henshall, B. D., & Roberts, R. (1985). Comparative assessment of tourist generating markets for New Zealand. *Annals of Tourism Research, 12*, 219–238.

Henshall, B. D., Roberts, R., & Leighton, A. (1985). Fly-drive tourists: Motivation and destination choice factors. *Journal of Travel Research* (Winter), 23–27.

Hindley, D. (1989). *New Zealand guides: Rotorua/Bay of plenty.* Wellington: Government Printing Office.

Holcolm, B. (1999). Marketing cities for tourism. In: D. R. Judd, & S. S. Fainstein (Eds), *The tourist city* (pp. 54–70). Newhaven: Yale University Press.

Hollingshead, K. (2001). Policy in paradise: The history of incremental politics in the tourism of island-state Fiji. *Tourism, 49*(4), 327–348.

Holloway, J. C. (1994). *The business of tourism.* Harlow, Essex: Longman.

Holloway, J. C., & Robinson, C. (1995). *Marketing for tourism* (3rd ed.). Harlow, Essex: Addison Wesley Longman.

Hooley, G. J., & Saunders, J. (1993). *Competitive positioning: The key to market success.* Hertfordshire: Prentice-Hall International.

Hooley, G., Saunders, J., & Piercy, N. (2004). *Marketing strategy and competitive positioning.* Harlow, Essex: Prentice-Hall.

Hoover (2003, 11 August). Industry execs appointed to new tourism board. www.bizjournals.com.

Hopper, P. (2002). Marketing London in a difficult climate. *Journal of Vacation Marketing, 9*(1), 81–88.

Horn, C., Fairweather, J. R., & Simmons, D. C. (2000). Evolving community response to tourism and change in Rotorua. Rotorua case study Report No. 14. Christchurch: Lincoln University.

Howard, J. A. (1963). *Marketing management: Analysis and planning.* Homewood, ILL: Irwin.

Howard, J. A., & Sheth, J. N. (1969). *The theory of buyer behavior.* New York: Wiley.

Howie, F. (2003). *Managing the tourist destination.* London: Continuum.

Hu, Y., & Ritchie, J. R. B. (1993). Measuring destination attractiveness: A contextual approach. *Journal of Travel Research, 32*(2), 25–34.

Hudson, S., & Shephard, G. W. H. (1998). Measuring service quality at tourist destinations: An application of importance – Performance analysis to an alpine ski resort. *Journal of Travel & Tourism Marketing, 7*(3), 61–77.

Hughes, H. L. (2002). Marketing gay tourism in Manchester: New market for urban tourism or destruction of 'gay space'? *Journal of Vacation Marketing, 9*(2), 152–163.

Hunt, J. D. (1975). Image as a factor in tourism development. *Journal of Travel Research* (Winter), 1–7.

ILO (2003, 14 May). *ILO sees further tourism job losses due to travel woes – SARS, economic doldrums cited as causes.* Media Release. International Labour Organization.

Inkson, K., & Kolb, D. (1998). *Management.* Auckland: Addison Wesley Longman.

Ioannides, D. (2003). The economics of tourism in host communities. In: S. Singh, T. J. Timothy, & R. K. Dowling (Eds), *Tourism in destination communities* (pp. 37–54). Oxon: CABI Publishing.

Ioannides, D., & Aspost, Y. (1998). Political instability, war, and tourism in Cyprus: Effects, management, and prospects for recovery. *Journal of Travel Research, 38*(August), 51–56.

Jacoby, J. (1984). Perspectives on information overload. *Journal of Consumer Research, 10,* 432–435.

Javalgi, R. G., Thomas, E. G., & Rao, S. R. (1992). U.S. pleasure travellers' perceptions of selected European destinations. *European Journal of Marketing, 26*(7), 45–64.

Jeffries, D. (1989). Selling Britain – A case for privatisation? *Travel & Tourism Analyst, 1,* 69–81.

Jeffries, D. (2001). *Governments and tourism.* Oxford: Butterworth-Heinemann.

Jenkins, C. L. (1991). Development strategies. In: L. J. Lickorish (Ed.), *Developing tourism destinations: Policies and perspectives* (pp. 59–118). Harlow, Essex: Longman.

Jenkins, C. L. (1999). Tourism academics and tourism practitioners – Bridging the great divide. In: D. G. Pearce, & R. W. Butler (Eds), *Contemporary issues in tourism development* (pp. 52–64). London: Routledge.

Jenkins, J. (1995). A comparative study of tourist organisations in Australia and Canada. *Australia-Canada Studies, 13*(1), 73–108.

Jenkins, J. (2000). The dynamics of regional tourism organisations in New South Wales, Australia: History, structures and operations. *Current Issues in Tourism, 3*(3), 175–203.

Jenkins, O. H. (1999). Understanding and measuring tourist destination images. *International Journal of Tourism Research, 1,* 1–15.

Johnson, G., & Scholes, K. (2002). *Exploring corporate strategy* (6th ed.). Harlow, Essex: Pearson Education.

Johnson, R. R., & Messmer, D. J. (1991). The effect of advertising on hierarchical stages in vacation destination choice. *Journal of Advertising Research* (December), 18–24.

Kearsley, G. W., Coughlan, D. P., & Ritchie, B. W. (1998). *Images of New Zealand holiday destinations: An international and domestic perspective.* Dunedin: University of Otago Centre for Tourism.

Kelly, I., & Nankervis, K. (2001). *Visitor destinations.* Milton, Qld: Wiley.

Keller, K. L. (1993). Conceptualizing, measuring, and managing customer-based brand equity. *Journal of Marketing, 57*(January), 1–22.

Keller, K. L. (2003). *Strategic brand management.* Upper Saddle River, NJ: Prentice-Hall.

Keller, P. (1998). Destination marketing: Strategic questions. In: P. Keller (Ed.), *Destination marketing – Reports of the 48th AIEST Congress, Marakech* (pp. 9–22).

Keller, P. (2000). Destination marketing: Strategic areas of inquiry. In: M. Manente, & M. Cerato (Eds), *From destination to destination marketing and management* (pp. 29–44). Venice: CISET.

Kerr, B., & Wood, R. C. (2000). Tourism policy and politics in a devolved Scotland. In: M. Robinson, N. Evans, P. Long, R. Sharpley, & J. Swarbrooke (Eds), *Management, marketing and the political economy of travel and tourism* (pp. 284–296). Sunderland: Centre for Travel & Tourism.

Kim, S., Crompton, J. L., & Botha, C. (2000). Responding to competition: A strategy for Sun/Lost City, South Africa. *Tourism Management, 21*(1), 33–41.

King, B. (1994). Australian attitudes to domestic and international resort holidays: A comparison of Fiji and Queensland. In: A. V. Seaton (Ed.), *Tourism: The state of the art* (pp. 347–358). Chichester: Wiley.

King, S. (1970). Development of the brand. *Advertising Quarterly* (Summer), 6–14.

King, S. (1991). Brand-building in the 1990s. *Journal of Marketing Management, 7,* 3–13.

Kleinman, M., & Bashford, S. (2002). BTA set for 40m blitz to tempt back tourists. *Marketing* (Feb 28), 6.

Kolb, D. A., Rubin, I. M., & Osland, J. S. (1995). *Organizational behavior – An experiential approach.* Englewood Cliffs, NJ: Prentice-Hall.

Kotler, P., Adam, S., Brown, L., & Armstrong, G. (2003). *Principles of marketing* (2nd ed.). Sydney: Prentice-Hall.

Kotler, P., Bowen, J., & Makens, J. (1999). *Marketing for hospitality and tourism* (2nd ed.). Upper Saddle River, NJ: Prentice-Hall.

Kotler, P., & Gertner, D. (2002). Country as brand, product, and beyond: A place marketing and brand management perspective. *Journal of Brand Management, 9*(4/5), 249–261.

Kotler, S. (1996, January 8). *The Kingdom of Jose Cuervo: Ad campaign or Republic?* www.wirednews.com.

Kubiak, G. D. (2002). Travel & tourism: Export of tomorrow. *Spectrum: The Journal of State Government* (Spring), 18–20.

Lasser, C. (2000). Implementing destination-structures: Experiences with Swiss cases. In: M. Manete, & M. Cerato (Eds), *From destination to destination marketing and management* (pp. 111–126). Venice: CISET.

Lavery, P. (1990). *Travel and tourism*. Huntington, UK: ELM Publications.

Lavery, P. (1992). The financing and organisation of national tourist offices. *EIU Travel & Tourism Analyst, 4*, 84–101.

Law, C. M. (1993). *Urban tourism – Attracting visitors to large cities*. London: Mansell.

Laws. E. (1995). *Tourist destination management*. London: Routledge.

Laws, E., & Ryan, C. (1992). Service on flights – Issues and analysis by the use of diaries. *Journal of Travel & Tourism Marketing, 1*(3), 61–70.

Lawton, G. R., & Page, S. J. (1997). Analysing the promotion, product and visitor expectations of urban tourism: Auckland, New Zealand as a case study. *Journal of Travel & Tourism Marketing, 6*(3/4), 123–142.

Leiper, N. (1979). The framework of tourism. *Annals of Tourism Research* (October/December), 390–407.

Leiper, N. (1995). *Tourism management*. Collingwood, Vic: TAFE Publications.

Lennon, J. J., & Foley, M. (1999). Interpretation of the unimaginable: The U.S. Holocaust Memorial Museum, Washington, DC, and "dark tourism". *Journal of Travel Research, 38*, 46–50.

Lennon, J., & Foley, M. (2000). *Dark tourism – The attraction of death and disaster*. London: Continuum.

Leslie, D. (1999). Terrorism and tourism: The Northern Ireland situation – A look behind the veil of certainty. *Journal of Travel Research, 38*, 37–40.

Lickorish, L. J. (1991). *Developing tourism destinations: Policies and perspectives*. Harlow, Essex: Longman.

Lilly, T. (1984). From industry to leisure in The Potteries. *Tourism Management, 5*(2), 136–138.

Liscom, B. (2003). Good news and bad news on newzealand.com. *Nigel Coventry's Inside Tourism* (Speakers' Corner – an occasional series), 70.

Litchfield, J. (2003, 30 July). French tourism counts cost as Americans stay away. www.eTurboNews.com.

Litvin, S. W., & Alderson, L. L. (2003). How Charleston got her groove back: A convention and visitors bureau's response to 9/11. *Journal of Vacation Marketing, 9*(2), 188–197.

Lohmann, M. (1990). Evolution of shortbreak holidays in Western Europe. In: W. Fache (Ed.), *Shortbreak holidays*. Rotterdam: Center Parcs.

Lohmann, M. (1991). Evolution of shortbreak holidays. *The Tourist Review, 46*(2), 14–23.

Long, J. (1994). Local authority tourism strategies – A British appraisal. *The Journal of Tourism Studies, 5*(2), 17–23.

Lovelock, C. (1991). *Services marketing*. Englewood Cliffs, NJ: Prentice-Hall.

Lovelock, C. H., Patterson, P. G., & Walker, R. H. (1998). *Services marketing: Australia and New Zealand*. Sydney: Prentice-Hall.

Lovelock, C. H., & Weinberg, C. B. (1984). *Marketing for public and nonprofit managers*. New York: Wiley.

Lundberg, D. E. (1990). *The tourist business*. New York: Van Nostrand Reinhold.

Lynch, K. (1960). *The image of the city*. Cambridge, MA: MIT Press and Harvard University Press.

MacCannell, D. (1976). *The tourist*. New York: Shocken Books.

MacInnes, D. J., & Price, L. L. (1987). The role of imagery in information processing: Review and extensions. *Journal of Consumer Research, 13*, 473–491.

Machiavelli, A. (2001). Tourist destinations as integrated systems. *Tourism Review, 54*(3/4), 6–11.

MacKay, K. J., & Fesenmaier, D. R. (1997). Pictorial element of destination in image formation. *Annals of Tourism Research, 24*(3), 537–565.

Manning, A. (2003, 25 July). WHO lifts last SARS travel warning. www.eTurboNews.com.

Mansfield, Y. (1992). From motivation to actual travel. *Annals of Tourism Research, 19*, 399–419.

Mansfield, Y. (1999). Cycles of war, terror, and peace: Determinants and management of crisis and recovery of the Israeli tourism industry. *Journal of Travel Research, 38*, 30–36.

Marshman, I. (1995). Challenge to Queensland as domestic market number 1. *Traveltrade* (19 Apr/02 May), 10–11.

Martinovic, S. (2002). Branding Hrvatska – A mixed blessing that might succeed: The advantage of being unrecognisable. *Journal of Brand Management, 9*(4/5), 315–322.

Masberg, B. A. (1999). What is the priority of research in the marketing and promotional efforts of convention and visitors Bureaus in the United States? *Journal of Travel & Tourism Marketing, 8*(2), 29–40.

Maslow, A. H. (1943). A theory of human motivation. *Psychological Review, 50*, 370–396.

May, C. (2001). From direct response to image with qualitative and quantitative research. Presentation at the 32nd annual conference of the Travel & Tourism Research Association. Fort Myers.

Mayo, E. J. (1973). Regional images and regional travel behaviour. *The Travel Research Association 4th Annual Proceedings*. Idaho.

Mayo, E. J., & Jarvis, L. P. (1981). *The psychology of leisure travel*. Massachusetts: CBI Publishing Company.

Mazanec, J. A. (1986). Allocating an advertising budget to international travel markets. *Annals of Tourism Research, 13*(4), 609–634.

Mazanec, J. A. (1997). Satisfaction tracking for city tourists. In: J. A. Mazanec (Ed.), *International city tourism* (pp. 75–100). London: Pinter.

Mazanec, J. A., & Schweiger, G. C. (1981). Improved marketing efficiency through multi-product brand names. *European Research* (January), 32–44.

McCabe, C. (1998). Short breaks counter tourism competition. *Australian. NSW: The 21st Century State Special Report* (10 Nov), 5.

McClellan, T. (1995). Restructuring a tourist industry to attract the British visitor: An examination of tourism marketing pressures in the Cherbourg peninsula. *Journal of Vacation Marketing, 2*(1), 67–75.

McClellan, T. (1998). Tourism marketing: A question of perception. *Journal of Vacation Marketing, 4*(4), 408–414.

McClelland, C. (2003, 18 June). Toronto tourism loses $190 million, says report. www.eTurboNews.com.

McEnnally, M., & de Chernatony, L. (1999). The evolving nature of branding: Consumer and managerial considerations. *Journal of Consumer and Market Research* [Online], *99*(02), www.jcmr.org.

McKercher, B. (1995). The destination-market matrix: A tourism market portfolio analysis model. *Journal of Travel and Tourism Marketing, 4*(2), 23–40.

McKercher, B. (1998). The effect of market access on destination choice. *Journal of Travel Research, 37*(August), 39–47.

McKercher, B. (2003). SIP (SARS induced panic) a greater threat to tourism than SARS (Severe Acute Respiratory Syndrome). *e-Review of Tourism Research (eRTR), 1*(1), www.ertr.tamu.edu.

McKercher, B., & Ritchie, M. (1997). The third tier of public sector tourism: A profile of local government tourism officers in Australia. *Journal of Travel Research, 36*(1), 66–72.

McWilliams, E. G., & Crompton, J. L. (1997). An expanded framework for measuring the effectiveness of destination advertising. *Tourism Management, 18*(3), 127–137.

Medlik, S., & Middleton, V. T. C. (1973). The tourist product and its marketing implications. *International Tourism Quarterly, 3,* 28–35.

Meethan, K. (2002). Selling the difference: Tourism marketing in Devon and Cornwall, South-west England. In: R. Voase (Ed.), *Tourism in Western Europe: A collection of case histories* (pp. 23–42). Oxon: CABI publishing.

Meler, M., & Ruzic, D. (1999). Marketing identity of the tourist product of the Republic of Croatia. *Tourism Management, 20,* 635–643.

Middleton, V. T. C. (1998). New marketing conditions, and the strategic advantages of products similar to destination. In: P. Keller (Ed.), *Destination marketing – Reports of the 48th AIEST Congress, Marakech* (pp. 153–165).

Middleton, V., & O'Brien, K. (1987). Short break holidays in the U.K. *Travel & Tourism Analyst* (May), 45–54.

Midgal, D. (1993). Getting the best from your bureau. *Meetings & Conventions* (February), 51–52, 70.

Mihali, T. (2000). Environmental management of a tourist destination: A factor of tourism competitiveness. *Tourism Management, 21*(1), 65–78.

Mill, R. C., & Morrison, A. M. (1985). *The tourism system: An introductory text.* Englewood Cliffs, NJ: Prentice-Hall.

Mill, R. C. & Morrison, A. M. (1992). *The tourism system: An introductory text* (2nd ed.). Englewood Cliffs, NJ: Prentice-Hall.

Miller, A. (2003). Leicester promotions: Destination management for maximising tourist potential. In: N. Evans, D. Campbell, & G. Stonehouse (Eds), *Strategic management for travel and tourism* (pp. 358–361). Oxford: Butterworth-Heinemann.

Miller, G. A. (1956). The magical number seven, plus or minus two: Some limits on our capacity for processing information. *The Psychological Review, 63*(2), 81–97.

Miller, K. E., & Ginter, J. L. (1979). An investigation of situational variation in brand choice behavior and attitude. *Journal of Marketing Research, 16*(February), 111–123.

Milman, A., & Pizam, A. (1995). The role of awareness and familiarity with a destination: The central Florida case. *Journal of Travel Research, 33*(3), 21–27.

Mollo-Bouvier, S. (1990). Short-break holidays: Where are the children? In: W. Fache (Ed.), *Shortbreak holidays.* Rotterdam: Center Parcs.

Morgan, A. (2003). *Eating the big fish – How challenger brands can compete against brand leaders.* New York: Wiley.

Morgan, M. (1991). Dressing up to survive – Marketing Majorca anew. *Tourism Management* (March), 15–20.

Morgan, N. J. (2000). Creating supra-brand Australia: Answering the challenges of contemporary destination marketing. In: M. Robinson, N. Evans, P. Long, R. Sharpley, & J. Swarbrooke (Eds), *Management, marketing and the political economy of travel and tourism* (pp. 352–365). Sunderland: Business Education Publishers.

Morgan, N., & Pritchard, A. (1998). *Tourism promotion and power: Creating images, creating identities.* Chichester: Wiley.

Morgan, N., Pritchard, A., & Piggot, R. (2002). New Zealand, 100% pure. The creation of a powerful niche destination brand. *Brand Management, 9*(4/5), 335–354.

Morgan, N., Pritchard, A., & Pride, R. (2002). *Destination branding – Creating the unique destination proposition*. Oxford: Butterworth-Heinemann.

Morley, P. (2003). Tiny town hope statue will be the ant's pants. *The Sunday Mail* (6 April), 19, Brisbane.

Morley, P., & Stolz, G. (2003). Gold Coast blunders by promoting wrong beach. *The Courier Mail*, 3, Brisbane.

Morrison, A. M., Braunlich, C. G., Kamaruddin, N., & Cai, L. A. (1995). National tourist offices in North America: An analysis. *Tourism Management, 16*(8), 605–617.

Morrison, A. M., Bruen, S. M., & Anderson, D. J. (1998). Convention and visitor bureaus in the USA: A profile of bureaus, bureau executives, and budgets. *Journal of Travel & Tourism Marketing, 7*(1), 1–19.

Moutinho, L. (1987). Consumer behaviour in tourism. *European Journal of Marketing, 21*(10), 1–44.

Moutinho, L. (1994). Positioning strategies. In: S. Witt, & L. Moutinho (Eds), *Tourism marketing and management handbook* (2nd ed., pp. 332–336). Hertfordshire: Prentice-Hall International.

Munro, C., & Taylor, A. (2003). The tourist trade. *The Courier Mail* (11 October), 34, Brisbane.

Murphy, L. (1999). Australia's image as a holiday destination – Perceptions of backpacker visitors. *Journal of Travel and Tourism Marketing, 8*(3), 21–45.

Murphy, P., Pritchard, M. P., & Smith, B. (2000). The destination product and its impact on traveller perceptions. *Tourism Management, 21*(1), 43–52.

Murphy, P. E. (1985). *Tourism: A community approach*. London: Methuen.

Murphy, P. E., & Pritchard, M. (1997). Destination price-value perceptions: An examination of origin and seasonal influences. *Journal of Travel Research, 35*(3), 16–22.

Myers, J. H. (1992). Positioning products/services in attitude space. *Marketing Research* (March), 46–51.

Myers, J. H., & Alpert, M. I. (1968). Determinant buying attitudes: Meaning and measurement. *Journal of Marketing, 32*(October), 13–20.

Myers, J. H., & Gutman, J. (1974). Validating multi-attribute attitude models. *American Marketing Association Proceedings*, 95–99.

Narayana, C. L., & Markin, R. J. (1975). Consumer behavior and product performance: An alternative conceptualisation. *Journal of Marketing, 39*(October), 1–6.

New Zealand Department of Tourist and Health Resorts (1902). *First annual report*. Wellington.

Nickerson, N. P., & Moisey, R. N. (1999). Branding a state from features to positioning: Making it simple? *Journal of Vacation Marketing, 5*(3), 217–226.

Nykiel, R. A., & Jascolt, E. (1998). *Marketing your city, USA*. New York: Haworth Hospitality Press.

NZTB (1992, July). *A review of Rotorua's tourism infrastructure*. Wellington: Policy, Planning and Investment Division, New Zealand Tourism Board.

NZTP (1989). *New Zealand Regional Tourism Summary*. Wellington: New Zealand Tourist & Publicity Department.

NZTP (1989/2). *The economic determinants of domestic travel in New Zealand*. Wellington: New Zealand Tourist & Publicity Department.

NZTPD (1976). *75 Years of tourism*. Wellington: New Zealand Tourist & Publicity Department.

O'Halloran, R. M. (1992). Tourism management profiles: Implications for tourism education. *FIU Hospitality Review, 10*(1), 83–91.

Olins, W. (2002). Branding the nation — The historical context. *Journal of Brand Management, 9*(4/5), 241–248.

O'Neill, M. A., & McKenna, M. A. (1994). Northern Ireland tourism: A quality perspective. *Managing Service Quality, 4*(2), 31–35.

Opanga, K. (2003). Kenya suffers for the U.S. and because of America. www.eTurboNews.com, 24 June.

Oppermann, M. (1996). Visitation of tourism attractions and tourist expenditure patterns — Repeat versus first-time visitors. *Asia Pacific Journal of Tourism Research*, *1*(1), 61–68.

Oppermann, M. (1996b). Convention destination images: Analysis of association meeting planners' perceptions. *Tourism Management*, *17*(3), 175–182.

Oppermann, M. (1999). Where psychology and geography interface in tourism research and theory. In: A. G. Woodside, G. I. Crouch, J. A. Mazanec, M. Oppermann, & M. Y. Sakai (Eds), *Consumer psychology of tourism, hospitality and leisure* (pp. 19–37). Oxon: CABI Publishing.

Oppermann, M. (2000). Tourism destination loyalty. *Journal of Travel Research*, *39*(August), 78–84.

Osti, L., & Pechlaner, H. (2001). Communication issues in NTO distribution strategies. In: D. Buhalis, & E. Laws (Eds), *Tourism distribution channels* (pp. 231–242). London: Continuum.

OSTP (2001). *New Zealand tourism strategy 2010: Summary of recommendations*. Wellington: Office of Tourism and Sport.

Owen, C. (1992). Building a relationship between government and tourism. *Tourism Management*, *13*(6), 358–362.

Page, S. (1995). *Urban tourism*. London: Routledge.

Page, S., & Lawton., G. (1997). The impact of urban tourism on destination communities: Implications for community tourism planning in Auckland. In: C. M. Hall, J. Jenkins, & G. Kearsley (Eds), *Tourism planning and policy in Australia and New Zealand* (pp. 209–226). Roseville, NSW: McGraw-Hill.

Page, S., & Wilks, J. (2004). *Managing tourist health and safety*. Oxford: Elsevier.

Page, S., Clift., & Clark, N. (1994). Tourist health: The precautions, behaviour and health problems of British tourists in Malta. In: A. V. Seaton, C. L. Jenkins, R. C. Wood, P. U. C. Dieke, M. M. Bennett, L. R. MacLellan, & R. Smith (Eds), *Tourism the state of the art* (pp. 799–817). Chichester: Wiley.

Palmer, A. (1998). Evaluating the governance style of marketing groups. *Annals of Tourism Research*, *25*(1), 185–201.

Passmore, D. (2003). Big pelican for tourism roost. *The Sunday Mail* (24 August), 24, Brisbane.

PATA (1996). *Annual report*. Bangkok: Pacific Asia Travel Association.

PATA (2002, February). *Issues & trends — Pacific Asia travel*, *7*(2).

PATA (2003). *Crisis — It won't happen to us!* Bangkok: Pacific Asia Travel Association.

Pattinson, G. (1990). Place promotion by tourist boards: The example of 'Beautiful Berkshire'. In: G. Ashworth, & B. Goodall (Eds), *Marketing tourism places* (pp. 209–226). New York: Routledge.

Pearce, D. (1992). *Tourist organizations*. Harlow, Essex: Longman.

Pearce, D. G. (1990). Tourism, the regions and restructuring in New Zealand. *The Journal of Tourism Studies*, *1*(2), 33–42.

Pearce, D. G. (1996a). Tourist organizations in Sweden. *Tourism Management*, *17*(6), 413–424.

Pearce, D. G. (1996b). Regional tourist organizations in Spain: Emergence, policies and consequences. *Tourism Economics*, *2*(2), 119–136.

Pearce, D. G. (1997). Competitive destination analysis in Southeast Asia. *Journal of Travel Research*, *35*(4), 16–24.

Pearce, P. L. (1982a). Perceived changes in holiday destinations. *Annals of Tourism Research*, *9*, 145–164.

Pearce, P. L. (1982b). *The social psychology of tourist behaviour*. Oxford: Pergamon Press.

Pearce, P. L. (1988). *The Ulysses factor*. New York: Springer-Verlag.

Pearce, P. L. (1994). Fundamentals of tourist motivation. In: D. Pearce, & R. Butler (Eds), *Tourism research: Critiques and challenges*. New York: Routledge.

Pearce, P. L., Morrison, A. M., & Rytledge, J. L. (1998). *Tourism — Bridges across continents.* Roseville, NSW: McGraw-Hill.

Pechlaner, H. (1999). The competitiveness of alpine destinations between market pressure and problems of adaptation. *Tourism, 47*(4), 332–343.

Pechlaner, H., & Abfalter, D. (2002). New challenges for NTOs — A multi-national perspective with the example of cultural tourism in Italy. *Tourism, 50*(1), 5–20.

Pedro Bueno, A. (1999). Competitiveness in the tourist industry and the role of the Spanish public administrations: The case of Valencia Region. *Tourism, 47*(4), 316–331.

Perdue, R. R. (1986). Traders and nontraders in recreational destination choice. *Journal of Leisure Research, 18*(1), 12–25.

Perdue, R. R., & Pitegoff, B. E. (1990). Methods of accountability research for destination marketing. *Journal of Travel Research* (Spring), 44–49.

Phelps, A. (1986). Holiday destination image — The problem of assessment. *Tourism Management* (September), 168–180.

Pike, S. (1998). *Destination positioning: Too many fingers in the pie?* NZ Tourism and Hospitality Research Conference Proceedings. Christchurch: Lincoln University.

Pike, S. (2002a). Destination image analysis: A review of 142 Papers from 1973–2000. *Tourism Management, 23*(5), 541–549.

Pike, S. (2002b). ToMA as a measure of competitive advantage for short break holiday destinations. *The Journal of Tourism Studies, 13*(1), 9–19.

Pike, S. (2002c). The use of importance-performance analysis to identify determinant short break destination attributes in New Zealand. *Pacific Tourism Review, 6*(1), 23–33.

Pike, S. (2003). The use of repertory grid analysis to elicit salient short break holiday attributes. *Journal of Travel Research, 41*(3), 326–330.

Pike, S. (2004). Spoilt for choice — Short break holiday preferences in the Brisbane market. The Council for Australian University Tourism and Hospitality Education (CAUTHE) Annual Conference. Brisbane: University of Queensland, February, 577–586.

Pike, S., & Ryan, C. (2004). Dimensions of short break destination attractiveness — A comparison of cognitive, affective and conative perceptions. *Journal of Travel Research, 42*(4).

Pitts, B. G., & Ayers. K. (2000). Sports tourism and the gay games: The emerging use of destination marketing with the gay games. In: M. Robinson, N. Evans, P. Long, R. Sharpley, & J. Swarbrooke (Eds), *Management, marketing and the political economy of travel and tourism* (pp. 389–401). Sunderland: Business Education Publishers.

Pizam, A. (1990). Evaluating the effectiveness of travel trade shows and other tourism sales-promotion techniques. *Journal of Travel Research* (Summer), 3–8.

Pizam, A. (1999). A comprehensive approach to classifying acts of crime and violence at tourism destinations. *Journal of Travel Research, 38*, 5–12.

Plog, S. T. (1974). Why destination areas rise and fall in popularity. *The Cornell HRA Quarterly, 14*(4), 55–58.

Plog, S. T. (2000, June). Thirty years that changed travel: Changes to expect over the next ten. Keynote address — 31st Travel and Tourism Research Association Conference. Burbank, CA.

Poetschke, B. (1995). Key success factors for public/private-sector partnerships in island tourism planning. In: M. V. Conlin, & T. Baum (Eds), *Island tourism*. Chichester: Wiley.

Poiesz, T. B. C. (1989). The image concept: Its place in consumer psychology. *Journal of Economic Psychology, 10*, 457–472.

Porter, M. E. (1980). *Competitive strategy.* New York: Free Press.

Porter, M. E. (1991). Towards a dynamic theory of strategy. *Strategic Management Journal, 12*, 95–117.

Portorff, S. M., & Neal, D. M. (1994). Marketing implications for post-disaster tourism destinations, Journal of Travel. *Journal of Travel & Tourism Marketing*, *3*(1), 115–122.

Pride, R. (2002). Brand Wales: 'Natural revival'. In: N. Morgan, A. Prichard, & R. Pride (Eds), *Destination branding* (pp. 109–123). Oxford: Butterworth-Heinemann.

Prideaux, B. (2000). The role of the transport system in destination development. *Tourism Management*, *21*(1), 53–63.

Pritchard, A., & Morgan, N. (1998). Mood marketing — The new destination branding strategy: A case of Wales the brand. *Journal of Vacation Marketing*, *4*(3), 215–229.

Pritchard, G. (1982). Tourism promotion: Big business for the States. *The H.R.A. Quarterly*, *23*(2), 48–57.

Pritchard, M. P., & Walkup, K. W. (2000). A qualitative approach to destination assessment: The case of Western Australia. *31st Annual TTRA Proceedings*. Travel & Tourism Research Association.

Prosser, G., Hunt, S., Braithwaite, D., & Rosemann, I. (2000). *The significance of regional tourism: A preliminary report*. Lismore: Centre for Regional Tourism Research.

Pyo, S., Song, S., & Chang, H. (1998). Implications of repeat visitor patterns: The Cheju Island case. *Tourism Analysis*, *3*, 181–187.

Quinn, J. B., Anderson, P., & Finkelstein, S. (1996). Managing professional intellect: Making the most of the best. *Harvard Business Review* (March–April), 71–80.

Rahman, F. (2003). *New visa rule to boost Man's tourism sector*. www.eTurboNews.com, 29 July.

Reggett, R. S. (1972). *The Tarawera eruption: Its effects on the tourist industry*. Unpublished MA Thesis. Dunedin: University of Otago.

Reich, A. (1997). Improving the effectiveness of destination positioning. *Tourism Analysis*, *2*, 37–53.

Reid, L. J., & Reid, S. D. (1993). Communicating tourism supplier services: Building repeat visitor relationships. *Journal of Travel and Tourism Marketing*, *2*(2/3), 3–19.

Reilly, M. D. (1990). Free elicitation of descriptive adjectives for tourism image assessment. *Journal of Travel Research* (Spring), 21–26.

Reisenger, Y., & Turner, L. (2000). Japanese tourism satisfaction: Gold Coast versus Hawaii. *Journal of Vacation Marketing*, *6*(4), 299–317.

Reynolds, W. H. (1965). The role of the consumer in image building. *California Management Review* (Spring), 69–76.

Richardson, J., & Cohen, J. (1993). State slogans: The case of the missing USP. *Journal of Travel & Tourism Marketing*, *2*(2/3), 91–109.

Richardson, S. L. (1987). An importance-performance approach to evaluating communication effectiveness. *Journal of Park and Recreation Administration*, *5*(4), 71–83.

Richardson, S. L., & Crompton, J. L. (1988). Cultural variations in perceptions of vacation attributes. *Tourism Management* (June), 129–136.

Richter, L. K. (1999). After political turmoil: The lessons of rebuilding tourism in three Asian countries. *Journal of Travel Research*, *38*, 41–45.

Ries, A. (1992). The discipline of the narrow focus. *Journal of Business Strategy* (November/December), 3–9.

Ries, A. (1996). *Focus — The future of your company depends on it*. New York: HarperCollins.

Ries, A., & Ries, L. (1998). *The 22 immutable laws of branding*. New York: HarperCollins.

Ries, A., & Trout, J. (1981). *Positioning: The battle for your mind*. New York: McGraw-Hill.

Ries, A., & Trout, J. (1982). The enormous competitive power of a selling product name. *Marketing Times*, *29*(5), 28–38.

Ries, A., & Trout, J. (1986). *Positioning: The battle for your mind*. New York: McGraw-Hill.

Riley, R., & Van Doren, C. (1998). Movies as tourism promotion: A push factor in a pull location. *Tourism Management*, *13*, 267–274.

Riley, R., Baker, D., & Van Doren, C. S. (1998). Movie induced tourism. *Annals of Tourism Research*, *25*(4), 919–933.

Riley, S., & Palmer, J. (1975). Of attitudes and latitudes: A repertory grid study of perceptions of seaside resorts. *Journal of the Market Research Society*, *17*(2), 74–89.

Ritchie, J. R. B. (1996). Beacons of light in an expanding universe: An assessment of the state-of-the-art in tourism marketing/marketing research, Journal of Travel. *Journal of Travel & Tourism Marketing*, *5*(4), 49–84.

Ritchie, J. R. B., & Crouch, G. I. (2000a). *Are destination stars born or made: Must a competitive destination have star genes?* Lights, Camera, Action — 31st Annual Conference Proceedings. San Fernando Valley, CA: Travel and Tourism Research Association.

Ritchie, J. R. B., & Crouch, G. I. (2000b). The competitive destination: A sustainability perspective. *Tourism Management*, *21*, 1–7.

Ritchie, J. R. B., & Crouch, G. (2003). *The competitive destination — A sustainable tourism perspective*. Oxon: CABI Publishing.

Ritchie, J. R. B., Johnston, E. E., & Jones, V. J. (1980). Competition, fares and fences — perspective of the air traveler. *Journal of Travel Research*, *18*, 17–25.

Ritchie, J. R. B., & Ritchie, R. J. B. (1998).The branding of tourism destinations — past achievements and future challenges. In: P. Keller (Ed.), *Destination marketing — Reports of the 48th AIEST Congress, Marrakech* (pp. 89–116).

Ritchie, R. J. B., & Ritchie, J. R. B. (2002). A framework for an industry supported destination marketing information system. *Tourism Management*, *23*, 439–454.

Ritchie, J. R. B., & Zins, M. (1978). Culture as determinant of the attractiveness of a tourism region. *Annals of Tourism Research*, *5*(2), 252–267.

Roehl, W. S. (1990). Travel agent attitudes toward China after Tiananmen square. *Journal of Travel Research* (Fall), 16–22.

Roper, P. (2001). The case against tourism: Doubters and sceptics. In: D. Jeffries (Ed.), *Governments and tourism* (pp. 27–50). Oxford: Butterworth-Heinemann.

Rosenberg, M. J. (1956). Cognitive structure and attitudinal affect. *Journal of Abnormal and Social Psychology*, *15*(5), 367–372.

Ross (2003). It's a wacky world out there. *The Sunday Mail* (27 July), 4–5, Brisbane.

Ruddy, J., & Flanagan, S. (1999). *Tourism destination marketing: Gaining the competitive edge*. Conference Proceedings. European Conference of the Travel and Tourism Research Association.

Russel, J. A. (1980). A circumplex model of affect. *Journal of Personality and Social Psychology*, *39*(6), 1161–1178.

Russel, J. A., Ward, L. M., & Pratt, G. (1981). Affective quality attributed to environments: A factor analytic study. *Environment and Behavior*, *13*(3), 259–288.

Ryan, C. (1983). *Modelling hotel strategies in the weekend break market*. Unpublished report. Nottingham: Clarendon College.

Ryan, C. (1991). *Recreational tourism: A social science perspective*. London: Routledge.

Ryan, C. (2002). Academia-industry tourism research links: States of confusion. *Pacific Tourism Review*, *5*(3/4), 83–97.

Ryan, C., & Pike, S. (2003). Maori based tourism in Rotorua — Perceptions of place by domestic visitors. *Journal of Sustainable Tourism*, *11*(4), 307–321.

Sandilands, B. (1997). The short break catches on. *Business Review Weekly*, *19*(29), 78–79.

Schoenbacher, D. D., di Benetto, C. A., Gordon, G. L., & Kaminski, P. F. (1995). Destination advertising: Assessing effectiveness with the split-run technique. *Journal of Travel & Tourism Marketing*, *4*(2), 1–21.

Schofield, L. (2002). Weaving monumental magic. *The Sunday Telegraph* (18 August), 96, Sydney.

Schultz, D., Tannenbaum, S., & Lauterborn, R. (1993). *Integrated marketing communications.* Lincolnwood, IL: NTC Publishing.

Schwartz, P. (1992). *The art of the long view.* London: Century Business.

Seaton, A. V. (1996). Guided by the dark: From thanatopsis to thanatourism. *International Journal of Heritage Studies, 2*(4), 234–244.

Selby, M., & Morgan, N. J. (1996). Reconstruing place image: A case study of its role in destination market research. *Tourism Management, 17*(4), 287–294.

Sharpley, R. (2002). Tourism: A vehicle for development? In: R. Sharpley, & D. Telfer (Eds), *Tourism and development — Concepts and issues.* Clevedon: Channel View Publications.

Sheehan, L. R., & Ritchie, J. R. B. (1997). Financial management in tourism: A destination perspective. *Tourism Economics, 3*(2), 93–118.

Sheldon, P. (1993). Destination information systems. *Annals of Tourism Research, 20,* 633–649.

Sigaux, G. (1966). *History of tourism.* London: Leisure Arts Ltd.

Sims, S. L. (1990). Educational needs and opportunities for personnel in convention and visitor bureaus. *Visions in Leisure and Business, 9*(3), 27–32.

Slater, J. (2002). Brand Louisiana: 'Come as you are. Leave different©'. In: N. Morgan, A. Pritchard, & R. Pride (Eds), *Destination branding* (pp. 148–162). Oxford: Butterworth-Heinemann.

Smith, G. (1999). Toward a United States policy on traveler safety and security: 1980–2000. *Journal of Travel Research, 38,* 62–65.

Smith, S. L. J. (1988). Defining tourism: A supply-side view. *Annals of Tourism Research, 15,* 179–190.

Smith, S. L. J. (2003). A vision for the Canadian tourism industry. *Tourism Management, 24,* 123–133.

Smith, V. L. (2001). Tourism issues of the 21st century. In: V. L. Smith, & M. Brent (Eds), *Hosts and guests revisited: Tourism issues of the 21st century* (pp. 333–353). New York: Cognizant.

Sonmez, S. F., Apostolopoulous, Y., & Tarlow, P. (1999). Tourism in crisis: Managing the effects of terrorism. *Journal of Travel Research, 38,* 13–18.

Spotts, D. M. (1997). Regional analysis of tourism resources for marketing purposes. *Journal of Travel Research* (Winter), 3–15.

Spiggle, S., & Sewall, M. A. (1987). A choice sets model of retail selection. *Journal of Marketing, 51*(April), 97–111.

Stafford, D. (1986). *The founding years in Rotorua: A history of events to 1900.* Auckland: Ray Richards.

Stafford, D. (1988). *The new century in Rotorua.* Auckland: Ray Richards.

Staniford, T., & Cheyne, J. (1994). *The search for the perfect organisation: A New Zealand case study.* Tourism Down-Under: A Tourism Research Conference Proceedings. Palmerston North: Massey University.

Stern, E., & Krakover, S. (1993). The formation of a composite urban image. *Geographical Analysis, 25*(2), 130–146.

STPB (1996). *Tourism 21: Vision of a tourism capital.* Singapore Tourism Promotion Board.

Stuart, J. (1986). Tourism in Scotland — Under new management. *Tourism Management, 7*(4), 298–301.

Supphellen, M., & Nygaardsvic, I. (2002). Testing country brand slogans: Conceptual development and empirical illustration of a simple normative model. *Journal of Brand Management, 9*(4/5), 385–395.

Tan, T. S. W., Barnes, D. J., & Smith, R. W. N. (1995). *An overview of quality management practice in the New Zealand tourism industry.* Unpublished report. Massey University.

Tapsell, E. (1972). *A history of Rotorua.* Published by the author.

Taylor, G. D., Rogers, J., & Stanton, B. (1994). Bridging the gap between industry and researchers. *Journal of Travel Research* (Spring), 9–12.

Teare, R., Davies, M., & McGeary, B. (1989). The operational challenge of hotel short breaks. *International Journal of Contemporary Hospitality Management, 1*(1), 22–24.

Thompson, J. R., & Cooper, P. D. (1979). Additional evidence on the limited size of evoked and inept sets of travel destination. *Journal of Travel Research, 17*(3), 23–25.

TNZ (2001). *100 years pure progress.* Wellington: Tourism New Zealand.

TNZ (2003). *SARS impacts on international arrivals to New Zealand.* Media Release. 20 June. Accessed at www.tourisminfo.govt.nz/cir_news, 25/6/03. Tourism New Zealand.

TNZ (2004). *Tourism New Zealand profile.* Wellington: Tourism New Zealand. Accessed on-line 4/4/04 at: http://www.tourisminfo.co.nz/doclibrary/Tourism_Profile_2003FINAL.pdf.

Tolhurst, C. (1999). Hunter Valley entices the two-day tripper. *Australian Financial Review* (December 8th), 33. Special Report: Hunter.

Tooke, N., & Baker, M. (1996). Seeing is believing: The effect of film on visitor numbers to screened locations. *Tourism Management, 17*(2), 87–94.

Tourelle, G. (2003). United tourism market mooted. *The New Zealand Herald* (29 July).

Tourism Auckland (2002, October). *Presentation to the Auckland City Council.*

Tourism Rotorua (1996). *Emergence of a new spirit: An introduction to Rotorua's brand identity process.* Rotorua District Council.

Tourism Strategy Group (2001, May). *New Zealand tourism strategy: 2010.* Tourism New Zealand. www.tourisminfo.co.nz.

Treacy, M., & Wiersema, F. (1995). *The discipline of market leaders.* London: HarperCollins.

Tribe, J. (1997). *Corporate strategy for tourism.* London: ITP.

Trout, J., & Ries, A. (1979). Positioning: Ten years later. *Industrial Marketing, 64*(7), 32–42.

Trout, J., & Rivkin, S. (1995). *The new positioning.* New York: McGraw-Hill.

Um, S., & Crompton, J. L. (1990). Attitude determinants in tourism destination choice. *Annals of Tourism Research, 17,* 432–448.

Urde, M. (1999). Brand orientation: A mindset for building brands into strategic resources. *Journal of Marketing Management, 15,* 117–133.

Uysal, M., Chen, J. S., & Williams, D. R. (2000). Increasing state market share through a regional positioning. *Tourism Management, 21*(1), 8996.

Van Middelkoop, M., Borgers, A. W. J., & Timmermans, H. J. P. (1999). Complimentarity, substitution and independence among tourist trips. *Tourism Analysis, 4,* 63–74.

Vaughan, D. R., & Edwards, J. R. (1999). Experiential perceptions of two winter sun destinations: The Algarve and Cyprus. *Journal of Vacation Marketing, 5*(4), 356–368.

Velas, F., & Bechell, L. (1995). *International tourism — An economic perspective.* Basingstoke: Macmillan Business.

Voase, R. (2002). *Tourism in Western Europe: A collection of case histories.* Wallingford: CABI Publishing.

Wahab, S., Crampon., L. J., & Rothfield, L. M. (1976). *Tourism marketing.* London: Tourism International Press.

Walmsley, D. J., & Jenkins, J. M. (1993). Appraisive images of tourist areas: Application of personal constructs. *Australian Geographer, 24*(2), 1–13.

Wanhill, S. (2000). Issues in public sector involvement. In: B. Faulkner, G. Moscardo, & E. Laws (Eds), *Tourism in the 21st century — Lessons from experience* (pp. 222–242). London: Continuum.

Ward, S. V., & Gold, J. R. (1994). *The use of publicity and marketing to sell towns and regions.* Chichester: Wiley.

Wason, G. (1998). Taxation and tourism. *Travel & Tourism Analyst, 2,* 77–95.

Wee, C. H., Hakam, A. N., & Ong, E. (1985). Temporal and regional differences in image of a tourist destination: Implications for promoters of tourism. *Service Industries Journal, 5,* 104–114.

Wicks, B. E., & Schutt, M. A. (1991). Examining the role of tourism promotion through the use of brochures. *Tourism Management* (December), 301–312.

Wilkie, W. L., & Pessemier, E. A. (1973). Issues in marketing's use of multi-attribute attitude models. *Journal of Marketing Research, 10*(November), 428–441.

Wilson, C. E. (1981). A procedure for the analysis of consumer decision making. *Journal of Advertising Research, 21*(2), 31–36.

Wind, Y. (1980). New twists for some old tricks. *The Wharton Magazine* (Spring), 34–39.

Wind, Y., & Robinson, P. J. (1972). Product positioning: An application of multidimensional scaling. *Attitude Research in Transition*, 155–175. American Marketing Association.

Wintermans, J. (1994). The problem of articulate incompetence. *Canadian Business Review* (Spring), 42–43.

Wöber, K. W. (2003). Information supply in tourism management by marketing decision support systems. *Tourism Management, 24*, 241–255.

Woodside, A. G. (1981). Measuring the conversion of advertising coupon inquirers into visitors. *Journal of Travel Research* (Spring), 38–41.

Woodside, A. G. (1982). Positioning a province using travel research. *Journal of Travel Research, 20*(Winter), 2–6.

Woodside, A. G. (1990). Measuring advertising effectiveness in destination marketing strategies. *Journal of Travel Research, 29*(2), 3–38.

Woodside, A. G. (1999). Theory and research on the consumer psychology of tourism, hospitality and leisure. In: A. G. Woodside, G. I. Crouch, J. A. Mazanec, A. Oppermann, & M. Y. Sakai (Eds), *Consumer psychology of tourism, hospitality and leisure*. Wallingford: CABI Publishing.

Woodside, A. G., & Carr, J. A. (1988). Consumer decision making and competitive marketing strategies: Applications for tourism planning. *Journal of Travel Research* (Winter), 2–7.

Woodside, A. G., & Lysonski, S. (1989). A general model of traveler destination choice. *Journal of Travel Research* (Spring), 8–14.

Woodside, A. G., & Reid, D. M. (1974). Tourism profiles versus audience profiles: Are upscale magazines really upscale? *Journal of Travel Research, 12*(4), 17–23.

Woodside, A. G., & Ronkainen, I. A. (1994). Improving advertising conversion studies. In: J. R. B. Ritchie, & C. R. Goeldner (Eds), *Travel, tourism, and hospitality research: A handbook for managers and researchers* (pp. 545–557). New York: Wiley.

Woodside, A. G., Ronkainen, I., & Reid, D. M. (1977). *Measurement and utilization of the evoked set as a travel marketing variable*. The Travel Research Association Eighth Annual Conference Proceedings. Salt Lake City: Travel and Tourism Research Association, 123–130.

Woodside, A. G., & Sakai, M. Y. (2001). Meta-evaluations of performance audits of government tourism-marketing programs. *Journal of Travel Research, 39*, 369–379.

Woodside, A. G., & Sherrell, D. (1977). Traveler evoked, inept, and inert sets of vacation destinations. *Journal of Travel Research, 16*, 14–18.

Woodside, A. G., & Wilson, E. J. (1985). Effects of consumer awareness of brand advertising on preference. *Journal of Advertising Research, 25*(4), 41–48.

WTO (1979). *Tourist images*. Madrid: World Tourism Organization.

WTO (1983a). *The framework of the state's responsibility for the management of Tourism*. Madrid: World Tourism Organization.

WTO (1983b). *Appraisal and social value of investments in domestic tourism*. Madrid: World Tourism Organization.

WTO (1994). *National and regional tourism planning*. Madrid: World Tourism Organization.

WTO (1995). *Concepts, definitions and classifications for tourism statistics. Technical manual no. 1*. Madrid: World Tourism Organization.

WTO (1996). *Towards new forms of public-private sector partnership*. Madrid: World Tourism Organization.

WTO (1999). *Budgets of national tourism administrations*. Madrid: World Tourism Organization.

WTO (2002). *Thinktank*. World Tourism Organisation. Accessed on-line: http://www.world-tourism.org/education/menu.html.

WTTC (2003). *Blueprint for new tourism*. London: World Travel & Tourism Council.

Yau, O. H. M., & Chan, C. F. (1990). Hong Kong as a travel destination in South-east Asia: A multidimensional approach. *Tourism Management* (June), 123–132.

You, X., O'Leary, J., & Fesenmaier, D. (2000). Knowledge management through the web: A new marketing paradigm for tourism organizations. In: B. Faulkner, G. Moscardo, & E. Laws (Eds), *Tourism in the 21st century – Lessons from experience* (pp. 181–197). London: Continuum.

Appendices

Appendix 1 — Position Description: New Zealand Tourism Board Member

Role of the New Zealand Tourism Board (NZTB)

The New Zealand Tourism Board, currently trading as Tourism New Zealand, was established by The New Zealand Tourism Board Act 1991 ". . . to ensure that New Zealand is so marketed as a visitor destination as to maximise long-term benefits to New Zealand."
   Subject to this object it has functions to: (a) develop, implement, and promote strategies for tourism; and (b) advise the Government and the New Zealand tourism industry on matters relating to the development, implementation, and promotion of those strategies.
   The current outputs purchased by the Government from Tourism New Zealand include:

- advertising (brand and tactical, including partnerships with tourism operators);
- other promotion activity such as public relations, events and trade shows;
- various information and advisory services; and
- marketing research.

The Board comprises nine members, including a Chair and Deputy Chair, appointed by the Minister of Tourism.

Working in the State Sector

The Government is both the owner and the main purchaser of services from Tourism New Zealand. The Government expects that Tourism New Zealand will operate in a manner consistent with the values of a public sector organisation, in particular:

- integrity;
- frugality and due care in the use of taxpayer money;
- advancing activities beneficial to the tourism sector and wider economy rather than to any individual business;
- focusing on medium to long term strategies rather than short term gains;
- showing openness and having good communication with the Minister, the Ministry of Tourism and other government agencies; and

- partnering with the private sector to add value rather than displace or duplicate private businesses.

Expectations of Members

The Tourism New Zealand Chair and Members are accountable to the Minister of Tourism for the good governance of the organisation. In particular Members are expected to contribute to:

- ensuring that Tourism New Zealand delivers its services;
- protecting the value of the Crown's investment in Tourism New Zealand (Statement of Intent);
- ensuring Tourism New Zealand acts within its statutory authority and meets its statutory responsibilities, including the Annual Statement (purchase agreement), Statement of Intent and Annual Report, and complies (if issued), with policy directives from the Government;
- ensuring Tourism New Zealand undertakes effective consultation with the tourism industry when planning and implementing marketing and other strategies, partners with the industry and maintains effective communications with the industry, and is committed to measuring the success of partnerships;
- the Board's oversight of the employment and performance of the Chief Executive.

Partnership with the Tourism Industry

One of the key principles of the New Zealand Tourism Strategy 2010 is strengthened partnerships between the public and private sectors. In taking a leadership role in destination brand development, international marketing, market research and product development, Tourism New Zealand needs to promote a high level of alignment between the public and private sectors through effective engagement and involvement. The Board should ensure Tourism New Zealand is effective in co-ordinating marketing effort and expenditure with the private sector.

The Government, in assessing the Board's performance, will look for evidence of effective engagement by Tourism New Zealand with industry in developing and implementing Tourism New Zealand programmes.

Terms of Appointment

The term of appointment is for up to three years. The Minister of Tourism may consider re-appointing a member for a further term of up to three years but there should be no expectation of such reappointment.

Skills and Experience

The candidate should have skills and experience in several of the following:

* the capability of having a wide perspective on issues;
* good oral and written communication;
* understanding of public sector governance and accountability;
* previous experience as a company director;
* an ability to work in a team and work collaboratively;
* strategic skills;
* experience in developing and maintaining partnerships with other organisations and companies;
* experience with financial statements;
* understanding of and/or experience in the tourism sector at a senior level;
* understanding the importance of value creation, innovation and international best practice comparisons; and
* experience of marketing issues.

Fees and Allowances

An annual fee of $15,000 is payable. Members are also eligible for some expense allowances.

Appendix 2 — NTO Slogans in 2003

National Tourism Office	Theme	WWW URL
Afghanistan		No web site
Albania	(No slogan)	http://www.albaniatourism.com
Algeria	(No slogan)	http://www.tourisme.dz/
American Samoa	American Samoa — America's South Pacific Paradise	http://www.tcsp.com/destinations/american_samoa/index.shtml
Andorra	(No slogan)	http://www.turisme.ad/
Angola	(No slogan)	http://www.angola.org/referenc/r_ttips.htm
Anguilla	Tranquillity wrapped in blue	http://anguilla-vacation.com/
Antigua	The Caribbean you've always imagined	http://www.antigua-barbuda.org/
Argentina	Visit Argentina the whole year	http://www.sectur.gov.ar/eng/menu.htm
Armenia		No web site
Aruba	Aruba is where happiness lives	http://www.aruba.com/
Ascension Island	(No slogan)	http://www.obsidian.co.ac
Australia	(No core slogan — differs between markets)	http://www.atc.net.au/brand.asp?sub=2OVE
Austria	Austria — holiday break away	http://www.austria-tourism.at/
Azerbaijan	(No slogan)	http://azerbaijan.tourism.az/
Bahamas	The Islands of the Bahamas — it just keeps getting better	http://www.bahamas.com/
Bahrain	Bahrain — island of golden smiles	http://www.bahraintourism.com/
Bangladesh		(No web site sourced)
Barbados	Barbados — just beyond your imagination	http://barbados.org/
Belarus	(No slogan)	http://www.touragency.by/ru/
Belgium	Welcome to Flanders, Belgium	http://www.visitflanders.co.uk/index.html
Belize	Belize — mother nature's best kept secret	http://www.travelbelize.org/
Benin	(No slogan)	http://www.tourisme.gouv.bj/
Bermuda	(No slogan)	http://www.bermudatourism.com
Bhutan	(No slogan)	http://www.kingdomofbhutan.com/
Bolivia	(No slogan)	http://www.mcei.gov.bo
Bonaire	(No slogan)	http://www.infobonaire.com/index.html
Bosnia & Herzegovina	Bosnia & Herzegovina — your next adventure	http://www.bhtourism.ba/
Botswana	Make your own picture of Botswana	http://www.botswana-tourism.gov.bw/tourism/index_f.html
Brazil	If travelling is your passion, Brazil is your destiny	http://www.brazil.org.uk/turismo/brazilbrochure.pdf
British Virgin Islands	British Virgin Islands — nature's little secrets	http://www.bvitouristboard.com
Brunei	(No slogan)	http://www.visitbrunei.com
Bulgaria	Bulgaria — a treasure to discover	http://www.bvitouristboard.com
Burkina Faso	Burkina — land of tradition	http://www.mtt.gov.bf
Burundi	(No slogan)	http://www.burundi.gov.bi/tourisme.htm
Cambodia	(No slogan)	http://www.tourismcambodia.com/
Cameroon	Cameroon — toute l'Afrique dans un pays (All of Africa in one country)	http://www.bcenter.fr/cameroun/index.php

National Tourism Office	Theme	WWW URL
Canada	Canada — discover our true nature	http://www.travelcanada.ca
Cape Verde		No web site
Cayman Islands	Could it be Cayman?	http://www.caymanislands.ky
Central African Republic		No web site
Chad		No web site
Chile	Chile — naturaleza que conmueve	http://www.sernatur.cl/
China	Come say "Nihau"! . . . and discover the glory of China	http://www.cnto.org.au
Colombia	(No slogan)	http://www.turismocolombia.com
Comoros		No web site
Congo		No web site
Cook Islands	Cook Islands — your recipe for true paradise	http://www.tcsp.com/destinations/cooks/index.shtml
Costa Rica	Costa Rica — no artificial ingredients	http://www.visitcostarica.com
Croatia	(No slogan)	http://www.croatia.hr
Cuba	Cuba — peaceful, safe and healthy tourism	http://www.cubatravel.cu/
Curacao	Curacao — in the Southern Caribbean. Real. Different.	http://www.curacao-tourism.com
Cyprus	Cyprus — irresistible for 9,000 years	http://www.cyprustourism.org/cyprus.html
Czech Republic	(No slogan)	http://www.czechtourism.com
Democratic Republic of Congo		No web site
Denmark	(No slogan)	http://www.visitdenmark.com
Djibouti	Djibouti — terre d'echanges et de rencontres (Land of exchanges and meetings)	http://www.office-tourisme.dj
Dominica	Dominica — welcome to the nature island	http://www.dominica.dm/
Dominican Republic	Dominican Republic — experience our Caribbean	http://www.dominicanrepublic.com/Tourism/index.htm
Dubai	Dubai — the Gulf destination	http://www.dubaitourism.co.ae
East Timor		No web site
Ecuador	Ecuador — nature, culture, adventure and travel	http://www.vivecuador.com/
Egypt	Egypt — where history began and continues	http://www.egypttourism.org/
El Salvador	El Salvador — no hay nada como lo tuyo! (There is nothing like your own)	http://www.elsalvadorturismo.gob.sv/
England	Enjoy England	http://www.visitengland.com
Equatorial Guinea		No web site
Eritrea		No web site
Estonia	Estonia — positively transforming	http://www.visitestonia.com/
Ethiopia	Ethiopia — 13 months of sunshine	http://www.tourismethiopia.org/
Falkland Islands	(No slogan)	http://www.tourism.org.fk/
Faroe Islands	(No slogan)	http://www.tourist.fo/
Fiji	Fiji — the truly relaxing tropical getaway	http://www.bulafiji.com/

National Tourism Office	Theme	WWW URL
Finland	Finland — naturally	http://www.finland-tourism.com/
France	(No slogan)	http://www.franceguide.com
French Guiana		(No web site)
Gabon	(No slogan)	http://www.gabontour.com/
The Gambia	The Gambia — welcome to your haven in Africa	http://www.visitthegambia.gm/
Georgia	(No slogan)	http://www.parliament.ge/tourism/
Germany	Germany — a country rich in experiences!	http://www.germany-tourism.de/
Ghana	(No slogan)	http://www.africaonline.com.gh/Tourism/ghana.html
Gibraltar	(No slogan)	http://www.gibraltar.gov.gi/
Greece	Greece — beyond words	http://www.gnto.gr/
Greenland	Greenland — out of this world	http://www.greenland.com
Grenada	Grenada — the spice of the Caribbean	http://www.grenada.org/
Guadelupe		No web site
Guam	(No slogan)	http://www.visitguam.org/
Guatemala	(No slogan)	http://www.terra.com.gt/turismogt/
Guinea		No web site
Guinea-Bassau		No web site
Guyana	Guyana — the land of many waters	http://www.sdnp.org.gy/mtti/guyana.html
Haiti	(No slogan)	http://www.haititourisme.org/
Honduras	Honduras — one small country, three worlds apart	http://www.letsgohonduras.com/web/
Hong Kong	Hong Kong — live it, love it!	http://webserv2.discoverhongkong.com/login.html
Hungary	(No slogan)	http://www.hungarytourism.hu
Iceland	Iceland — discoveries, the whole year round	http://www.icetourist.is
India	Incredible India	http://www.tourismofindia.com
Indonesia	Indonesia — your genuine experience	http://www.indonesia-tourism.com/
Iran	(No slogan)	http://www.irantourism.org/
Iraq		(No web site)
Ireland	Ireland — live a different life	http://www.ireland.travel.ie
Israel	(No slogan)	http://www.tourism.gov.il/english/default.asp
Italy	Pin Italia — che mai!	http://www.enit.it/default.asp?Lang=UK
Jamaica	Jamaica — one love	http://www.visitjamaica.com
Japan	Explore Japan	http://www.jnto.go.jp/
Jersey	Enjoyment begins with Jersey	http://www.jersey.com
Jordan	(No slogan)	http://www.see-jordan.com/
Kazakhstan	(No slogan)	http://www.kazsport.kz/
Kenya	Kenya — creation's most beautiful destinations, all in one country	http://www.magicalkenya.com
Kiribati	(No slogan)	http://www.tcsp.com/destinations/kiribati/index.shtml
Kuwait	(No slogan)	http://www.kuwaittourism.com
Kyrgyzstan		No web site
Laos	Sabbai dee and welcome!	http://visit-laos.com/

National Tourism Office	Theme	WWW URL
Latvia	Latvia — the land that sings	http://www.latviatourism.lv
Lebanon	(No slogan)	http://www.lebanon-tourism.gov.lb
Lesotho	Welcome to the mountain Kingdom	http://www.lesotho.gov.ls/lstourism.htm
Liberia		No web site
Libya		No web site
Liechtenstein	Liechtenstein — princely moments	http://www.tourismus.li/
Lithuania	(No slogan)	http://www.tourism.lt/
Luxemburg	Grand Duchy of Luxemburg	http://www.ont.lu/
Macau	More than ever Macau is a festival	http://www.macautourism.gov.mo
Macedonia	(No slogan)	http://www.economy.gov.mk
Madagascar	(No slogan)	http://www.madagascar-contacts.com
Malawi	Malawi — the land of smiles and laughter	http://www.tourismmalawi.com/
Malaysia	Malaysia — truly Asia	http://tourism.gov.my/
Maldives	Maldives — the sunny side of life	http://www.visitmaldives.com.mv/
Mali	(No slogan)	http://www.tourisme.gov.ml
Malta	Malta — welcome to the heart of the Mediterranean	http://www.visitmalta.com
Marshall Islands		(No web site)
Martinique	Martinique — the French Caribbean Haven	http://www.martinique.org
Mauritania	(No slogan)	http://www.mauritania.mr
Mauritius	Mauritius — an invitation to paradise	http://www.mauritius.net/
Mexico	The timeless experience - Mexico	http://www.visitmexico.com
Micronesia	Dive into the heart of exotic Micronesia	http://www.visit-fsm.org/
Moldova	(No slogan)	http://www.turism.md
Monaco	Monaco — an exceptional destination	http://www.monaco-tourisme.com
Mongolia	(No slogan)	http://www.mongoliatourism.gov.mn
Montenegro	Montenegro — art of nature	http://www.visit-montenegro.com
Monteserrat	Monsteserrat — one hundred thousand welcomes	http://www.visitmontserrat.com
Morocco	(No slogan)	http://www.tourism-in-morocco.com
Mozambique	Mozambique — new for you	http://www.mozambique.mz/
Myanmar	(No slogan)	http://www.myanmar.com/Ministry/Hotel_Tour/usefullink.htm
Namibia	Namibia — Africa's gem	http://www.met.gov.na/
Nepal	(No slogan)	http://www.welcomenepal.com
Netherlands	(No slogan)	http://www.holland.com/global/
Netherlands Antilles		No web site
New Caledonia	Discover Caledonia — France's best kept secret	http://www.new-caledonia-tourism.nc/
New Zealand	100% pure NZ	http://www.purenz.com
Nicaragua	Nicaragua — a water paradise	http://www.intur.gob.ni/
Niger		No web site
Nigeria	Nigeria — beauty in diversity	http://www.nigeriatourism.net/
Norfolk Island	Norfolk Island — paradise discovered	http://www.norfolkisland.com
Northern Ireland	Discover Northern Ireland	http://www.discovernorthernireland.com
Northern Marianas	My Marianas	http://www.mymarianas.com/
North Korea	(No slogan)	http://www.dprknta.com

National Tourism Office	Theme	WWW URL
Norway	Norway — a pure escape	http://www.visitnorway.com/foreign_offices/great_britain/
Nuie	Nuie — rock of Polynesia	http://www.niueisland.com/
Oman		No web site
Pakistan	(No slogan)	http://www.tourism.gov.pk/
Palestine	Palestine — the Holy land	http://www.visit-palestine.com/
Palau	Experience the wonders of Palau	http://www.visit-palau.com
Panama	Panama — the path less travelled	http://www.visitpanama.com
Papua New Guinea		(No web site)
Paraguay	(No slogan)	http://www.senatur.gov.py
Peru	Pack your six senses — come to Peru	http://www.peru.org.pe/perueng.asp
Philippines	Philippines — more than the usual	http://www.tourism.gov.ph/
Pitcairn Islands	(No slogan)	http://www.government.pn
Poland	(No slogan)	http://www.travelpoland.com/
Portugal		
Puerto Rico	Go to Puerto Rico	http://www.gotopuertorico.com
Qatar		No web site
Reunion		No web site
Romania	Romania — come as a tourist, leave as a friend	http://www.romaniatourism.com/
Russia	(No slogan)	http://www.russia-tourism.ru/
Rwanda		No web site
Saba	Saba — the unspoiled queen . . . in the Dutch Caribbean	http://www.sabatourism.com
Samoa	Samoa — the treasured islands of the South Pacific	http://www.visitsamoa.us
San Marino	(No slogan)	http://www.visitsanmarino.com/
Sao Tome and Principe	Sao Tome & Principe — paradise on Earth	http://www.saotome.st/
Sark	(No slogan)	http://www.sark.info
Saudi Arabia	(No slogan)	http://www.sct.gov.sa/
Scotland	Live it — visit Scotland	http://www.visitscotland.com/
Senegal	No slogan	http://www.dakarville.sn/tourisme
Serbia	Serbia — three times love	http://www.serbia-tourism.org/
Seychelles	Seychelles — as pure as it gets	http://www.aspureasitgets.com
Sierra Leone		No web site
Singapore	Singapore roars	http://www.visitsingapore.com
Slovakia	Slovakia — your choice	http://www.slovakiatourism.sk/
Slovenia	Slovenia — the green place of Europe	http://www.slovenia-tourism.si/
Solomon Islands	Solomon Islands — the treasured islands of Melanesia	http://www.tcsp.com/destinations/solomons/index.shtml
Somalia		No web site
South Africa	Discover South Africa	http://www.southafrica.net/
South Korea	No slogan	http://www.tour2korea.com
Spain	(No slogan)	http://www.spain.info/Portal/EN
Sri Lanka	Sri Lanka — a land like no other	http://www.lanka.net/ctb/
St. Barthelemy	(No slogan)	http://www.st-barths.com/homeeng.html
St. Helena	Discover St. Helena — emerald isle of the South Atlantic Ocean	http://www.sthelenatourism.com

National Tourism Office	Theme	WWW URL
St. Kitts and Nevis	St. Kitts and Nevis — two islands, one paradise	http://www.interknowledge.com/stkitts-nevis/
St. Lucia	St. Lucia — simply beautiful	http://www.stlucia.org/
St. Maarten	St. Maarten — a little European, a lot of Caribbean!	http://www.st-maarten.com/
St. Martin	St. Martin — French Caribbean	http://www.st-martin.org/
St. Vincent and the Grenadines	St. Vincent and the Grenadines — jewels of the Caribbean	http://www.svgtourism.com
Sudan		No web site
Surinam	Surinam — the drum beat of the Amazon	http://www.surinam.net
Swaziland	Swaziland — the royal experience	http://www.mintour.gov.sz/
Sweden	(No slogan)	http://www.visit-sweden.com
Switzerland	Switzerland — get natural	http://www.myswitzerland.com/
Sudan		No web site
Syria	(No slogan)	http://www.syriatourism.org
Tahiti	Tahiti — islands beyond the ordinary	http://www.tahiti-tourisme.com/
Taiwan	Taiwan — touch your heart	http://www.taiwan.net.tw/index.jsp
Tajikistan	Adventure on the roof of the world	http://www.traveltajikistan.com
Tanzania	(No slogan)	http://www.tanzania-web.com
Thailand	(No slogan)	http://www.tourismthailand.org/
Togo		No web site
Tokelau Islands		No web site
Tonga	The ancient Kingdom of Tonga	http://www.tongaholiday.com/
Trinidad & Tobago	(No slogan)	http://www.visittnt.com/
Tunisia	(No slogan)	http://www.tourismtunisia.com
Turkey	Go with the rhythm . . . enjoy Turkey	http://www.turizm.gov.tr/
Turkish Republic of Northern Cyprus	(No slogan)	http://www.trncwashdc.org/c000.html
Turkmenistan		(No web site)
Turks & Caicos Islands	Turks & Caicos Islands — get lost	http://www.turksandcaicostourism.com/
Tuvalu	Tuvalu — timeless!	http://www.tcsp.com/destinations/tuvalu/index.shtml
Uganda	Uganda — the pearl of Africa	http://www.visituganda.com/
Ukraine	(No slogan)	http://www.tourism.gov.ua/
United Arab Emirates	(No slogan)	http://www.uae.org.ae/tourist/index.htm
United Kingdom	(No slogan)	http://www.visitbritain.com
Uruguay	Uruguay — natural	http://www.turismo.gub.uy/
United States of America	(No slogan)	http://www.tinet.ita.doc.gov
U.S. Virgin Islands	U.S. Virgin Islands — America's Caribbean	http://www.usvitourism.vi/en
Uzbekistan	(No slogan)	http://www.uzbektourism.uz/
Vatican City	(No slogan)	http://www.vatican.va
Vanuatu	Vanuatu — another time, another place	http://www.vanuatutourism.com
Venezuela	(No slogan)	http://www.turismoparatodos.org.ve
Vietnam	Vietnam — a destination for the new millennium	http://www.vietnamtourism.com/

National Tourism Office	Theme	WWW URL
Wales	Be inspired by Wales	http://www.visitwales.com
Wallis and Futuna	(No slogan)	http://www.wallis.co.nc/adsupwf/
West Sahara		No web site
Yemen	Yemen — be ready to be astounded	http://yementourism.com/index.htm
Zambia	Zambia — the real Africa	http://www.zambiatourism.com/
Zimbabwe	(No slogan)	http://www.zimbabwetourism.co.zw

Author Index

Subject Index